HD
5713
J63
2013

The Job Guarantee.

MT SAN JACINTO COLLEGE
SAN JACINTO CAMPUS
1499 N STATE ST
SAN JACINTO, CA 92583

The Job Guarantee

The Job Guarantee

Toward True Full Employment

Edited by
Michael J. Murray
and Mathew Forstater

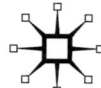

THE JOB GUARANTEE
Copyright © Michael J. Murray and Mathew Forstater, 2013.
All rights reserved.
First published in 2013 by
PALGRAVE MACMILLAN®
in the United States—a division of St. Martin's Press LLC,
175 Fifth Avenue, New York, NY 10010.

Where this book is distributed in the UK, Europe and the rest of the world, this is by Palgrave Macmillan, a division of Macmillan Publishers Limited, registered in England, company number 785998, of Houndmills, Basingstoke, Hampshire RG21 6XS.

Palgrave Macmillan is the global academic imprint of the above companies and has companies and representatives throughout the world.

Palgrave® and Macmillan® are registered trademarks in the United States, the United Kingdom, Europe and other countries.

ISBN: 978–1–137–28610–9 (paperback)
ISBN: 978–1–137–28609–3 (hardcover)

Library of Congress Cataloging-in-Publication Data

    The job guarantee : toward true full employment / edited by Michael J. Murray and Mathew Forstater.
     p. cm.
     ISBN 978–1–137–28609–3 (alk. paper)—
     ISBN 978–1–137–28610–9 (alk. paper)
    1. Full employment policies. 2. Manpower policy. 3. Employment (Economic theory) 4. Unemployment. I. Murray, Michael J. II. Forstater, Mathew, 1961–

HD5713.J63 2013
331.12′0424—dc23
                                                    2012028026

A catalogue record of the book is available from the British Library.

Design by Newgen Imaging Systems (P) Ltd., Chennai, India.

First edition: January 2013

10 9 8 7 6 5 4 3 2 1

Contents

List of Tables	vii
List of Figures	ix
Introduction *Michael J. Murray and Mathew Forstater*	1
1. Rising Job Complexity and the Need for Government Guaranteed Work and Training *Jon D. Wisman and Nicholas Reksten*	5
2. Wage Policies and Funding Strategies for Job Guarantee Programs *Philip Harvey*	39
3. The Low Cost of Full Employment in the United States *Fadhel Kaboub*	59
4. The Costs and Benefits of a Job Guarantee: Estimates from a Multicountry Econometric Model *Scott T. Fullwiler*	73
5. Effective Demand, Technological Change, and the Job Guarantee Program *Michael J. Murray*	95
6. Transformational Growth, Endogenous Demand, and a Developmental ELR Program *Edward J. Nell and George Argyrous*	125
7. The Euro Crisis and the Job Guarantee: A Proposal for Ireland *L. Randall Wray*	161
Notes on Contributors	179
Index	183

Tables

3.1	Three-year ELR plan	67
5.1	Hypothetical base-model input output table; initial period	100
5.2	Base-model coefficient matrix; initial period	101
5.3	Base-model distribution of the social surplus; initial period	102
5.4	Input-output base-model simulations; periods one–seven	107
5.5	Hypothetical ELR-model input output table; initial period	114
5.6	Hypothetical ELR-model input output table; period = 1	116

Figures

1.1	Total college enrollment as percentage of population 18–25 years old, 1869–2009	12
1.2	Public and private portions of student enrollment in higher education, 1963–2009	13
1.3	Accounting for changes in wage inequality: the role of globalization, technology, and labor market policies and institutions (average annual percentage changes)	14
1.4	Expenditures on education by type of institution as a percentage of GDP, 1929–2009	15
1.5	Public primary and secondary education expenditures per pupil in constant 1982–1984 dollars, 1869–1996	15
1.6	Total cost of undergraduate education by type of institution in constant 2008–2009 dollars, 1965–2009	16
1.7	Gap between average undergraduate costs of college attendance and student aid per full-time equivalent student per year, constant 2008–2009 dollars	17
1.8	Human capital tree	18
1.9	Percentage of persons 25 and over having completed high school or college, 1910–2010	20
1.10	Average duration of unemployment, United States, 1947–2011	22
1.11	Average duration of unemployment, 1948–2007 around trend line	23
2.1	US unemployment rate 1933–1940	42
3.1	US GDP with and without the ELR program ($ trillions)	66
4.1	Job guarantee employees (millions)	80
4.2	Annualized nominal GDP for JG program less base data ($ billions)	81
4.3	Annualized real GDP for JG program less base data ($ billions)	81
4.4	Quarterly annualized inflation for JG program less base data	82

4.5	Capacity use (fairmodel-specific measure) for JG program less base data	83
4.6	Value of US$ for JG program less base data (percent difference)	84
4.7	Total spending on JG program as a percent of GDP	85
4.8	Federal government deficit/surplus as a percent of GDP for JG program less base data	85
4.9	State/local government surplus/deficit as a percent of GDP for JG program less base data	87
4.10	Sector financial balances as a percent of GDP for JG program less base data	88
4.11	Financial balances for household and firm sectors as a percent of GDP for JG program less base data	89
4.12	Private sector employment (millions) for JG program less base data	90
4.13	Private sector jobs created per $1 billion in JG program spending	91
4.14	Real private sector capital stock ($ billions) for JG program less base data	92
4.15	Increase in nominal private sector capital stock per $1 in JG program spending	92
5.1	Reduction in labor coefficients over seven simulated periods	104
5.2	Retained earnings through simulated time	105
5.3	GDP and unemployment rates	106
5.4	Real personal disposable income (2005 chained dollars)	110
5.5	US corporate profits (2000–2012)	110
6.1	Occupations as a percentage of the labor force	138
7.1	Monthly overdraft loans to nonfinancial businesses, 2004:1–2011:1	164

Introduction
Michael J. Murray and Mathew Forstater

The essays that make up this volume begin from a set of shared premises. Involuntary unemployment is a normal feature of capitalist economies. There is no "natural" rate of unemployment or NAIRU (nonaccelerating inflation rate of unemployment), so it is unnecessary for millions of workers to remain jobless in order to maintain price stability. Unemployment and underemployment are associated with tremendous social and economic costs, including loss of output and income, financial insecurity, and a host of social problems, including crime, family disruption, physical and mental health problems, drug addiction, and many others. Since the private sector will never create enough jobs to employ all those who want and need to be working, it is the responsibility of government to use policy to promote true full employment, which means zero involuntary unemployment. Conventional fiscal and monetary policies are incapable of attaining and maintaining true full employment with price stability. The policy approach known variously as "Employer of Last Resort" (ELR), "Public Service Employment" (PSE), or the "Job Guarantee" (JG), if properly designed, can provide for true full employment.

The idea of a government-sponsored job guarantee is not a new one. Since 1996, however, there has been a revival of the policy approach, with institutes in the United States, Australia, and Europe and a variety of conferences and publications developing, promoting and debating the JG. Much, though not all, of this work has been within a framework dubbed MMT (Modern Monetary Theory) combining the JG with the chartalist approach to monetary history, theory, and policy and the functional finance approach to managing government budgets and the national debt.

There is general agreement among supporters of the JG regarding the basic outline of the program. Government offers a public service job to anyone ready and willing to work, no means tests or time limits. The federal government pays the basic JG wage-benefits package, but community groups, NGOs, nonprofit enterprises, and local governments administer and manage the program. There are always enough jobs to employ all those who need one, as government provides an infinitely elastic demand for labor. The program creates a strong, countercyclical stabilizer, expanding when the economy goes into a downturn and contracting as the private sector demand for labor rises.

In addition to providing full employment and macroeconomic stability, and reducing the social and economic costs of unemployment, the JG has numerous other potential benefits. Staying employed maintains the skills of workers, whose productivity declines during periods of joblessness. The JG can provide training and education, which may open opportunities for employment in new occupations and industries. Businesses benefit from hiring workers who have been able to maintain and even enhance their capabilities. By guaranteeing high and stable incomes and demand, the uncertainty characterizing investment decisions is reduced, and firms will have the resources and incentives to retool and make use of the latest technologies.

In addition to creating jobs, income, and demand, and developing skills and offering opportunities for training and education, the JG also supports the provision of public services. Suddenly there is no labor constraint for providing services often in short supply and for addressing unmet social and community needs. Libraries and community centers can stay open every night, and additional helping hands are available for playgrounds, nursing homes, and recycling centers. Revitalized infrastructure reduces costs and stimulates productivity.

The JG is also the only real means of achieving the right to employment found in numerous government and other documents, such as the United Nations' "Universal Declaration of Human Rights." The right to employment is also the most important means to many other economic and social rights, such as the right to food, housing, and health care.

While conventional fiscal stimulus is unlikely to provide true full employment or to reconcile full employment and price stability, the JG addresses unemployment due to both insufficient effective demand and ongoing structural and technological change. In addition, the JG approach deals with the functionality of unemployment, which is completely unaddressed by traditional Keynesian policies.

Initial research on the JG has largely focused on developing the theoretical framework underlying the program, addressing concerns and criticisms, examining historical precedents, and country studies and policy applications. Further extensions of the JG paradigm include:

- history of JG schemes by Rose (1994; 1995), and Harvey (2012);
- simulations by Fullwiler (2007), Majewski (2004), Murray (2012), and Nell et al. (2012);
- evaluations of JG-inspired programs in Argentina by Tcherneva and Wray (2005b; 2005c);
- relevance of the JG framework to gender issues by Tcherneva and Wray (2005a), Todorova (2009), and Antonopoulos (2009);
- JG as a means of promoting human rights and social justice by Harvey (1989), Wray and Forstater (2004), and Forstater (2012);
- the JG and ecological sustainability by Forstater (2004), and Godin (2012).

This list is not exhaustive, but provides a general idea of previous work. The purpose of *The Job Guarantee: Toward True Full Employment* is to provide an outlet for additional contributions to this "second stage" of JG research.

The book addresses three broad areas of further development of the JG: (1) new theoretical developments; (2) modeling and simulations; and (3) case studies and empirical evidence. In elaborating the JG literature in these directions, the motivation remains the same as guided the initial development of the approach: that of constructing an effective policy program for eliminating unemployment and underemployment.

REFERENCES

Antonopoulos, Rania. 2009. "Promoting Gender Equality through Stimulus Packages and Public Job Creation." *Public Policy Brief 101*, Annandale-on-Hudson, NY: The Levy Economics Institute (June).

Forstater, Mathew. 2004. "Green Jobs: Addressing the Critical Issues Surrounding the Environment, Workplace and Employment." *International Journal of Environment, Workplace and Employment* 1(1): 53–61.

———. 2012. "Jobs and Freedom Now! Functional Finance, Full Employment, and the Freedom Budget." *Review of Black Political Economy* (20 January 2012), pp. 1–16, doi:10.1007/s12114-011-9125-z.

Fullwiler, Scott T. 2007. "Macroeconomic Stabilization through an Employer of Last Resort." *Journal of Economic Issues* 41(1): 93–134.

Godin, Antoine. 2012. "Guaranteed Green Jobs: Sustainable Full Employment" Working Paper No. 722, Annandale-on-Hudson, NY: The Levy Economics Institute (May).

Harvey, Philip. 1989. *Securing the Right to Employment: Social Welfare Policy and the Unemployed in the United States*. Princeton, NJ: Princeton University Press.

Harvey, Philip. 2012. "Learning from the New Deal." *Review of Black Political Economy,* forthcoming.

Majewski, Ray. 2004. "Simulating an Employer of Last Resort Program." In George Argyrous, Mathew Forstater, and Gary Mongiovi, eds., *Growth, Distribution, and Effective Demand: Alternatives to Economic Orthodoxy: Essays in Honor of Edward J. Nell.* Armonk, NY: M. E. Sharpe.

Murray, Michael J. 2012. "The Regional Benefits of the Employer of Last Resort Program." *Review of Radical Political Economics* (September).

Nell, Edward J., Ray Majewski, and Michael J. Murray. 2012. *Maintaining Full Employment,* forthcoming.

Rose, Nancy E. 1994. *Put to Work: The WPA and Public Employment in the Great Depression.* New York: Monthly Review Press.

———. 1995. *Workfare or Fair Work: Women, Welfare, and Government Work Programs.* Newark, NJ: Rutgers University Press.

Tcherneva, Pavlina R. and L. Randall Wray. 2005a. "Employer of Last Resort: A Case Study of Argentina's *Jefes* Program." Working Paper 41, Center for Full Employment and Price Stability, University of Missouri—Kansas City.

———. 2005b. "Gender and the Job Guarantee: The Impact of Argentina's *Jefes* Program on Female Heads of Households." Working Paper 49, Center for Full Employment and Price Stability, University of Missouri—Kansas City.

———. 2005c. "Is Argentina's *Jefes de Hogar* an Employer of Last Resort Program?" Working Paper 43, Center for Full Employment and Price Stability, University of Missouri—Kansas City.

Todorova, Zdravka. 2009. "Employer of Last Resort Policy and Feminist Economics: Social Provisioning and Socialization of Investment." Working Paper 56, Center for Full Employment and Price Stability, University of Missouri—Kansas City.

Wray, L. Randall and Mathew Forstater. 2004. "Full Employment and Social Justice.' In D. P. Champlin and J. T. Knoedler, eds., *The Institutionalist Tradition in Labor Economics.* Armonk, NY: M. E. Sharpe.

CHAPTER 1

Rising Job Complexity and the Need for Government Guaranteed Work and Training

Jon D. Wisman and Nicholas Reksten[1]

> There is no extravagance more prejudicial to the growth of national wealth than that wasteful negligence which allows genius that happens to be born of lowly parentage to expend itself in lowly work.
>
> Marshall 1920, 176

> Give a man a fish and you feed him for a day. Teach a man to fish and you feed him for a lifetime.
>
> Chinese Proverb, credited to Lao Tzu, founder of Taoism, fourth to sixth century BC

> (The) real problem, fundamental yet essentially simple (is) to provide employment for everyone.
>
> Keynes 1980, 267

Introduction

Government, as Adam Smith pointed out over two centuries ago, must provide for certain public goods that would not be provided in adequate quantity by the private sector. He identified education as among these public goods (1981[1776], 651). Until fairly recent times, however, government was controlled by a small elite whose members mistakenly did not generally recognize greatly expanding educational opportunity as in their own interest. Myopically, their more immediate short-term interest blinded them to how, in a longer term, a better educated workforce would make everyone, including members of their own class, richer.

In today's wealthy countries, a surge in the democratization of education evolved toward the end of the nineteenth century, along with an extension of the franchise and labor reform in response to threats from below of violence and revolution (Acemoglu and Robinson 2000). As the twentieth century unfolded, democratic pressures led to the progressive extension of years of publicly provided education. Even higher education became increasingly democratized, especially between the end of World War II and the mid-1970s.

However, over the past 35 years, inequality has dramatically increased in almost all wealthy societies, and substantially in a good number of them, challenging the expectations set forth by Kuznets (1955) that mature economic development would witness declining inequality. This reversal suggests a new "reversal" inflection point on the Kuznets curve. In the United States, the erosion of working class power and fraying of social safety nets since the mid-1970s has led to persistent educational achievement gaps, causing the poor to increasingly be locked out of educational opportunities. The educational achievement gap between children from rich and poor families is roughly 30–40 percent greater for those born in 2001 than those born in the mid-1970s and is now more than twice as large as the black-white achievement gap (Reardon 2011). This means that the formal education that society provides to some of its future workers is not adequate for the job market demands created by an ever-increasing pace of change.[2]

Further, in an evermore complex economy, the training most receive when young is not adequate for their full work lives. More and more need, and will need, continual retraining. While much of this training has been and will continue to be on the job, some workers will lose their jobs and for lack of necessary skills, not find comparable new ones. Although publicly provided formal schooling might provide some of the necessary reskilling, some workers who perform poorly in school settings learn well when training is part of their jobs.

The traditional model—that future workers receive their formation when young and any future reskilling occurs on the job—no longer suffices. To maintain skills and full employment in increasingly sophisticated workplaces, a new model is needed, one that provides those who do poorly in school with needed skills while continually retraining those who become and remain unemployed because of obsolete skills. This chapter argues that it is in the best interest not only of workers but also of society generally that a critical component of a new model be a government employer of the last resort program that ensures not only continuous employment but also the necessary skills for workers to successfully enter and reenter the private labor market.

This chapter is organized as follows. After briefly surveying worker formation in premodern societies in which formal schooling was nonexistent or was provided for political and religious reasons to a small elite, it turns to the rising need for public education that accompanies industrialization. An examination is then provided of the intensified pace of churn and technological change in modern economies that leave an increasing number of workers with inadequate levels of human capital.[3] The result is greater job insecurity, higher long-term unemployment and its attendant loss of human capital, a polarized labor market, and the consequent high personal and social costs. The study concludes with an overview of how provision of guaranteed employment with a robust training component would provide workers with adequate human capital throughout their lifetimes, resulting in a healthier economy and more just society.

THE EARLY EVOLUTION OF EDUCATION

Due to low levels of technology and specialization, premodern agricultural societies had little need for formal education. Occupations were usually inherited, and children began participating in agricultural work at a young age, progressively learning the needed skills. Urban children often became apprentices within craft industries, picking up the needed skills to eventually become masters themselves. Beyond education given to the Church's priests or to Mandarins in China, some portion of the elite often received some formal education, but much of this served as a status signifier and method of socialization.

This small amount of formal education prior to modern times was, as Galor puts it, "motivated by a variety of reasons, such as religion, enlightenment, social control, moral conformity, sociopolitical stability, social and national cohesion, and military efficiency" (2005, 194). For instance, by the eleventh century, the Medieval Church in most of Europe had established schools to provide a small cohort with the necessary skills to manage its activities (Boyd 1966, 100). With the expansion of commerce, reading or song schools evolved in most small European towns and villages, while grammar schools developed in larger towns (Boyd

1966, 155). However, attendance was voluntary, and most parents could not afford having their children, among their most important economic assets, attend for very long. Incentives for investment in education were small.

With the rise of Protestantism, the demand for education expanded. Martin Luther and other early Protestant leaders were advocates of universal education, regardless of sex or class (Boyd 1966, 188–189). For them it was vital that all members of the community be able to read the Bible, and thereby have equal access to God's word. They also sought a transfer of authority over education from the Church to the state throughout a large portion of Western Europe (Boyd 1966, 183).

With the rise of industrialization, formal education became more economically important. Although it played but a minor role in the driving industry of textiles, Becker, Hornung, and Woessman argue that its role in other industries was more important, and that this importance only increased as the industrial revolution progressed.[4] Among economically and militarily competing nations, education was important for "technological catch-up" (2009, 2).

Yet except for a few intellectuals such as Adam Smith,[5] providing education to the working class was not generally viewed as an important end. Even the somewhat progressive Bernard de Mandeville argued that workers would work harder if they were kept not only poor, but also uneducated, or as he put it, it is "requisite that great Numbers of them should be Ignorant as well as Poor" (1924, 288).[6] Even the enlightened Voltaire feared that education would erode the deference of the poor for their superiors (Viner 1968, 33). It should also be noted that creating human capital would absorb part of the surplus that only the elite possessed.

The general failure to recognize the importance of human capital is not surprising in light of the fact that the first industrial revolution did not generally need highly trained workers.[7] Factories paired large amounts of physical capital with raw material, which enabled the replacement of the highly skilled artisans of the handicraft era with relatively unskilled workers.[8] Rather than complement human capital, physical capital became its substitute (Goldin and Katz 1998, 694–697). Indeed, in factories, workers under a regime of divided labor were generally de-skilled, a downward turn in worker welfare that did not go unnoticed by Adam Smith, who claimed that this form of work rendered them "as stupid and ignorant as it is possible for a human creature to become ... unless government take some pains to prevent it" (1776: II, 782).[9] Although the second industrial revolution evolved upon a greater marriage of science and technology, many workers continued to be de-skilled well into the twentieth century (Braverman 1974).

Working People Fight for Universal Education

The evolution of capitalism created an industrial working class that became increasingly organized and aware of its political power as the nineteenth century unfolded. Through strikes and revolts it increasingly threatened the existing power structure. By the latter part of that century it achieved considerable advances in work reform, in franchise rights, and in publicly providing education for its children.

Providing for education—creating human capital—is expensive.[10] Because the incomes of workers generally barely exceeded subsistence, they were not financially capable of bearing the full costs. Funds would have to come from the wealthier classes. Understandably, the wealthy would resist giving up some of their incomes through higher taxes, even when some might recognize the long-term benefits because of stronger economic growth. Their short-term interests generally trumped their long-term interests. It took rising working class power to force a state, predominantly controlled by the wealthy until the state become more democratized, to extend educational opportunity.

The extent of these gains in education can be seen in England, where, as elsewhere, the state had been reluctant to enter into the business of educating the population well into the nineteenth century. The schools that were available for the poor depended heavily on donations from the wealthy for their existence, and the education they provided emphasized social control (Carpentier 2003, 9). However, popular demands increased such that by the 1860s, even some capitalists supported government provision of universal public education (Galor 2005, 208). The demands for universal education became so forceful that enrollment of ten-year-olds soared from 40 percent in 1870 to 100 percent in 1900 (Acemoglu and Robinson 2000, 1191). Public expenditure on education rose from about 0.1 percent of GDP in 1870 to roughly 1 percent by 1900 and almost 3 percent in the 1930s (Carpentier 2003, 5).

This occurred, evidence suggests, concomitantly with the inflection point of the Kuznets curve, whereby the rising inequality that accompanied early economic growth began to reverse. Acemoglu and Robinson find that for the countries they examine (Britain, France, Germany, and Sweden) "inequality peaked approximately at the time of the major political reforms, and fell sharply after the extension of the franchise.... in large part due to major redistributive efforts including increased taxation, investment in education of the poor, and labor market reform" (2000, 1193, 1180). Easterlin has also viewed the democratization of education as a response by the elites to the threat of violence and revolution: "To judge from the historical experience of the world's twenty-five largest nations, the establishment and experience of formal schooling has depended in large part on political conditions and ideological influences.... A major commitment to mass education is frequently symptomatic of a major shift in political power and associated ideology in a direction conductive to greater upward mobility for a wider segment of the population" (1981, 1, 14).

The evolution of educational opportunities in the United States differed in important ways, although many of the same forces were at work. Protestants for whom education had religious importance had predominantly settled in the territory. Literacy rates were also higher among immigrants than the literacy rates of populations they left behind. Engerman and Sokoloff suggest that the development story of the United States be considered an anomaly among New World economies. Compared to other countries in the Western Hemisphere, Canada and the United States were extremely egalitarian (1994, 3). Notions of equity pervaded both the economic and governmental spheres in the United States, with titles of nobility specifically prohibited in its Constitution (article I, section 9). In addition to providing an incentive to develop a deep manufacturing base, with a working class that could afford cheap manufactured goods, greater equality meant that elites could not stymie efforts to provide education, at least outside of the American South. There was a belief that "schooling would help equip men for self-governance and participation in a democracy, as well as provide an avenue for self-improvement and upward mobility" (Black and Sokoloff 2006, 74). As a result, primary school enrollment rates in the United States passed Germany in the 1840s to become the highest in the world at the time (among the free population) (Easterlin 1981, 8).[11]

This occurred as US states gradually abolished property ownership requirements to vote, thereby extending the franchise to the (white male) working class. By 1815, seven out of twenty states had universal white male suffrage (Black and Sokoloff 2006, 77), and all states had abolished property requirements by 1856[12] (Engerman and Sokoloff 2005, 898). Such suffrage laws allowed local governments to raise money for schools primarily through property taxes, which fell disproportionately upon the wealthy (Black and Sokoloff 2006, 78).

The rural setting of much of the country also played a key role in the development of schools. In the Northeast, small farms dotted the countryside, and elites were relatively weak at the local level. School funding was tied to local trade networks among neighbors (Beadie 2008, 8). "Social capital appears to have been the handmaiden of human capital" (Goldin and Katz 1999, 684), and the first schools appeared where close-knit communities permitted the organizing of funding. Community funding of schools served to build trust, enabling coordination that resulted in further community investments (Beadie 2008, 10–11). As markets expanded into the countryside, rural participants needed business and social skills to avoid being taken in by more savvy urban traders.

As industrialization advanced, primary schooling in urban settings in the United States had differing objectives. In Boston, for example, it was designed largely to pacify the lower classes, socialize rural migrants seeking factory work, and absorb Irish Catholic immigrants into Protestant Whig society (Urban and Wagoner Jr. 2004, 96–97). Many advocates of universal education at the time were also concerned about a perceived breakdown of the family accompanying agricultural migration into the manufacturing economy.

Educational opportunities continued to spread throughout the century. For example, in 1863, the Morrill Act began the creation of Land Grant Universities. Advocates for these universities argued that the government would reap the rewards of greater revenues by improving the skills of agricultural and industrial workers. By that time, "these colleges were needed because, just as the professions... needed training grounds, farmers and mechanics required special skills and appropriate literature" (Key 1996, 215).

The dominance of the state as a provider of education at all levels continued to evolve with the pace of the industrial revolution. Yet, until the early twentieth century, most children finished their formal education upon completing primary school. The relatively slow pace of technological change meant that on-the-job training sufficed. Further, a still large agricultural sector and the availability of low skilled manufacturing jobs meant that the opportunity cost of additional schooling was high (Goldin 1998, 368). In 1900, in the United States, secondary schools were still seen largely as preparatory institutions for college, emphasizing Latin, French, history, mathematics, and some science (Goldin 1998, 351).

An explosion in secondary school completion accompanied the surge of the United States toward industrial preeminence between 1910 and 1940. Whereas in 1910 less than 10 percent of youths graduated from high school, by 1940, 51 percent had done so (US Census Bureau 2006). Driving this additional schooling was a rise in white-collar jobs requiring higher levels of human capital and specific skills such as typing and bookkeeping (Goldin 1998, 352). Blue-collar occupations were also becoming more skilled, requiring training in subjects like chemistry, geometry, or mechanical drawing (Galor 2005, 212). The role of secondary schooling in the United States changed from preparing an elite minority of students for college to preparing a majority of pupils for work life. Vocational courses increasingly replaced courses in the traditional classical curriculum (Goldin 1998, 352).

It is noteworthy that this "high school movement" in the United States disproportionately occurred in relatively egalitarian areas where elites were not powerful enough to resist the taxes required for funding of schools. Goldin notes that by 1924, "the graduation rate in California or Nebraska was twice that in New Jersey and New York...as an institution [the secondary school] was rooted in egalitarianism and was often a by-product of the extensive state university systems in the United States" (1998, 349–350). As more opportunities for high school graduates became available, it was these more equal areas that first prepared their graduates to meet educational demands.

The extraordinary expansion of educational opportunity during the first half of the twentieth century came forth as physical and human capital were becoming more complementary, whereas during early industrialization they had generally been substitutes. With the advent of batch operations, assembly lines, and continuous-process methods in factories, the demand fell for unskilled workers to haul and assemble goods (Goldin and Katz 1999, 694–697). Changing technology quickly and decisively altered the model of education that was needed, and a more egalitarian political system created the wherewithal to produce huge numbers of high-school educated workers.

The growing and increasingly sophisticated economies of the industrialized countries continued to require more human capital. In the United States, following the World War II, the G.I. Bill began an era of dramatically increasing college enrollment, especially during the 1960s and

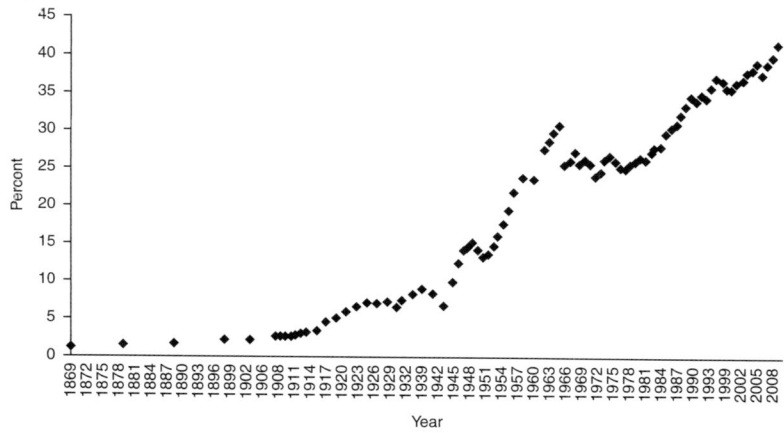

Figure 1.1 Total college enrollment as percentage of population 18–25 years old, 1869–2009.

Source: US Census Bureau and US Department of Education 2010, Table 212.[13]

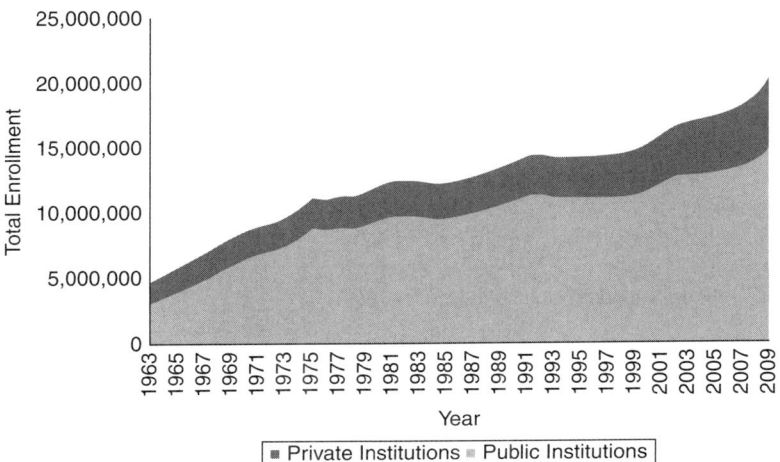

Figure 1.2 Public and private portions of student enrollment in higher education, 1963–2009.
Source: National Center for Education Statistics 2010, Table 198.

the mid-1980s to early 1990s (figure 1.1), mostly at public institutions (figure 1.2).

Such trends show that taxpayer supported public institutions, not on-the-job learning, have been the primary formal creators of human capital, ensuring that workers possess appropriate workplace skills. As technology and job demands advanced, these better-educated workers were generally able to gain needed new skills through on-the-job training.

POST 1975: LABOR BUSTED AND EDUCATIONAL STAGNATION

Political pressure to expand educational opportunity has varied with the relative political power possessed by labor, and the latter can readily be gauged by trends in income distribution. For instance, over the three decades following World War II, the United States became a more egalitarian society. Between 1946 and 1976, inflation-adjusted per capita income increased by about 90 percent. For the bottom 90 percent of households it increased by 83 percent, but for the top 1 percent only by 20 percent. Educational opportunity significantly expanded during this period. However, over the following three decades—between 1976 and 2006—whereas inflation-adjusted per capita income increased by 64 percent, for the bottom 90 percent of households it increased by only 10 percent. And over this latter period,

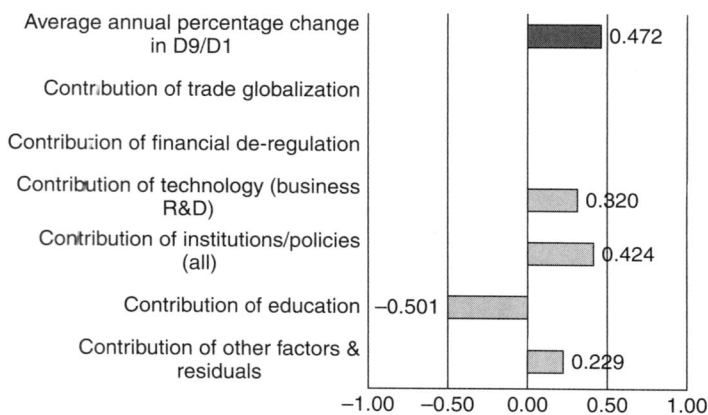

Figure 1.3 Accounting for changes in wage inequality: the role of globalization, technology, and labor market policies and institutions (average annual percentage changes).
Source: OECD 2011, 124, Figure 2.3

educational opportunities failed to keep pace with the economy's, and hence workers' needs (Baker 2007).[14]

A recent OECD (2011) report shows that this is the case throughout the developed world. Universally, education is the main inhibitor of increasing wage inequality, while policy, institutional, and technological changes have exacerbated it in recent decades. Figure 1.3 shows the OECD's estimates of the contributors to wage inequality between the top and bottom 10 percent of incomes (the "D9/D1 ratio") in recent decades. As Goldin and Katz (2008) suggest by the title of their book, whether wage inequality grows is largely determined by the winner of this "race between education and technology." The OECD report "firmly identifies *upskilling* of the workforce as one of the most powerful instruments at the disposal of governments to counter rising inequality. *Upskilling* is singled out as the only force which succeeds in not only reducing wage dispersion but also in increasing employment rates" (emphasis in original; 19).

Across the OECD, but especially in the United States, educational support has not been winning the race against forces generating greater inequality. While per-pupil public spending on primary and secondary education in the United States has continued to increase over time, as can be seen in Figure 1.4, support for education as a percentage of GDP has been relatively stagnant over the past 40 years. Figure 1.5 shows the increasing real costs of higher education in the United States since 1870. Especially important to note is that the real cost of attending a public college or university has more

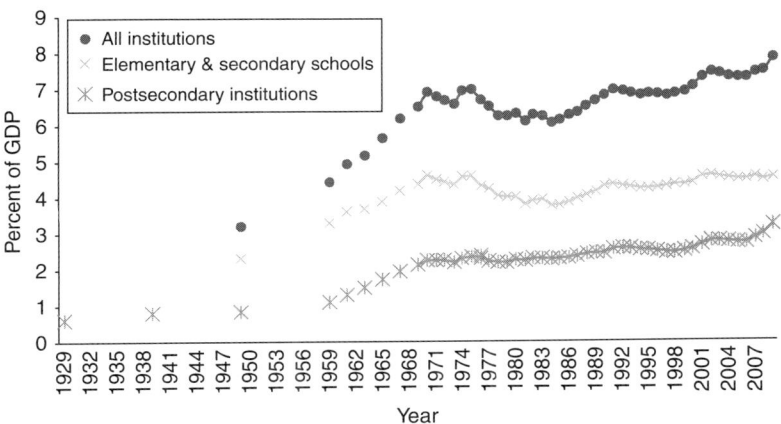

Figure 1.4 Expenditures on education by type of institution as a percentage of GDP, 1929–2009.
Source: National Center for Education Statistics 2010, Table 28.

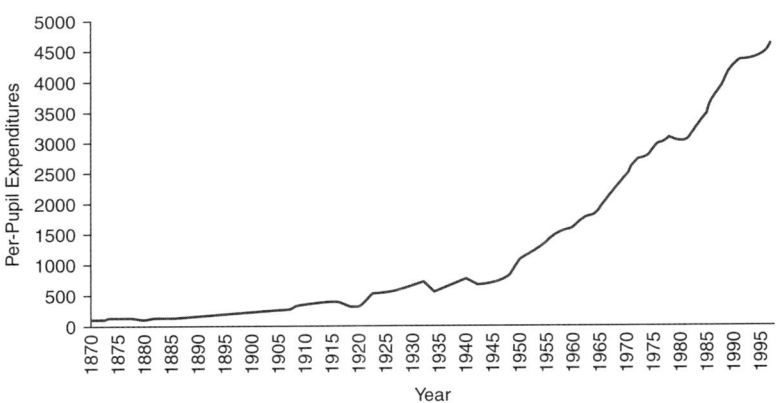

Figure 1.5 Public primary and secondary education expenditures per pupil in constant 1982–1984 dollars, 1869–1996.
Source: US Census Bureau 2006, Table Bc924.

than doubled since the early 1980s, from an average cost of $6,440 per year in 1982 to $12,861 in 2009 (in constant 1982–1984 dollars).

Figure 1.6 shows that while much of these cost increase has been offset by increase in student aid, most of this has taken the form of student loans, contributing to an exploding burden of student debt for graduates and their

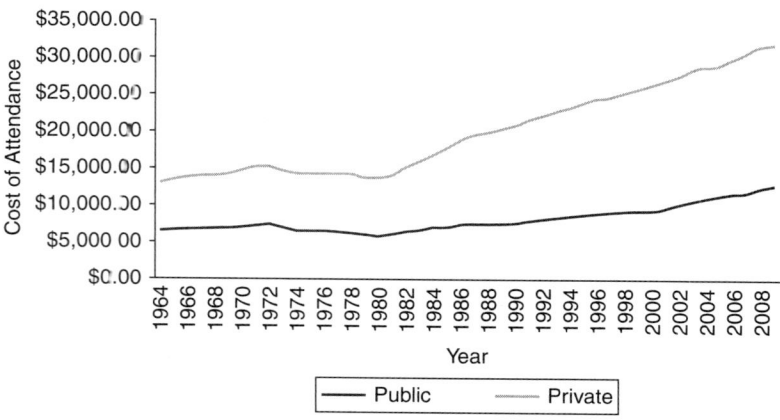

Figure 1.6 Total costs of undergraduate education by type of institution in constant 2008–2009 dollars, 1965–2009.
Source: National Center for Education Statistics 2010, Table 345.

families, and shifting some benefits of a degree from the student to the college or university. Since the early 1990s, when the earliest data are available, the average federal loan per full-time equivalent student has increased from about $1,600 per year to about $4,900 per year in the 2009–2010 school year. Over the course of four years, this amounts to a debt burden that is about $13,000 higher in real terms than it was in 1990; and this includes only *federal* student loans. Not included are private loans or other means families have drawn upon to meet the increasing costs of higher education, such as taking out a second mortgage on a home or simply paying a higher percentage of income as fees. Figure 1.7 shows that the gap between attending the cost of attending college and non-loan financial aid packages has been growing over the past two decades. Such cost increases have also occurred in the face of drastically rising income inequality, with real wages stagnating for most families since the early 1970s.[15]

Additionally, college completion rates in the United States have been falling since at least the early 1990s, when the first reliable data are available.[16] Five-year completion rates for first-time college students at both two- and four-year institutions were 51.2 percent for the cohort entering school in 1990, falling to 47.3 percent for the 1996 cohort, and 41.3 percent for the 2004 cohort. Six-year completion rates are only available for the latter two cohorts, but they tell a similar story. Completion rates for full-time students in the 1996 cohort were 65.3 percent and for the 2004 cohort, 62.6 percent (National Center for Education Statistics 2010). The cost to students of not completing is considerable. Investing in only half a degree's requirements may confer half the costs on a student, but it does not provide half the benefits in

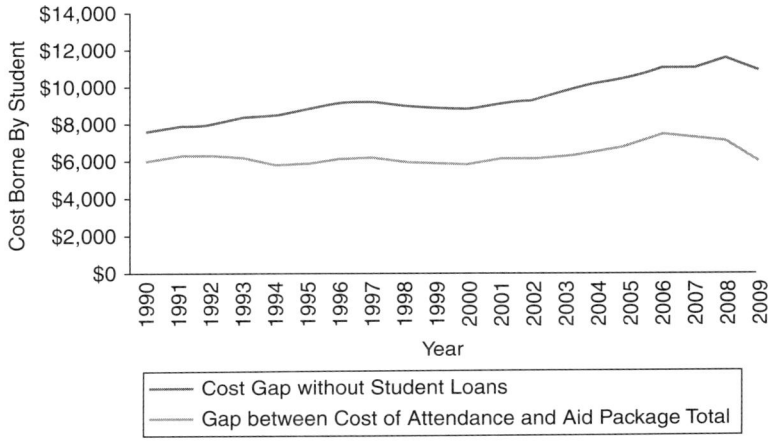

Figure 1.7 Gap between average undergraduate costs of college attendance and student aid per full-time equivalent student per year, in constant 2008–2009 dollars.

Sources: Authors' calculations from National Center for Education Statistics 2010, Table 345; College Board 2010, Table 3a.

terms of earnings. Stagnation in support paired with skyrocketing costs and increasing student loan burdens have occurred as the pace at which the United States is becoming a knowledge economy has been dramatically accelerating. With less pressure from below, educational expansion has become anemic. An assault has been made on public spending at all levels, heavily impacting education budgets, increasing inequality and handicapping the economy's performance.[17] Inequality reduces the effective pressure for further educational advances while the relative stagnation in educational advancement exacerbates inequality—a vicious destructive cycle.

ROBUST CREATIVE DESTRUCTION AND THE CHALLENGE OF MAINTAINING ADEQUATE WORKER SKILLS

Increasingly robust technological change, rising capital mobility, and globalization generally, combined with decreases in the rate of improvement of educational attainment in the United States, have led to decreasing job security, increasing long-term unemployment and underemployment, and a hollowing-out of the labor market.

AUTOMATION AND OUTSOURCING

Technological change and globalization continually augment specialization and an increasing international division of labor. When industrial

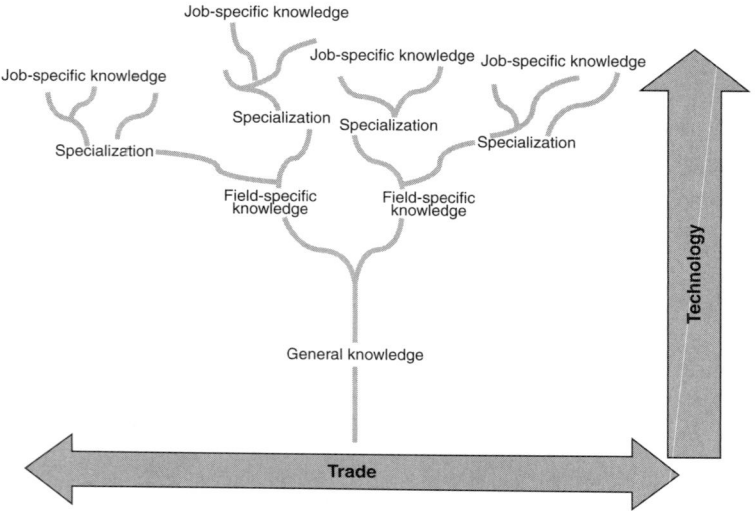

Figure 1.8 Human capital tree.

workers were unskilled, displaced workers could often find relatively similar work at another nearby firm. However, more advanced technology and increasing specialization have led to more specific investments in human capital that are inherently riskier. Hacker notes that the return on such specific investments increasingly depends on the performance of specific firms, industries, and occupations instead of the economy as a whole (2006, 79).

The idea of a human capital "tree" (figure 1.8) for any given set of jobs in the economy provides graphic clarity. Jobs require a certain amount of general knowledge, such as reading or a basic knowledge of mathematics, and they require a certain amount of specialized knowledge, but some can still be shared among occupations. Skill-biased technological change creates jobs that are more complex. That is, they have more branches and the skills required to perform them overlap with fewer other jobs as a result of specialization.

When a worker loses a job, there will be several jobs that he/she can qualify for in the same region of branches as the one lost. If he/she gets one of these jobs, the firm can train him/her to build up any specific human capital needed, in addition to any firm-specific human capital required. This happens in the vast majority of cases of reemployment. However, as technology becomes more advanced and specialization continues, the skills required for jobs increasingly branch off and differ. Technology can also render some occupations obsolete through automation, removing a larger branch of the tree. Additionally, outsourcing can remove a large branch in a certain geographic area.

This leaves workers who are too far removed from the branches of the jobs that exist in that area, and they may be unable to migrate to an area that contains that branch, resulting in long-term unemployment. This is when additional education becomes necessary. Firms will only be willing to engage in a certain amount of on-the-job training for workers, since not only is additional training costly, but workers may also take their additional skills to competitors.

SLOWING EDUCATIONAL ATTAINMENT

Goldin and Katz (2007) have examined the rate of skill-biased technological change and found that it has been fairly constant for much of the twentieth century. However, because the total "stock" of technology is growing, workers must learn even more to still be considered highly skilled.[18] Skill-biased technological change increases demand for high-skilled high-wage jobs, leaving many middle-skill jobs to be automated or outsourced. The number of menial and low-skill jobs has also tended to grow, although at a slower rate than high-skill jobs (Autor 2010a, 2–3). These jobs are those involving nonroutine manual tasks, primarily in the service sector such as food preparation and service, cleaning and janitorial work, and maintenance that cannot be readily automated or outsourced (Autor 2010b, 4).

Goldin and Katz point to the increasing college-wage premium as evidence that the United States is not keeping up with the increasing demand for high-skilled jobs. Further evidence of the slowing of educational expansion is the fact that in the first half of the twentieth century, each generation of Americans had about two more years of schooling on average than their parents. Those born in 1975, however, had only 0.74 year more schooling on average than their parents' generation (Goldin and Katz 2007, 155). Figure 1.9 documents this attainment growth slowdown.

The wage premium of skilled over nonskilled workers is at its highest level since the early twentieth century (Goldin and Katz 2007, 32). From 1915 to 1980, the supply and demand for college educated workers grew at more or less the same pace, with supply growing an average of 3.1 percent and demand 2.9 percent. Between 1990 and 2010, however, supply grew at 1.5 percent whereas demand grew by 2.0 percent (Carnevale and Rose 2011, 18). The result has been a surge in the premium of a college degree over a high school degree from 40 percent to 74 percent (17). Carnevale and Rose project that if current supply trends continue, that

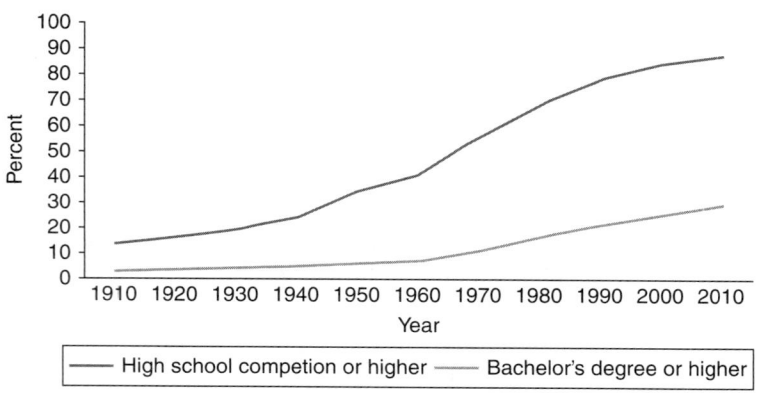

Figure 1.9 Percentage of persons 25 and over having completed high school or college, 1910–2010.
Source: National Center for Education Statistics 2010, Table 8.

premium will rise to 96 percent by 2025 due to a shortage of 20 million college degrees (10, 17).

Automation and outsourcing, combined with this shortage of highly trained labor, has created a polarized labor market. Thus, whereas between 1979 and 2007 real hourly earnings of college-educated workers rose between 10 percent and 37 percent, depending on their level of postbaccalaureate education, real earnings for workers with a high school diploma or less stagnated or declined (Autor 2010a). Among males, earnings fell by 12 percent for high school graduates and 16 percent for high school dropouts (6).

Part of the reason for the slowdown in the rate of increase in educational attainment in recent years can be attributed to the skyrocketing costs of higher education in the United States along with a failure of public support to grow at the same rate.

JOB INSECURITY

Aggregated statistics on the performance of the US economy in recent decades paint a deceptive picture of life for many workers. While there have been net job gains over the past 25 years, there has also been a large increase in job insecurity as jobs created in some sectors were partially offset by massive displacements of workers in others (Gosselin 2008, 113). Between 1977 and 2009, an annual average of 17.3 percent of jobs were created and 15.3 percent were destroyed (US Census Bureau 2011).

Though this hides the variations that exist across time and especially across industry, it shows that millions of workers are changing jobs as a result of this process of creative destruction. As such, this looks healthy: more new jobs are created than destroyed and presumably the new jobs have higher productivity.

However, workers have gained little from these productivity gains. Whereas productivity increased by 62.5 percent between 1989 and 2010, real hourly wages increased by only about 12 percent (Mishel and Shierholz 2011), which, for a 20-year period, is not far from full wage stagnation.

Creative destruction was conceptualized by Schumpeter as a "process of industrial mutation...that incessantly revolutionizes the economic structure from *within*, incessantly destroying the old one, incessantly creating a new one. The process of creative destruction is the essential fact about capitalism" (1962, 83). Indeed, this process of continuous churn occurs in modern economies at an accelerating rate, contributing to lower levels of job security.

Farber, for instance, has found that the average job tenure for men in the private sector fell by about 25 percent between 1973 and 2006 (2008, 9–10). In an earlier study he found that mean job tenure has been declining since at least 1920 for men and that the path has been approximately the same for male and female workers since the 1970s (2007, 9, 18).

Farber also examines another measure of churn: the relationship between the unemployment rate and the job loss rate. He finds that while the unemployment rate and job loss tended to move jointly in the past, beginning in the late 1990s, the job loss rate increased while unemployment was still falling. This led to a large increase in the gap between the two. In the period between 2001 and 2003, roughly 6 percent of workers were unemployed, while 12 percent lost their jobs involuntarily. This gap between the job loss rate and the unemployment rate became larger than at any other time in the previous two decades, leading Farber to conclude that "the structure of jobs in the private sector has moved away from long-term relationships" (2005, 14; 2008, 12).

Involuntarily displaced workers suffer lost human capital and face reduced bargaining power and hence lower wages. Since the early 1980s, this earnings decline has fluctuated between 10 percent and 20 percent. Not unexpectedly, the decline was 20 percent in the "recession" year of 2010 (Farber 2011, 6, 20). This level of churn, combined with earnings decline, suggests that either firms are responding to continuously changing market conditions and new technologies by changing workers and skill requirements or firms themselves are failing and being replaced by new firms tooled with different technologies. Apparently many workers do not possess the skill sets necessary to keep up.

LONG-TERM UNEMPLOYMENT AND UNDEREMPLOYMENT

While employers in the modern economy have been shedding workers more frequently, the average unemployment spell has gone from 12 to 16 weeks since the 1960s (figures 1.10, 1.11), and the probability of an average family experiencing an income drop of half or more jumped from 7 percent in the early 1970s to 17 percent in 2007[19] (www.hamiltonproject.org). This trend suggests that while some of the current unemployment is cyclical—caused by a lack of demand—a rising share is also structural, the result of a skill mismatch between workers and firms.

A survey of manufacturing by Deloitte for the Manufacturing Institute finds that "high unemployment is not making it easier to fill positions, particularly in the areas of skilled production and production support" (cited in Whoriskey 2012, A14). According to Martin Schmidt, companies such as Apple report that "the challenge in setting up U.S. plants is finding a technical work force" (cited in Duhigg and Bradsher 2012). A current Apple executive has claimed: "We shouldn't be criticized for using

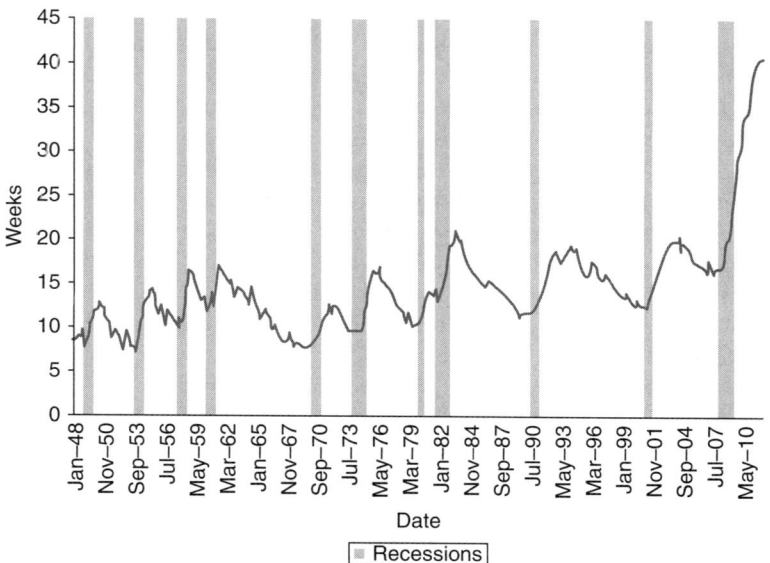

Figure 1.10   Average duration of unemployment, United States, 1947–2011.
Source: Bureau of Labor Statistics, 2012.

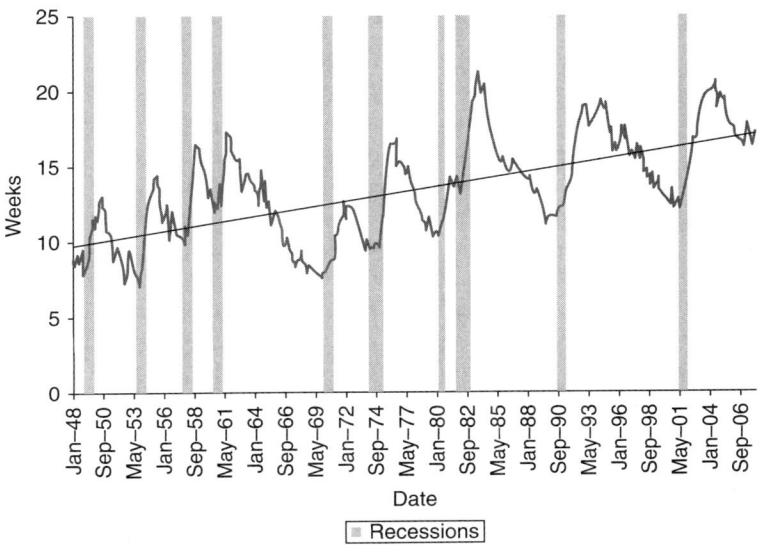

Figure 1.11 Average duration of unemployment, 1948–2007 around trend line.
Source: Authors' calculations with data from Bureau of Labor Statistics, 2012.

Chinese workers [in China]...The U.S. has stopped producing people with the skills we need" (ibid). This has led more and more companies to lobby for visa reform to permit more foreign highly trained workers to enter the United States. Doing so, however, lowers the pressure on the United States to produce the educated workers the economy needs.

These employment statistics do not take account of those who do not participate in the labor force. With their inclusion, the unemployment rate would be considerably higher. During the 1990s, more than half of high school dropouts (excluding the high percent of high school dropouts in prison) did not participate in the labor force, even though the economic expansion of the decade at its most robust reduced the official aggregate unemployment rate to 3.9 percent (Wray and Forstater 2004, 265).

Men have tended to be more impacted by these changes in employment and tenure than women. Juhn and Potter document the fall in labor force participation rates among prime-aged (25–54) men, which they attribute to a decline in demand for less-skilled workers (2006, 37). Between 1969 and 2004, total male participation rates fell by about 6 percent from 96 percent to 90 percent, a substantial decline considering they made up nearly 40 percent of the civilian labor force in 1969 and about 36 percent in 2004.

THE COSTS OF LONG-TERM UNEMPLOYMENT

Much of mainstream economics focuses primarily on the pecuniary costs to workers of being unemployed (e.g., Feldstein 1978). These principally include lost income and thus lower consumption, depreciation of human capital, and in some instances, loss of health insurance. These costs are substantial. Notably, because extended unemployment destroys human capital, it serves as an antieducation force, reducing the benefits of education.

Human capital—the full complement of skills and capabilities that a worker possesses in the labor market—generally depreciates during periods of unemployment. As Amartya Sen puts it, unemployment "may generate a loss of cognitive abilities as a result of the unemployed person's loss of confidence and sense of control" (1997, 161). Or, as he goes on to argue, "The discouragement that is induced by unemployment can lead to a weakening of motivation and make the long-term unemployed more resigned and passive...There is...considerable evidence suggesting that the typical effect, especially of long-term unemployment, is one of motivational decline and resignation. This can yield a hardening of future poverty and further unemployment" (1997, 162–163). Price et al. (1992) also note how unemployment can lower self-confidence, leading to lower social assertiveness that impairs effective job search. As the duration of unemployment grows, there is a decline in the perseverance needed to solve problems (Baum, Fleming, and Reddy 1986).[20] Kelvin and Jarrett report that the unemployed are preoccupied with time yet find themselves unable to use time effectively or productively (1985, Chapter 5). Calvo-Armengol finds that "long unemployment spells can generate a desocialization process leading to a progressive removal from labor market opportunities and to the formation of unemployment traps.... [Thus the] average probabilities of finding employment [are] on the order of 0.30 after one week of unemployment, 0.08 after eight weeks of unemployment and 0.02 after a year of unemployment" (2004, 443, 428; see also, Darity and Goldsmith 1993; 1996).

There are, however, many other costs than those noted by mainstream economics that are either consequent to these costs or in addition to them that receive less attention. Indeed, it has been claimed that these "nonpecuniary" costs drastically outweigh the monetary and consumption costs of not possessing a job (Winkelman and Winkelman 1998, 66). These additional personal costs of unemployment to its victims are well-documented. They include poorer health, mental distress, alcohol abuse, lowered social status, lowered self-esteem, marital instability, proneness to violence and crime, increased vulnerability to suicide, loss of networking opportunities, and lower levels of personal fulfillment.[21]

It should be noted that most if not all of these "other costs" of unemployment not only reduce human capital, but also impair ability to augment it. Indeed, there is an intergenerational cost insofar as it reduces the potential of the children of unemployed parents to do well in school.[22]

THE CURRENT CRISIS AND THE URGENCY FOR A NEW MODEL

A striking characteristic of the Great Recession is that the long-term unemployed—those unemployed for at least 27 weeks—make up 43 percent (as of February 2012) of the total unemployed in the United States (Bureau of Labor Statistics 2012). This level is by far the highest the country has seen since the Great Depression. Even in the severe "Reagan" recession, the long-term unemployed comprised only about 24 percent of the total number of unemployed (Congressional Budget Office 2007, 3).

The severity of the current crisis has forced an inordinate number of firms into bankruptcy. The new firms that are being and will continue to be created will generally deploy the most recent technological advances, often meaning that workers released by the defunct firms will not possess the skill mix needed by the new ones. Not only does this prolong their unemployment, but also the enhanced demand for more highly skilled workers augments the polarization referred to above.

The traditional model which has been based primarily on providing future workers with education when they are young is no longer adequate for our increasingly complex economies. It is no longer sufficient for two reasons: first, there are fewer jobs available for those who fail to finish secondary schooling. Second, for more and more workers, the skills learned when young are no longer sufficient for a full work life. The severity of the current crisis has magnified these two reasons.

The only viable long-term solution to unemployment and skill obsolescence is to guarantee employment and retraining. It is true that evaluations of job retraining programs in developed economies have produced mixed results, showing that the structure of the program can make a large difference in its effectiveness.[23] However, numerous evaluations of retraining programs in different countries have shown that it is possible to structure them so that they are effective. Moreover, no country has fully implemented an Employer of the Last Resort program (ELR) with a long-term commitment.[24]

Such a program might work as follows. Government offers employment to anyone who seeks work but would otherwise be without a job.[25] Government, as Mitchell and Wray put it, "hires off the bottom" (2005, 236). The offered wage serves as a price floor, a minimum wage for labor, presumably providing a "living wage."[26] After losing a job, unemployment insurance could cover a set number of weeks for the individual's job search. If at the end of this period a job has not been located, then the individual could join the ELR program.[27]

It is important to note that for many, a universal training or reskilling program alone would not work well. This may help account for why much evidence on the success of training programs is ambiguous. Too many people do not fare well in classrooms when that is all they are doing. Plus, just having a job instills discipline and self-respect.

No other form of public support—welfare—need be available to unemployed able workers. Thus, those who would not accept such employment would be revealing that the offered wage is below their reservation wage (the lowest acceptable wage) and thus they could be considered voluntarily unemployed.[28]

Entering into the ELR program would entail working in a government created or supported job and/or receiving training. The goal would be to keep the entire workforce at work or in training and to move workers into the regular economy as quickly as possible. A job placement component could facilitate reentry. The fundamental goal is that all have socially useful jobs, with skills upgraded as needed in an evermore complex economy such that everyone winds up being a productive member of the human community![29]

The program could be decentralized so as to better meet local needs.[30] For instance, states could receive an ELR budget from the federal government relative to their rate of unemployment (Wray 1999, 485).[31] If the program were to be administered by states or even smaller political jurisdictions, then the ELR wage could be set in terms of the local cost of living. Further, the local ELR wage could be set lower the higher the percent of the local labor force absorbed into the program, so as to preserve incentives for mobility.[32]

CONCLUSION

A new model of education is needed to adapt to evolving contemporary economic conditions, just as in the past new education models have been implemented to meet changing industrial needs. There was little need for formal education when most people were peasant farmers, and the required human capital was formed on the job within the family and craft shops. Although the need for formal schooling slowly increased with the evolution of capitalism, the surge came as the second phase of the industrial revolution created large numbers of moderately skilled blue- and white-collar jobs. In response, workers demanded publicly provided formal education for their children, first in primary schools, then in secondary schools, and eventually postsecondary education.[33]

Rising educational levels have had a self-reinforcing or feedback effect. Not only did they increase productivity, but they also fueled evermore robust creative destruction, thereby requiring evermore sophisticated education and retraining. The traditional model of providing the youth with education and counting upon on the job training to take care of future training needs is no longer adequate.[34] A new model is needed, one that responds to the ever-quickened pace of capitalism that increasingly renders old skills obsolete or inadequate. It must address this challenge by creating an institutional structure that ensures continuous employment and the requisite education and retraining. An ELR program in which employment is socially guaranteed to everyone willing and able to work that includes a training component could constitute the key component of such a model.

FINAL REFLECTION: CAN IT HAPPEN?

The silver lining of the current prolonged crisis is that it creates new opportunities. As Milton Friedman put it, "Only a crisis—actual or perceived—produces real change (1962, ix). It was not until 1933, four years into the Great Depression, that worker power began to assert itself, resulting in a number of unprecedented acts that benefited labor.[35] It took time for workers to fully realize how unfair the system had been to their interests and that there were alternatives. Today, workers face a dual problem: they have lost relative political power, and the more robust process of creative destruction has made their employment less secure. Yet this second problem, along with the continuing crisis, creates an opportunity: to insist upon a fairer system that guarantees employment and retraining for those who are not given adequate skills in youth or whose skills become inadequate later in a dynamic economic world. Might the Occupy Wall Street movement be the harbinger of an awakening?

The crisis might also awaken those who have been instrumental in impeding the expansion of adequate education—generally the wealthy—to better grasp their own long run interest. Although the proposal might strike some in the current climate of conservatism as radical, it is actually, as noted above, a further extension of measures that have been taken over the course of modern history as the educational requirements of the economy expanded. Further, it is far less radical than the measures taken to combat the pains of the Great Depression. Moreover, in that it would eliminate welfare for able workers, it reaffirms a widely embraced value that all should work.[36]

But against such optimism, Jared Diamond reminds us that in past civilizations elites pursued their own immediate self-interest even when they had before them the evidence of severe environmental decline, their civilization's decline, and thus the long-run ruin of the foundation upon which their own privileges and livelihoods depended (2005). However, the severe costs of unemployment and the benefits of education for economic performance are more readily visible and less in question than the consequences of ecological devastation. Guaranteeing employment and expanding educational opportunity promise to make the economy more robust, thereby raising living standards for the society as a whole, including that of the wealthy.

Finally, beyond the needs of a robust economy, there is something morally amiss in a rich economy that leaves a portion of its workforce unemployed and without adequate skills to readily find employment. That is, there is a moral imperative to guarantee employment and retraining (Wisman 2010). No matter the unemployment rate, it is morally wrong for an overwhelming majority of the population to condemn a portion of society—usually the least privileged—to a life of unemployment and underemployment.[37] The personal and social costs are far too high.[38]

NOTES

1. The authors are professor of Economics and PhD candidate respectively at American University, Washington, DC. Helpful comments from Stephen Rose and an anonymous referee are gratefully acknowledged.
2. Among 25–34 year olds with university degrees, the United States had sunk to twelfth place in 2010. The World Economic Forum ranked the United States fifty-second among 139 nations in the quality of its university math and science instruction in 2010. Almost half of all science graduates in the United States are foreigners.
3. Due to space constraints, after a brief discussion of the early evolution of education, this chapter focuses primarily on the United States during the twentieth century. Common elements are at work in other countries and where instructive, these will be briefly addressed.
4. As Mokyr notes, "the Industrial Revolution and the subsequent technological developments after 1760 led to many production processes that required a level of competence that was beyond the capability of the household" (2002, 140).
5. Smith is generally recognized as the father not only of modern economics, but also of the subfield of human capital.
6. If they received instruction, there was the danger that they be discontent with menial and demanding labor. Thus, humans, or at least their overwhelming majority, were viewed as mere means, to be maintained practically as beasts of burden and little more.
7. Most contemporary economic historians divide the industrial revolution into two major phases; the first saw skill-saving technological change, while the

second required more human capital as it played an increasing role in the manufacturing process (Becker, Hornung, and Woessman 2008, 4). Galor dates the first phase between 1760 and 1830 (2005, 206). Entry into the second phase varied across countries, not truly taking over until the late nineteenth or early twentieth century.
8. Much of the education that these factories provided, Mokyr points out, "was not technical in nature but social and moral... [workers] had to be taught to follow orders, to respect the space and property rights of others, and to be punctual, docile, and sober" (2002, 129).
9. Specifically, Smith advocated universal public schooling, mostly at government expense.
10. In the United States today, about 6 percent of GDP is spent on education. About 3 percent of GDP is spent on advertising, which many business interests also view as education.
11. As noted earlier, advances in education were not exclusively due to rising working class power. National interests have also been influential. For instance, educational expansion on the Continent was stimulated by state competition, especially in response to the industrial surging ahead of England. France established artillery schools in the 1720s and for training military officers, the École du Génie in the 1740s (Mokyr 2002, 46). The US educational reaction to Sputnik is another significant example.
12. However, Massachusetts, Rhode Island, Delaware, North Carolina, and Pennsylvania maintained requirements until 1860 that citizens pay taxes in order to be eligible to vote (Engerman and Sokoloff 2005, 898).
13. Data includes enrollment in both two-year and four-year institutions. Because they include enrollment in professional degree programs, the data between 1940 and 1967 are believed to be inflated. Before the 1940s, a baccalaureate degree was not necessary for entrance into professional degree programs (Goldin 1995).
14. The manner in which the increasing inequality of the last several decades influences public expenditure on public goods such as education was addressed by Christopher Lasch in his last major work, *The Revolt of the Elites* (1996). He noted that as economic elites take an ever-greater share of income and wealth, they tend to isolate themselves in social enclaves such as gated communities, exclusive clubs, and private schools. They tend to work in jobs, live in neighborhoods, and move in circles where they literally do not see those struggling to stay on their feet. Because of elites' disproportionate political power, this withdrawal from the wider society and from direct contact with the concerns of other citizens erodes support for public services on which those further down the economic ladder depend—services such as public schools, parks, transportation, public safety, and a clean environment. As secretary of Labor during the Clinton administration, Robert B. Reich has put it, "members see no reason why they should pay to support families outside the gates when members are getting everything they need inside" (Reich 2001, 199).

15. Between 1973 and 2005, the average income of the bottom 90 percent of households fell by 11 percent in real terms, in spite of the fact that worker productivity grew by over 80 percent. Thus the top 10 percent gained all of the benefits of this productivity gain (Baker 2007).
16. *The Chronicle of Higher Education* reports that about 28 percent of Americans over the age of 25 have graduated with four years of college (Richards 2011). However, although "the United States used to lead the world in the number of 25- to 34-year-olds with college degrees, as of 2010 it ranks 12th among 36 developed nations" (Lewin 2010).
17. State support for public universities has drastically declined. For instance, over the past 20 years, state support for the University of Virginia has declined from 26 percent to 7 percent of the operating budget; at the University of Michigan, from 48 to 17 percent; at Berkley, from 47 to 11 percent (De Vise 2011, A1). Over these same two decades, states have spent six times more on prisons than on higher education (Gopnik 2012, 73).
18. The rate of technological change is very difficult to measure across all of society since it can be many different things. For example, one could consider the number of research breakthroughs, or one could attempt to determine how many of those breakthroughs are incorporated into production processes. One crude way to measure technological change is Moore's Law (1965), which predicted (correctly) that the number of transistors that can be placed on an integrated circuit at a reasonable cost doubles roughly every two years. Another measure is the number of patents issued per capita. In the United States, this number is higher than ever before, at about 40 per 100,000 people per year, though this has fluctuated throughout the twentieth century as government research laboratories have played a larger role in R&D (Engerman and Wright 2006). However, the United States with 232,000 patents in 2010 now rates second behind Japan in worldwide patent applications, with China rapidly catching up with 195,000. In any event, a report by the RAND Corporation for the US Department of Labor predicts that the pace of technological change will continue to increase unabated at least in the near future (Karoly and Panis 2004, 105).
19. Some of the increase in the chance of an income drop is the result of increasing medical costs and higher levels of indebtedness, in addition to increased job insecurity. Such increases in insecurity have occurred broadly across all demographic groups (see Hacker et al. 2011,13; 16).
20. This may help account for the fact that job ads have started to appear that stipulate that the unemployed need not apply.
21. For a fuller discussion of these costs, see Wisman 2010.
22. Adolescent boys with unemployed parents are less likely to be confident about the future or to be independent and hopeful than are boys from families that "were not plagued with unemployment" (Storm 2003, 399). Neighborhoods with high unemployment present bad role models for children. Further, adolescents who attempt suicide are more likely to have an unemployed father than adolescents who do not attempt suicide (Storm 2003, 401).

23. For a review of retraining program evaluations through the 1990s, see Heckman, LaLonde, and Smith (1999).
24. The closest approximation in a wealthy country to an ELR program is the so-called Danish Flexicurity program. The understanding behind the Danish model is that whereas the unemployed are expected to seek jobs, the government is expected to ensure that adequate jobs exist and that workers are adequately trained for the available jobs. To the extent that adequate jobs do not exist, the government is expected to provide them. Denmark's model could be seen as a hybrid approach that blends Anglo-Saxon flexible labor markets with state-supplied unemployment benefits, hence the name "flexicurity" (Madsen 2006, 139). After World War II, Sweden embraced a right to work, but it was dismantled by neoliberal EU policy (Gould 1999).
25. Or, in technical terms, the program would operate so as to provide an infinitely wage-elastic demand for labor. The price of labor in the program would be set independent of market conditions, and the program would absorb all redundant labor at that price. That is, the market sets the quantity, but not the price.
26. Given Adam Smith's stature as the widely acknowledged father of modern economics, it is noteworthy that he suggested a living wage: "By necessaries I understand, not only the commodities which are indispensably necessary for the support of life, but whatever the custom of the country renders it indecent for a creditable people, even of the lowest order, to be without" (Smith 1981, 869–870). In the United States, the low level of the current minimum wage does not provide adequate income for a one-earner family to rise above the official poverty level. Although this state of affairs is widely lamented, it is alleged that the minimum wage cannot be raised without causing further unemployment. An ELR could circumvent this scenario. In a transitional period, those losing jobs as the minimum wage is slowly lifted would fall back into the buffer-employment sector where training would attempt to raise their skill level such that their productivity would make the higher wages profitable for their future employers. (Technically, the value of their marginal product would be raised to equal a higher wage level.)
27. An ELR program could also be crafted to provide part-time work for those who are able to find only part-time work in the private sector or who can only work part-time due to family responsibilities such as child or parental care.
28. Forecasting the long run costs of an ELR program would be difficult. It would entail estimating the value produced by ELR workers, the enhanced productivity of ELR-trained workers when they enter the non-ELR work sphere, the resulting increase in tax revenues and the decrease in current social costs resulting from unemployment. Unemployment benefits would disappear and social support cost would decline. Unemployment-generated health costs borne by Medicaid would be reduced, if not eliminated. Unemployment-generated crime would all but disappear.

29. Keynes argued that the "real problem, fundamental yet essentially simple [is] to provide employment for everyone." The goal is to create "a reduction of the unemployed to the sort of level we are experiencing in wartime, that is to say, an unemployed level of 120,000... or less than 1 percent unemployed at the present time (Keynes 1980, 267, 303).

30. Seemingly unknown to most Keynesians, Keynes advocated a permanent "on-the-spot" employment program (jobs that meet local needs and the qualifications of those in need of jobs) that would ensure full employment (1982).

31. Wray summarizes his idea of such a program as follows:

    Program wages and benefits will be federally funded; the wage will be periodically adjusted to reflect inflation and rising average labor productivity to prevent erosion of purchasing power and to allow workers to share in rising national productivity so that real living standards will rise. Program administration and operation will be decentralized. All state and local governments and registered not-for-profit organizations can propose projects submitted to a Federal office for final approval and funding. Project proposals will be evaluated on the following criteria: a) value to the community, b) value to the participants, c) likelihood of successful implementation of project, and d) contribution to preparing workers for nonprogram employment (2011, 17).

32. For a discussion of different ELR program designs, see Wray 2007.

33. In most countries, the state pays for most of the costs of higher education. Even in the United States, with its huge number of private universities and colleges, over two-thirds of all university and college students attend public institutions, although the decline in working class political power has meant that an increasing portion of the costs are borne by students and their families, most often as debt.

34. If it ever was, since it almost always left some portion of the workforce beyond those changing jobs ("frictional unemployment") unemployed. In any event, the inadequacy is glaring today. For instance, about 13 percent of US adults have not completed high school, and of these, about half are not employed even when the economy is in a boom phase (Wray and Forstater 2004, 268). The inadequacy of many high school graduates is evident in that, as The Education Trust reports, 23 percent of recent high school graduates do not get the minimum qualifying score on the military entrance exams (Theokas 2010, 1).

35. The momentum gave its most significant results in 1935 when the Works Progress Administration (WPA) was created by executive order. It offered government jobs to the unemployed on an unprecedented scale. Also coming forth in 1935 was the National Labor Relations Act that set up a process for collective bargaining and the Old-Age, Survivors, and Disability Insurance (Social Security Act). Three years later, the Fair Labor Standards Act established the first minimum wage in the United States.

36. Practically everyone agrees with Keynes that in providing the unemployed with unemployment insurance, nothing is created, and thus we "have nothing to show for it except more men on the dole" (1982, 149). In his memoir, Ronald Reagan praised the WPA as "one of the most productive elements" of Roosevelt's New Deal, among the largest jobs programs of all time (cited in Frank 2011, 10). Indeed, in 1971, as governor of California, he proposed a WPA sort of program to replace the state's welfare system. Created in 1933, the Civil Works Administration (CWA) found jobs for 4 million people within two months. Indeed, Jack Reagan, Ronald Reagan's father, found employment in the CWA. The WPA created three million jobs per year between 1933 and 1938.

37. When unemployment declines to a certain level—the so-called natural rate of unemployment, the people's government hits the breaks of restrictive monetary policy so that it not decline further, lest inflation result. In this manner, the unemployed are sacrificed for the greater good. Incidentally, Keynes noted the difficulty of achieving full employment by increasing aggregate demand, especially when approaching full employment (Keynes 1964 (1936, 118), and it was for this reason that he was especially concerned that structural unemployment "be treated as something to be handled forcibly and not something to be defeatist about" (Keynes 1980, 357). The response is public works and these must be targeted to those geographic areas—the "special" or "distressed" areas—where unemployment is highest. Keynes was more concerned with the deficient demand for labor than the inadequate demand for output. To achieve full employment, we are "more in need...of a rightly distributed demand than of greater aggregate demand" (Keynes 1982, 395).

38. Avner Offer notes that "the strongest determinant of low life satisfaction is absence of social connection, particularly unemployment and separation..." (2007, 7). In his new book, professor of psychiatry, James Gilligan claims that the inability to find a job is the foremost driver of shame and worthlessness (2011).

References

Acemoglu, Daron and James A. Robinson. 2000. "Why Did the West Extend the Franchise? Democracy, Inequality, and Growth in Historical Perspective." *The Quarterly Journal of Economics* November: 1167–1199.

Autor, David. 2010a. "The Polarization of Job Opportunities in the U.S. Labor Market." Center for American Progress and The Hamilton Project, Washington, DC.

———. 2010b. "U.S. Labor Market Challenges over the Longer Term." Paper prepared for the Federal Reserve Board of Governors, October 5.

Baker, Dean. 2007. "The Productivity to Paycheck Gap: What the Data Show." Center for Economic and Policy Research, Washington, DC.

Baum, Andrew, Raymond Fleming, and Diane M. Reddy. 1986. "Unemployment Stress: Loss of Control, Reactance and Learned Helplessness." *Social Science and Medicine* 5(11): 509–516.

Beadie, Nancy. 2008. "Education and the Creation of Capital: or What I have Learned from Following the Money." *History of Education Quarterly* 48(1): 1–29.

Becker, Sascha O., Erik Hornung, and Ludger Woessmann. 2009. "Catch Me If You Can: Education and Catch-Up in the Industrial Revolution." *Stirling Economics Discussion Paper* 2009–2019.

Black, S. E. and K. L. Sokoloff. 2006. "Long-Term Trends in Schooling: The Rise and Decline (?) of Public Education in the United States." In *Handbook of the Economics of Education*. Edited by E. A. Hanusek and F. Welch. Volume 1, Chapter 2.

Boyd, William. 1966. *The History of Western Education*. 8th Edition. New York: Barnes & Noble.

Braverman, Harry. 1974. *Labor and Monopoly Capital: The Degradation of Work in the Twentieth Century*. New York: Monthly Review Press.

Bureau of Labor Statistics. 2012. *The Employment Situation—February 2012*. News Release. Washington, DC: US Department of Labor.

Calvo-Armengol, Antoni. 2004. "The Effects of Social Networks on Employment and Inequality." *American Economic Review* 94(3), June: 426–454.

Carnevale, Anthony P. and Stephen J. Rose. 2011. "The Undereducated American." *Center on Education and the Workforce*. Washington, DC: Georgetown University.

Carpentier, Vincent. 2003. "Public Expenditure on Education and Economic Growth in the UK, 1833–2000." *History of Education* 32(1): 1–15.

College Board Advocacy & Policy Center. 2010. *Trends in Student Aid 2010*. The College Board, New York.

Congressional Budget Office. 2007. *Long-Term Unemployment*. Washington, DC: The Congress of the United States.

Darity, William Jr. and Arthur Goldsmith. 1993. "Unemployment, Social Psychology, and Unemployment Hysteresis." *Journal of Post Keynesian Economics* 16, Fall: 55–73.

———. 1996. "Social Psychology, Unemployment and Macroeconomics." *Journal of Economic Perspectives* 10(1), Winter: 121–140.

De Vise, Daniel. 2011. "Investment in Public's Ivory Towers is Eroding." *Washington Post*, December 27: A1, A10.

Diamond, Jared. 2005. *Collapse: How Societies Choose to Fail or Succeed*. New York: Viking Penguin.

Duhigg, Charles and Keith Bradsher. 2012. "How the U.S. Lost Out on iPhone Work." *New York Times*, January 21. http://www.nytimes.com/2012/01/22/business/apple-america-and-a-squeezed-middle-class.html?pagewanted=all. Accessed January 21, 2012.

Easterlin, Richard A. 1981. "Why Isn't the Whole World Developed?" *Journal of Economic History* XLI: 1–19.

Engerman, Stanley L. and Gavin Wright. 2006. "Science and Technology." In *Historical Statistics of the United States*. Cambridge: Cambridge University Press: 3-415–3-418.

Engerman, Stanley L. and Kenneth L. Sokoloff. 1994. "Factor Endowments, Institutions, and Differential Paths of Growth among New World Economies: A

View From Economic Historians of the United States." Historical Paper No. 66. National Bureau of Economic Research.

———. 2005. "Colonialism, Inequality, and Long-Run Paths of Development." Working Paper w11057. National Bureau of Economic Research.

Farber, Henry S. 1998. "Employment Insecurity: The Decline in Worker-Firm Attachment in the United States." CEPS Working Paper No. 172.

———. 2005. "What Do We Know about Job Loss in the United States? Evidence from the Displaced Workers Survey, 1984–2004." *Economic Perspectives* 2Q: 13–28.

———. 2007. "Is the Company Man an Anachronism? Trends in Long-Term Employment in the U.S., 1973–2006." Working Paper #518, Industrial Relations Section, Princeton University.

———. 2008. "Shorter Schrift: The Decline of the Worker-Firm Attachment in the United States." In *Risky Business Political and Economic Consequences of Employment Insecurity* (SSRC Series on the Privatization of Risk. New York: Columbia University Press.

———. 2011. "Job Loss in the Great Recession: Historical Perspective from the Displaced Workers Survey, 1984–2010." Working Paper #564, Industrial Relations Section, Princeton University.

Feldstein, Martin. 1978. "The Private and Social Costs of Unemployment." *The American Economic Review* 68(2): 155–158.

Frank, Thomas. 2011. "Easy Chair: More Government, Please." *Harper's Magazine* December: 8–12.

Friedman, Milton. 1962. *Capitalism and Freedom*. Chicago: University of Chicago Press.

Galor, Oded. 2005. "From Stagnation to Growth: Unified Growth Theory." In *Handbook of Economic Growth*. Vol 1A. Edited by Philippe Aghion and Steven N. Durlauf. Amsterdam and New York: Elsevier.

Gilligan, James. 2011. *Why Some Politicians Are More Dangerous Than Others*. New York: Polity Books.

Goldin, Claudia. 1995. "Education." In *Historical Statistics of the United States*. Millennial Edition Online. US Census Bureau. Washington, DC.

———. 1998. "America's Graduation from High School: The Evolution and Spread of Secondary Schooling in the Twentieth Century." *The Journal of Economic History* 58(2): 345–374.

Goldin, Claudia and Lawrence F. Katz. 1998. "The Origins of Technology-Skill Complementarity." *The Quarterly Journal of Economics* 113(3): 693–732.

———. 1999. "Human Capital and Social Capital: The Rise of Secondary Schooling in America, 1910–1940." *Journal of Interdisciplinary History* 29(4), "Patterns of Social Capital: Stability and Change in Comparative Perspective: Part II": 683–723.

———. 2007. "Long-Run Changes in the Wage Structure: Narrowing, Widening, Polarizing." *Brookings Papers on Economic Activity* 2: 135–165.

———. 2008. *The Race between Education and Technology*. Cambridge, MA: Harvard University Press.

Gopnik, Adam. 2012. "The Caging of America." *The New Yorker* January 30: 72–77.
Gosselin, Peter. 2008. *High Wire: The Precarious Financial Lives of American Families*. Philadelphia: Basic Books.
Gould, Arthur. 1999. "The Erosion of the Welfare State: Swedish Social Policy and the EU." *Journal of European Social Policy* 9(2): 165–174.
The Hamilton Project. 2011. http://www.hamiltonproject.org. The Brookings Institution, Washington, DC. Accessed December 21, 2011.
Hacker, Jacob S. 2006. *The Great Risk Shift: The Assault on American Jobs, Families, Health Care, and Retirement and How You Can Fight Back*. Oxford: Oxford University Press.
Hacker, Jacob S. et al. 2011. *Economic Insecurity and the Great Recession: Findings from the Economic Security Index*. New Haven, Connecticut: Institution for Social and Policy Studies.
Heckman, James J., Robert J. LaLonde, and Jeffrey A. Smith. 2009. *The Economics and Econometrics of Active Labor Market Programs*. Vol. 3A. In *Handbook of Labor Economics*. Edited by Orley Ashenfelter and David Card, 1865–2095. Amsterdam and New York: Elsevier.
Juhn, Chinhui and Simon Potter. 2006. "Changes in Labor Force Participation in the United States." *Journal of Economic Perspectives* 20(3): 27–46.
Karoly, Lynn A. and Constantijn W. A. Panis. 2004. "The 21st Century at Work." Prepared for the US Department of Labor, RAND Corporation.
Kelvin, Peter and Joanna E. Jarrett. 1985. *Unemployment: Its Social Psychological Effects*. Cambridge: Cambridge University Press.
Key, Scott. 1996. "Economics or Education: The Establishment of American Land-Grant Universities." *The Journal of Higher Education* 67(2): 196–220.
Keynes, John Maynard. 1936. *The General Theory of Employment, Interest, and Money*. New York: Harcourt-Brace and World, 1964.
———. 1980. *Activities 1940–46. Shaping the Post-War World: Employment and Commodities*. Vol. XXVII of *Collected Works*. Edited by D. Moggridge. London: Macmillan.
———. 1982. *Activities 1931–39. World Crises and Policies in Britain and America*. Vol. XXI of *Collected Works*. Edited by D. Moggridge. London: Macmillan.
Kuznets, Simon. 1955. "Economic Growth and Income Inequality." *American Economic Review* 45(March): 1–28.
Lasch, Christopher. 1995. *The Revolt of the Elites: and the Betrayal of Democracy*. New York: W. W. Norton.
Lewin, Tamar. 2010. "Once a Leader, U.S. Lags in College Degrees." *New York Times* July 23: A11.
Madsen, Per Kongshøj. 2006. "Labour Market Flexibility and Social Protection in European Welfare States: Contrasts and Similarities." *Australian Bulletin of Labour* 32(2): 139–160.
Mandeville, Bernard. 1924. *The Fable of the Bees*. Oxford: Oxford University Press.
Marshall, Alfred. 1920. *Principles of Economics*. London: Macmillan.

Mishel, Lawrence and Heidi Shierholz. March 2011. "The Sad but True Story of Wages in America." Issue Brief #297, Economic Policy Institute, Washington, DC.

Mitchell, William and L. Randall Wray. 2005. "Full Employment through Job Guarantee: A Response to Critics." Working Paper No. 39. Center for Full Employment and Price Stability.

Mokyr, Joel. 2002. *The Gifts of Athena: Historical Origins of the Knowledge Economy.* Princeton: Princeton University Press.

Moore, Gordon E. 1965. "Cramming More Components Onto Integrated Circuits." *Electronics* April 18: 4–8.

Muller, Jerry Z. *The Mind and the Market: Capitalism in Modern European Thought.* New York: Alfred A. Knopf.

National Center for Education Statistics. 1993. "120 Years of American Education: A Statistical Portrait." Edited by Thomas D. Snyder. US Department of Education, Washington DC.

———. 2010. "Digest of Education Statistics: 2010." http://nces.ed.gov/programs/digest/d10/. Accessed June 15, 2011.

———. 2011. "Trends in Attainment among Student Populations at Increased Risk of Noncompletion: Selected Years, 1989–90 to 2008–09." US Department of Education, Washington, DC.

Offer, Avner. 2007. "The Challenge of Affluence." Interview, *Challenge* 50(2), March/April: 6–19.

Organization for Economic Cooperation and Development. 2011. *Divided We Stand: Why Inequality Keeps Rising*, OECD Publishing. http://dx.doi.org/10.1787/9789264119536-en.

———. 2011. "Education at a Glance 2011: OECD Indicators." OECD Publishing. http://dx.doi.org/10.1787/eag-2011-en.

Price, Richard H., Michelle van Ryn, and Amiram D. Vinokur. 1992. "Impact of a Preventive Job Search Intervention on the Likelihood of Depression among the Unemployed." *Journal of Health and Social Behavior* 33(2): 158–167.

Reardon, S. F. 2011. "The Widening Socioeconomic Status Achievement Gap: New Evidence and Possible Explanations." In *Whither Opportunity? Rising Inequality and the Uncertain Life Chances of Low-Income Children.* Edited by Richard Murnane and Greg Duncan. New York: Russell Sage Foundation.

Reich, Robert B. 2001. *The Future of Success.* New York: Alfred A. Knopf.

Richards, Alex. 2011. "Census Data Show Rise in College Degrees, but also in Racial Gaps in Education." *The Chronicle of Higher Education* January 23. http://chronicle.com/article/Census-Data-Reveal-Rise-in/126026/. Accessed December 26, 2011.

Schumpeter, Joseph. 1962. *Capitalism, Socialism, and Democracy.* 3rd Edition. New York: Harper Perennial.

Sen, Amartya. 1997. "Inequality, Unemployment and Contemporary Europe." *International Labour Review* 136(2): 155–172.

Smith, Adam. 1981 (1776). *An Inquiry into the Nature and Causes of the Wealth of Nations.* Vols. I and II. Indianapolis: Liberty Classics.

Storm, Sara. 2003. "Unemployment and Families: A Review of Research." *The Social Science Review* 77(3): 399–401.
Theokas, Christina. 2010. "Shut out of the Military: Today's High School Education Doesn't Mean You're Ready for Today's Army." The Education Trust, Washington, DC.
US Census Bureau. 2006. "Table Bc258–264." *Historical Statistics of the United States*. Millenial Edition Online. Washington, DC.
———. 2011. *Business Dynamics Statistics*. Washington, DC.
US Department of Education. 1999. *College for All? Is there Too Much Emphasis on Getting a 4-year College Degree?* National Library of Education, Washington, DC.
Urban, Wayne J. and Jennings L. Wagoner Jr. 2004. *American Education: A History*. 3rd Edition. New York: The McGraw-Hill Companies.
Viner, Jacob. 1968. "Man's Economic Status." In *Man Versus Society in Eighteenth Century Britain*. Edited by J. Clifford. Cambridge: Cambridge University Press, 23–53.
Washington Post. 2010. "Military: Recruits Failing Army Entrance Exam." December 22: A2.
Whoriskey, Peter. 2012. "Wanted: Skilled Factory Workers," *Washington Post* February 20: A1, A14.
Willis, Jonathan L. and Julie Wroblewski. 2007. "What Happened to the Gains from Strong Productivity Growth?" *Economic Review* Q1: 5–23.
Winkelman, L. and R. Winkelman. 1998. "Why Are the Unemployed so Unhappy? Evidence from Panel Data." *Economica* 65(257): 1–15.
Wisman, Jon D. 2010. "The Moral Imperative and Social Rationality of Government-Guaranteed Employment and Reskilling." *Review of Social Economy* 68(1), March: 35–67.
Wray, Randall L. 1999. "Public Service Employment—Assured Jobs Program: Further Considerations." *Journal of Economic Issues* 33(2), June: 483–490.
———. 2007. "The Employer of Last Resort Programme: Could It Work for Developing Countries?" *Economic and Labour Market Papers*. Geneva: International Labor Office, August: 43.
———. 2011. "Lessons We Should Have Learned from the Global Financial Crisis but Didn't." Levy Economics Institute, Working Paper 681, August.
Wray, Randall L. and Mathew Forstater. 2004. "Full Employment and Social Justice." In *The Institutionalist Tradition in Labor Economics*. Edited by Dell P. Champlin and Janet T. Knoedler, 253–272. New York: M. E. Sharpe.

CHAPTER 2

Wage Policies and Funding Strategies for Job Guarantee Programs

Philip Harvey

As the contributions to this volume illustrate, most of the scholarly literature produced in recent years on the subject of job guarantees has been produced by people working within the Keynesian/post-Keynesian theoretical tradition. Within this theoretical framework, a job guarantee is seen as an economic measure that promises to remedy a critical weakness in conventional Keynesian aggregate demand management policies. That weakness is the inability of those policies to achieve full employment—and the benefits associated with it—without sacrificing price stability.

There is an older tradition, though, which views the job guarantee idea from a somewhat different perspective. I shall refer to this as the social welfare/right-to-work tradition. From the perspective of this tradition, a job guarantee is seen as a social welfare measure whose purpose is to secure the right to work.[1]

Does this difference in perspective matter? In this chapter I argue that it doesn't have to, but only if the distinct contributions of the Keynesian/post-Keynesian and social welfare/right-to-work traditions to the development of the job guarantee idea are recognized and their disparate contributions to the design of job guarantee programs are respected. The principle contribution of the social welfare/right-to-work tradition lies in its conceptualization of the normative goals a job guarantee should serve and its specification of the requirements a job guarantee would have to satisfy to achieve those goals. The principle contribution of the Keynesian/post-Keynesian theoretical tradition lies in its sophisticated analysis of the ways in which a job guarantee program would affect the functioning of a market economy, and its consequent ability to inform decisions concerning the optimal design of job guarantee initiatives.

There is no necessary conflict or contradiction between the contributions that each of these traditions can make to the design of effective job guarantee initiatives. Each of the traditions enhances the value of the other. Still, it is necessary for representatives of these two traditions to communicate with and learn from one another in order to realize these benefits. It is the purpose of this chapter to take a step in that direction with a discussion of two features commonly found in post-Keynesian job guarantee proposals that I believe would benefit from input provided by the social welfare/right-to-work tradition. The first of these two features is the proposal that a job guarantee program should pay all participants a uniform basic wage set at or close to the statutory minimum wage. The second feature is the linkage of the job guarantee idea with proposals to reform the fiscal policy regime of market economies along neochartalist lines.

It is important to emphasize once again that my criticism of these two features of post-Keynesian job guarantee proposals is not intended to cast doubt on the importance of the post-Keynesian contribution to the job guarantee idea. My goal is simply to challenge post-Keynesian job-guarantee advocates to reconsider these two features of their proposals in light of the criticisms expressed in this chapter and, to the extent they reject those criticisms, to explain their views on these matters more fully than they have in the past.

THE SOCIAL WELFARE/RIGHT-TO-WORK TRADITION

The claim that access to work is a human right that governments have a duty to secure (with direct job creation if necessary) dates back to the French revolution. Support for the idea has been intermittent since then and has assumed a variety of forms—frequently developed independently of one another (Harvey 1998; Siegel 1994). The modern history of the idea can be traced to proposals developed by the cabinet-level Committee on Economic Security (CES) that President Roosevelt appointed in June 1934 to develop a comprehensive set of legislative proposals to address the economic security needs of the American people (Roosevelt 1934). Chaired by secretary of

Labor Frances Perkins,[2] the CES described the goal of its mandate in the following terms:

> The one almost all-embracing measure of security is an assured income. A program of economic security, as we vision it, must have as its primary aim the assurance of an adequate income to each human being in childhood, youth, middle age, or old age—in sickness or in health. It must provide safeguards against all of the hazards leading to destitution and dependency. (Committee on Economic Security 1935)

The CES proposed a two-legged social welfare strategy to realize this goal. First the federal government should provide everyone who is expected to be self-supporting with "employment assurance" by (a) doing what it could to stimulate private employment, and (b) providing publicly funded jobs for any workers the private sector is unable to employ. Furthermore, the CES made it clear that it was proposing this strategy for use in "normal times" as well as during economic contractions.

> Since most people must live by work, the first objective in a program of economic security must be maximum employment. As the major contribution of the Federal Government in providing a safeguard against unemployment we suggest employment assurance—the stimulation of private employment and the provision of public employment for those able-bodied workers whom industry cannot employ at a given time. Public-work programs are most necessary in periods of severe depression, but may be needed in normal times, as well, to help meet the problems of stranded communities and overmanned or declining industries. (Committee on Economic Security 1935)

The second leg of the CES strategy consisted of the establishment of non-stigmatizing income assistance programs for people who were either unable or not expected to be self-supporting.

All of the CES's published recommendations were implemented by Congress, to some degree or another, in the first half of 1935.[3] The Social Security Act of 1935 was the vehicle used to implement the income security leg of the CES strategy,[4] while the employment assurance leg was implemented by an executive order establishing the Works Progress Administration (WPA) accompanied by a legislated budget authorization to pay for the program.

Unfortunately, President Roosevelt did not propose that the WPA be funded at the level required to achieve the CES's goal of providing "employment assurance" to all workers. Instead, he requested only enough funding to offer work to those among the unemployed who qualified as "needy." In accord with this mandate, the WPA, along with the New Deal's other direct job creation programs, provided work for an average of about a third of the nation's unemployed during the balance of the 1930s.

The effectiveness of this intervention has been obscured by the unemployment statistics normally cited for the New Deal period. These statistics count workers employed in the New Deal's direct job creation programs as unemployed. In contrast, workers employed by private contractors on projects funded by the Public Works Administration (PWA) are counted as employed, even though their employment was just as dependent on public funding as that of WPA workers. If workers employed in direct job-creation programs are counted as employed (as they are in unemployment statistics today), the effectiveness of the WPA is readily apparent, with the nation's unemployment rate dropping from 20.3 percent to 10.8 percent during the first full year of WPA operations—rather than to the 17.0 percent level commonly reported.

Figure 2.1 shows both the commonly reported and the actual unemployment rate in the United States from 1933 through 1939—with the difference between the two time series depending on nothing more than whether persons employed in the New Deal's direct job creation programs are counted as unemployed or employed. It also should be noted, of course, that the decline in private sector unemployment portrayed by the top line in figure 2.1 is also at least partly attributable to the federal government's deficit spending on these programs. Evidence of this latter effect can be seen in the upward spike in unemployment that occurred in 1937 when President Roosevelt cut back on federal government spending—including spending on direct job creation programs—in an ill-conceived attempt to balance the federal budget. Thus, the overall job creation effect of the New Deal's direct job creation programs includes part of the decline shown in the top

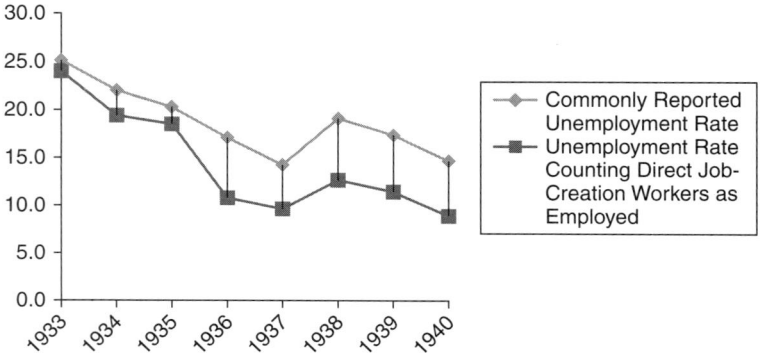

Figure 2.1 US unemployment rate 1933–1940.

line of figure 2.1 as well as the decline measured by the difference between the two lines.

During World War II, New Deal progressives made a concerted effort to promote the social welfare entitlements the CES's recommendations were designed to secure as a new category of human rights that governments had a duty to strive to secure for all members of society. President Roosevelt himself was principally responsible for this initiative, beginning with his 1941 "Four Freedoms" speech and culminating in his 1944 "Second Bill of Rights" speech (Roosevelt 1941, vol. 9, 663–678; 1950, vol. 13, 40–41). Embraced by progressives throughout the world, the expanded human rights vision Roosevelt promoted achieved formal recognition following the end of the war in the Universal Declaration of Human Rights—the text of which was drafted by a United Nation's committee chaired by Eleanor Roosevelt, the president's widow and tribune of New Deal values (United Nations 1948; Glendon 2001).

The right to work recognized in the Universal Declaration has three primary aspects. The *quantitative* aspect requires that there be enough paid jobs available in an economy to provide freely chosen employment for everyone who wants it. The *distributive* aspect requires that equal employment opportunity be guaranteed to all members of society. The *qualitative* aspect requires that these jobs pay fair wages capable of supporting a dignified existence for the worker and the worker's family (with social supplementation when needed) and that the jobs also satisfy minimum standards of decency in terms of benefits, hours of work, working conditions, workplace governance, protection from unfair treatment, and opportunities for individual development (Harvey 2007).[5]

At the same time the New Deal's expanded Human Rights vision was taking shape in the early 1940s, progressive reformers also embraced full employment as an economic policy goal. Although never defined authoritatively, as the right to work was in the Universal Declaration, the achievement of full employment was generally viewed at that time as virtually synonymous with securing the right to work. This was plainly the understanding of full employment that the founders of the United Nations had in mind when they included its promotion as one of the purposes (another being the realization of human rights) that all members of the organization "pledge themselves to take joint and separate action in co-operation with the Organization" to achieve (United Nations 1945, arts. 55 and 56). It also is plainly what people working in the social welfare/right-to-work tradition have in mind when they advocate the achievement of full employment, and it remains an enduring goal among progressive full-employment advocates today (Goldberg, Harvey, and Ginsburg 2007).

The contribution that people working in the Keynesian/post-Keynesian tradition can make to the achievement of the normative goals articulated by people working in the social welfare/right-to-work tradition should be obvious from this account. They can help devise economic policies that would help achieve full employment defined as it was defined in the 1940s. President Roosevelt's misguided decisions regarding the implementation of the CES's employment assurance proposal show that people who want to secure the right to work don't necessarily understand how to go about achieving the goal. The federal government spent 2.2 percent of GDP on direct job creation programs in 1936. If it had increased that spending to 5.3 percent (the equivalent of about $750 billion in 2009) the nation's unemployment rate could have been reduced from over 20 percent to 2 percent by 1936, and because of the multiplier effect of that additional spending, the private sector's full recovery from the Great Depression would have been accelerated by several years.

The contribution that people working in the social welfare/right-to-work tradition can make to their counterparts working in the Keynesian/post-Keynesian tradition also should be obvious. They can help insure that normative considerations are not given short shrift in the work of people who develop and/or advocate full-employment policies. It is the contention of this chapter that designing job guarantee programs that are both normatively acceptable and economically effective requires input from both the social welfare/right-to-work and the Keynesian/post-Keynesian traditions.

WHAT WAGES SHOULD A JOB GUARANTEE PROGRAM PAY?

The economists principally responsible for the development of the post-Keynesian version of the job guarantee idea have consistently proposed that the job guarantee program's wage policy should have the following three characteristics:

(1) Everyone hired pursuant to the job guarantee should be paid the same hourly wage,
(2) This wage rate should be set at or near the statutory minimum of the jurisdiction in which the job guarantee is offered, and
(3) This guaranteed wage rate should remain fixed in the short run, with adjustments being made only occasionally.

(Minsky 1986, 308; Mitchell and Watts 1997, 441–442; Mosler 1997–1998, 177–179; Wray 1998, 540–541; Wray 2012, 9–10; Center of Full Employment and Equity n.d.)

Wray (1999, 483–484) has stated that the program also should provide "full medical coverage and free child care," sick leave and vacation time after a minimum service requirement is met, and additional benefits over time, with the goal in mind of raising the level of compensation provided by the program "sufficiently so that anyone working full time in [the program] would be able to obtain a standard of living above a reasonably defined poverty threshold." Borrowing from Wray, I shall refer to a wage policy embodying these features as the "uniform basic wage" policy, Wray (2012, 10).

Post-Keynesian advocates of the uniform basic wage policy propose the establishment of a jobs program that would offer employment to any and all job seekers willing to work for the uniform basic wage. Because demand for labor at this wage would be infinitely elastic, it would function as a de facto minimum wage in the economy—along with any benefits provided with the wage. Because the program wage rate would remain fixed over the short run, the supply of labor available to private sector employers also would be infinitely elastic, up to the full employment level, at a wage level slightly above that paid by the job guarantee program. This latter effect would cause the program's labor force to perform a buffer stock function that would stabilize the price of labor in the private sector. Finally, demand-pull inflation also would be restrained by the automatic stabilization effect of the program's inherent tendency to shrink as unemployment rates fall. With all of these effects in mind, post-Keynesian advocates of the job guarantee strategy argue that it would achieve full employment (in the sense that everyone willing to work for the uniform basic wage would be guaranteed employment) without sacrificing price stability.

In contrast to this model, the wage policy I have proposed for a job-guarantee program is intended to secure all aspects of the right to work while still taking into account the macroeconomic considerations that inform the uniform basic wage policy. With that goal in mind, I have argued that a job guarantee program should offer unemployed workers jobs that are comparable in both pay and responsibility to those occupied by similarly qualified and experienced workers in the regular labor market—but with two caveats. The first caveat is that supplemental income-assistance benefits and/or job training should be provided to workers whose level of skill and experience does not qualify them for a good enough job to earn an adequate standard of living (whether they are employed in the job guarantee program or through the regular labor market). The second caveat is that persons filling managerial and professional positions in the program should be offered wages commensurate with public sector wage scales for positions of the type in question, rather than with private sector wage scales (Harvey 1989, 30–38; Harvey 2011a, 11, 15–16). As for benefits, I have argued that program participants should be provided (1) the same health insurance benefits as other public sector employees (the equivalent of which will soon become available to all workers in the United States under the terms of health insurance reform legislation enacted in 2010), (2) the same paid holiday, vacation, and sick leave benefits as other public sector employees, (3) child care on a sliding fee basis in child care centers operated as a project of the job guarantee program for the benefit of workers employed outside the program as well as program employees, and (4) access to the same income-enhancing social welfare benefits as other workers in the economy (with adjustments to the extent necessary to insure that all workers, both inside and outside the program, receive a real income that conforms to the human rights standards set forth in articles 22–25 of the Universal Declaration of Human Rights). In the United States, the latter would include the Earned Income Tax Credit (EITC), Supplemental Nutritional Assistance Program (SNAP) benefits (still generally described as Food Stamps), and section 8 Housing Choice vouchers (which would be offered on an entitlement basis, like EITC and SNAP benefits, to all households) (Harvey 2011a, 16).

This wage policy obviously differs from the uniform basic wage policy, but there is one characteristic of the latter that could be included in my proposal—and should be included if it proved necessary to achieve price stability. That is, the job program's wage scale could be fixed in the short run to enhance the program's buffer stock effect. The reason I take the view that this may or may not be necessary is because of two other anti-inflationary features of the job guarantee strategy. First, depending on the funding mechanism used to pay for a job guarantee program (see below), and the additional tax revenues and savings it would generate (Harvey 1995; 2006; 2011b, 14–17), the program's fiscal impact could be neutral or negative at the top of the business cycle, thereby eliminating demand-pull inflationary pressures. Second, the natural targeting of the strategy's job creation effect on communities and population groups with higher than average unemployment rates would diminish its competitive impact on market wage rates, thereby restraining cost-push inflationary pressures. If the program's buffer stock effect needed to be reinforced to provide adequate inflation control, the program's wage scale could be held constant, but it might not be necessary (Harvey 2006, 130–131 n. 6).

From the perspective of the social welfare/right-to-work theoretical tradition, the problem with the uniform basic wage policy is that the type of full employment it would achieve is a crabbed version that would not realize the full employment goal the UN Charter obligates its members to strive to achieve. As noted above, the conception of full employment that informed the drafters and ratifiers of the Charter (and which still animates advocates of full employment outside the economics profession today) is more or less synonymous with securing the right to work.

The income security rights recognized in the Universal Declaration are intended to do more than prevent destitution. They are intended to secure for all persons an income sufficient to secure their dignity and the free development of their personhood (United Nations 1948, art. 22). For the right to work to be secured, all workers must have access to jobs that are consistent with that goal, which means they must be paid fair wages consistent with their skills and experience. The type of full employment achieved by a job creation program that paid a uniform basic wage would fall short of that goal—even if it did guarantee that program participants could earn an income above a reasonable poverty threshold.

Workers whose skills and experience qualify them for no more than a minimum wage job are much more likely to suffer unemployment than other workers, but that doesn't mean they are representative of unemployed workers in general or that their need for work is greater than that of other unemployed workers. Between December 2000 and December 2011, the real earnings of Unemployment Insurance (UI) recipients before they lost their jobs averaged about twice what they could earn in a job guarantee program that paid the uniform basic wage originally proposed by Mosler (1997–1998, 168) and Wray (1998, 540).[6] Unemployed workers who do not qualify for UI benefits probably have fewer skills and less experience, on average, than workers who do qualify for benefits. In estimating the budgeted cost of a job guarantee program designed to secure the right to work, I have generally assumed that the average hourly wage for which this group of unemployed workers could qualify is equal to that of employed part-time workers (Harvey 2011a, 11). Based on this assumption, unemployed workers who do not qualify for UI benefits probably have sufficient skills and experience to qualify for jobs in the private sector that pay a third higher, on average, than the uniform basic wage proposed by Mosler and Wray.[7]

What these figures demonstrate is that the vast majority of unemployed workers would not be offered jobs commensurate with their earning capacity in a job guarantee program that paid a uniform basic wage. Nor can this shortcoming be remedied by increasing the uniform basic wage. As advocates of the policy are quick to note, the program's uniform basic wage would function in practice as a de facto minimum wage; and that being the case, increasing it would cause upward adjustments in the wages of other workers as employers sought to maintain differentials in their wage structure. Existing wage differentials might shrink, but they would not disappear. The great majority of unemployed workers would still not be able to find work commensurate with their qualifications.

The question that has to be asked in light of this is whether post-Keynesian advocates of the uniform basic wage policy have good reasons to prefer it over a wage policy designed to secure the right to work. This is hard to determine, since they have provided little guidance as to the reasons for their preference. Wray (2012, 10) has offered the following explanation:

> The advantage of the uniform basic wage is that it would limit competition with other employers as workers could be attracted out of the [job guarantee] program by paying a wage slightly above the program's wage. Obviously, higher skilled workers and those with higher educational attainment will be hired first. In an economic boom, employers will lower hiring standards to pull lower-skilled workers out of the program. The residual pool of workers in the program provides a buffer stock of employable labor, helping to reduce pressures on wages—and as wages for high skilled workers are bid up, the buffer stock becomes ever more desirable as a source of cheaper labor.

What Wray says is certainly true. The question is whether there is any need for a job guarantee program to adopt the uniform basic wage policy to achieve the goals he identifies. First, beyond insuring that employers are able to attract the workers they need from the ranks of the unemployed, there is no readily apparent reason why it would be desirable to limit labor market competition between the job guarantee program and other employers.

Nor is there any reason to believe that the payment of a uniform basic wage is necessary to insure private sector access to the program labor pool. Two separate mechanisms would insure private sector employers the access they need to the program's labor force. First, assuming the program wage scale mimicked that found in the regular labor market, employers should be able to hire workers away from the program by offering them marginally better wages, benefits, or working conditions. If this mechanism provided employers adequate access to minimum wage workers employed in the program, why wouldn't it be sufficient to give them adequate access to better qualified workers employed in the program? Second, a job guarantee program could require its employees to accept suitable job offers by private employers or forfeit their program eligibility—just as UI recipients are required to accept suitable job offers or lose their UI eligibility. If post-Keynesian job guarantee advocates believe that these mechanisms would be inadequate to insure private employers access to needed workers, they should explain why.

It also is unclear why the payment of a uniform basic wage would be necessary for the program's buffer stock function to work. As with the goal of insuring employer access to the program's labor force, the key to the success of this function is the relative constancy of the program's wage scale, not the fact that all program workers are paid the same wage or that the program wage is set at or near the lawful minimum. If the program wage scale mimics that found in the regular labor market but remains fixed over the short run, it will inhibit wage inflation for all grades of labor for which adequate supplies exist in the program relative to private sector labor demand. Once again, if post-Keynesian job guarantee advocates disagree, they should explain why.

In short, the justification offered for the uniform basic wage policy is unpersuasive. The functions ascribed to this policy would be performed just as well by the alternative policy I have proposed with an eye to securing the right to work. Moreover, the latter policy also would generate a range of other benefits that the uniform basic wage policy would not.

First, a program that employed workers of varying skill levels and assigned them fairly compensated work based on their level of skill could produce a wider range of better quality goods and services than a program that employed only persons willing to accept minimum wage work. In short, it would enrich society by more fully utilizing its labor resources.

Second, a program that employed and fairly compensated unemployed workers in accord with their skills and experience could also furnish much better job training opportunities to its work force—opportunities that combined instruction with on-the-job training—and which culminated in actual employment in jobs that utilize the workers' newly acquired skills.

Third, a program that assigned, compensated, and evaluated workers based on their qualifications would provide far better information to prospective private sector employers concerning the workers' qualifications and performance. I have proposed that all persons seeking employment in the job guarantee program should be required to register with the state employment service. The employment service would counsel them concerning their eligibility to participate in the program and evaluate their qualifications for different types of jobs both in and outside the program (Harvey 2011b, 22–23). While employed in the program they would continue to be listed as available for employment by the employment service, and information concerning the nature of their job assignment would be included in the data the employment service made available to prospective employers. With state employment services positioned in this way to provide prospective employers reliable information about the qualifications of all persons working in the job guarantee program, employers would have a much stronger incentive than they currently do to list their job openings with the employment service and work with it in seeking suitable candidates for employment. This would finally fulfill another goal articulated in the CES's 1935 report: "Above all, the employment offices should strive to become genuine clearing houses for all labor, at which all unemployed workers will be registered and to which employers will naturally turn when seeking employees" (Committee on Economic Security 1935).

Fourth, a program that provided jobs and compensation to unemployed workers commensurate with their qualifications could be administered in a wider variety of ways. As I have explained elsewhere, such a program could adopt the New Deal model in which program workers are employed on freestanding projects administered by the program separately from the regular operations of government. Alternatively, program employees could be integrated into the regular public sector workforce, the model adopted by the Public Service Employment program that operated during the 1970s under the Comprehensive Employment and Training Act (CETA). Finally, the program could furnish not-for-profit agencies with workers paid in part or in whole by the government—a model exemplified by the College Work Study program in the United States (Harvey 2011a, 18–21), A job guarantee program that paid a uniform basic wage would have more limited administrative choices because of the difficulties in providing work for an undifferentiated mass of minimum wage workers.

Finally, a program that embodied these characteristics would be far less likely to stigmatize the workers it employed than a program that treated its entire workforce as though it lacked the skills and experience to do anything but unskilled labor. A program that stigmatized its workforce would not only fail to secure their right to work; it also would have trouble garnering public support. In other words, creating a job program that does not stigmatize its workforce is important for both normative and practical reasons.

All these considerations argue strongly in favor of rejecting the uniform basic wage policy in favor of its human-rights-based alternative.

How Should a Job Guarantee Program Be Funded?

Proposals to fund a job guarantee program naturally give rise to concerns about the cost of such an initiative. Post-Keynesian supporters of the job guarantee idea have responded to these concerns by challenging the conventional view that the fiscal capacity of governments is limited by their ability to raise taxes and borrow money. This claim goes beyond the familiar Keynesian point that deficit spending by government is necessary to maintain adequate levels of aggregate demand in a market economy. It involves an embrace of the less familiar argument that currency-issuing governments should base their spending, taxing, and borrowing decisions on their macroeconomic effects rather than on the false belief that government spending must be financed with taxes or borrowing. This does not mean that the spending decisions of currency-issuing governments should be viewed as unconstrained, only that the constraints on their spending are political and macroeconomic rather than budgetary (Mosler 1997–1998; Wray 1999; Mitchell and Wray 2005; Mitchell and Watts 2005).

From this perspective, the proper question to ask about the funding of a job guarantee program is not how a government would pay for it. A currency-issuing government can always do so by writing checks, and it can write those checks whether it first collects the requisite funds to cover the spending or simply credits the accounts on which the checks are drawn with fiat (i.e., "modern") money. The important question to ask is what the macroeconomic effects would be of establishing and paying for a job guarantee program with or without counterbalancing increases in tax collections or government borrowing.

The macroeconomic effect of most concern to post-Keynesian advocates of the job guarantee idea is the possibility that spending on a job guarantee program, combined with the program's tightening of labor market conditions, would cause inflation rates to rise. This is why the buffer stock effect of a job guarantee program is so important in their view. By creating a pool of qualified labor available for hire at a fixed wage level (as explained above), they argue that a job guarantee program could achieve full employment without causing the wage inflation that normally occurs when labor markets tighten; and this, in turn, would constrain upward pressure on costs of production and product prices. For this reason, they believe the cost of the program should not concern policy makers. If the aggregate level of deficit spending by the government (not just deficit spending on the job guarantee program) induced enough private sector growth that employment levels in the job guarantee program shrank to the point that the program's buffer-stock effect was compromised, the government could simply take steps to slow the rate of economic growth—thereby reducing private sector employment enough to restore the job guarantee program's buffer-stock effect. The government could do this either by raising taxes to reduce aggregate demand or by raising interest rates via sales of government bonds and/or other monetary interventions.

As a practical matter, though, the federal government is legally prohibited from funding a job guarantee program—or any other type of federal spending—in this manner. The Secretary of the Treasury (the federal government's disbursing agent) is authorized to make payments only by warrants, checks, and drafts payable from public money on deposit in the US Treasury, 33 USC § 3321 et. seq. The only sources from which the required public money can be obtained consist of government receipts (from tax collections, fees, sales of assets, etc.) and government borrowing (from sales of bonds and other government securities). The federal government also lacks the legal authority to fund government expenditures—either by simply crediting government accounts with the needed funds, 12 USC § 342, or by purchasing government securities other than in the open market, 12 USC § 355(1).

Of course Congress can remove these barriers to the adoption of the fiscal strategy favored by post-Keynesian job guarantee advocates. Selling that idea, though, may be even harder than selling the job guarantee idea itself; and that being the case, it seems appropriate to ask whether there is any necessary linkage between the two reform proposals.

Job guarantee advocates working in the social welfare / right-to-work tradition have no trouble answering that question in the negative. From their perspective, a job guarantee is a social welfare benefit designed to secure the right to work, and the task of funding the benefit can be approached in any of the ways used to fund other social welfare benefits. The shortcomings of President Roosevelt's response to the CES's employment assurance recommendation demonstrates the importance of macroeconomic considerations in evaluating these options, but the effect of Keynes's teaching is to expand rather than limit the options available for funding government expenditures of all types. The fiscal strategy favored by post-Keynesian job guarantee advocates for funding government expenditures may be the best strategy from a purely economic perspective, but it doesn't mean it's the best from a political perspective. President Roosevelt's economic thinking may have been backward looking, but no one has ever questioned his political acumen, a fact illustrated by his famous response to the suggestion that it was a mistake to levy a payroll tax to pay for social welfare benefits in the 1930s.

> I guess you're right on the economics. They are politics all the way through. We put those pay roll contributions there so as to give the contributors a legal, moral, and political right to collect their pensions and their unemployment benefits. With those taxes in there, no damn politician can ever scrap my social security program. Those taxes aren't a matter of economics, they're straight politics. (Gulick 1941)

A comparison of the funding needs of a job guarantee program to those of the UI program to which Roosevelt refers in the above quote is instructive in this regard, because job guarantee expenditures would fluctuate over the course of the business cycle in exactly the same way that UI expenditures do. The principle source of funding for the UI benefit program in the United States is a federal payroll tax against which employers can credit up to 90 percent of the taxes they pay to fund a state unemployment insurance scheme that complies with federal standards. All taxes collected by the federal government and state governments under this arrangement are deposited in a trust fund administered by the US Department of the Treasury. All deposits into this trust fund are mingled for purposes of investment, but the federal government and each state has its own account to which their share of the trust fund is credited. Each state administers its own UI system pursuant to state law, certain features of which must comply with federal requirements as a condition for the state's participation in the overall scheme (Social Security Administration 1997, 25–26).

The details of this taxing scheme are not important to our inquiry. The important point is the system's reliance on a trust fund mechanism to allow program expenditures that fluctuate over the course of the business cycle to be paid from a fixed tax levy. The same mechanism could be used to fund a job guarantee program with the further advantage that the program could be established by state or local governments as well as by the federal government (Harvey 2011b, 14–17). The trust fund mechanism also could be used to accumulate resources that were drawn from other sources to pay for a job guarantee program. The viability of the trust fund mechanism doesn't depend on the nature of the taxes or other funding sources used to replenish the fund. A levy on the income of millionaires or on financial transactions would work just as well as a payroll tax.

Nor is this the only way a job guarantee program could be funded without resorting to unconventional fiscal measures. If account is taken of the additional tax revenues and savings a job guarantee program would generate, there is good reason to believe that securing the right to work might cost tax payers less than they already are spending to address the many social and economic problems that unemployment either causes or aggravates (Harvey 1989, 45–50; 1995; 2011a; 2011b). If I am correct in this assessment, funding a job guarantee program may only require a reallocation of existing government expenditures rather than a net increase in government spending. No trust fund would be needed to effect such a reallocation, of course, but it could be used to accumulate the savings and revenues needed to fund job guarantee program across the business cycle.

It also is important to note that a job guarantee program should be funded in such a way that it would not increase aggregate demand above the level at which inflationary tendencies would begin to be problematic. One way of achieving this goal would be to use a dedicated payroll tax to fund the program in the same manner that UI benefits are funded. Another possibility would be to use different funding sources to support different portions of the job guarantee program budget. Program funding required to secure the right to work when private sector employment levels were at the optimum level could be provided from general government revenues. Additional program expenditures—required only when further stimulation of private sector growth would be helpful—could be funded using additional deficit spending. Nor would it matter for the effectiveness of this funding strategy whether the additional deficit spending was linked to additional government borrowing—as existing law requires—or relied instead on the more flexible fiscal strategy advocated by post-Keynesian job guarantee advocates.

My general point is a straightforward one. There is nothing exotic about providing a job guarantee that would prevent it from being funded in conventional ways—provided appropriate account is taken of the program's macroeconomic effects (Harvey 2011a; 2011b). It is perfectly all right that post-Keynesian job guarantee advocates have other fish to fry in macroeconomic policy debates; but it's important that they do not confuse what's desirable with what's necessary (or what's economically desirable with what's politically desirable) in describing funding options for a job guarantee program. Keeping the social welfare/right-to-work tradition in mind could be helpful in maintaining this perspective.

Conclusion

Macroeconomists have an entirely appropriate tendency to assess public policy based on its macroeconomic effects. Still, it is important to recognize that the job guarantee idea has conceptual roots that are older, and in some respects richer than those associated with macroeconomic policy debates. The social welfare/right-to-work tradition from which the job guarantee idea originally emerged has something to teach post-Keynesian job guarantee advocates—just as Keynesian and post-Keynesian economic theory has something to teach job guarantee advocates steeped in the social welfare/right-to-work tradition. To advance that mutual learning, this chapter identifies two specific areas in which post-Keynesian job guarantee proposals tend to diverge from those rooted in the social welfare/right-to-work tradition. I believe these differences are important and should be discussed, but they in no way suggest any fundamental disagreement or incompatibility between the disparate theoretical traditions that gave rise to the differences in question. The chapter's goal is emphatically not to drive a wedge between these two theoretical traditions, but to promote the beneficial influence of each on the other.

Notes

1. In this context, the right to work means a right of access to decent employment that is capable of supporting a dignified standard of living (United Nations 1948, art. 23). This usage is to be distinguished from the use of the right-to-work designation to refer to legislation prohibiting employers and unions from concluding union security agreements (Hogler 2006).
2. The other members of the CES were secretary of the Treasury Henry Morgenthau Jr., Attorney General Homer Cummings, secretary of Agriculture (and later vice president) Henry A. Wallace, and Federal Emergency Relief Administrator Harry Hopkins.
3. The CES developed proposals for a range of public health initiatives, including the establishment of a national health insurance program that would have

provided wage replacement benefits for sick workers as well as reimbursement for health care expenses that were beyond a family's means; however, due to the strength of opposition to the latter proposal by health care professionals, President Roosevelt directed the CES not to release that portion of its report.

4. In addition to the Social Security Old Age and Survivors Insurance (OASI) system, the programs proposed by the CES included a means-tested Old Age Assistance (OAA) program designed to provide support to the elderly until the Social Security system matured (and which survives today as a component of the Supplemental Security Income (SSI) program); the nation's Unemployment Insurance (UI) system; an Aid for Dependent Children (ADC) program that the CES argued should be designed to free the mothers of needy children from having to work outside the home; a system of state-funded and administered disability assistance programs that would operate pursuant to federal guidelines (a system that eventually evolved into another component of today's federally funded SSI program); a variety of public health initiatives; and an expanded public employment service (Committee on Economic Security, 1935).

5. Because the question of what qualifies as "work" is not answered expressly in the Universal Declaration of Human Rights, I have described a fourth aspect of the right to work as its *scope*. This aspect of the right to work refers to the extent of its application to persons who engage in nonwaged work (Harvey 2007). I believe it can be assumed that all aspects of the right to work attach to persons engaged in nonwaged labor for their own support and the support of their families (e.g., sharecroppers). The harder question is whether and to what extent the right attaches to persons engaged in forms of nonwaged work that are more tenuously connected to the self and family support purpose of recognizing the right to work. In some cases (e.g., reasonably necessary family care work) the connection is clear enough that very strong claims can be made that persons engaged in such work are entitled to material support, conditions of work, and opportunities for personal development that are consistent with those to which wage workers are entitled—even if these guarantees are secured by means other than those that apply to wage employment. In other cases (e.g., volunteer community service work) the connection is less clear but presumably would apply in some cases. Finally, in cases where the work clearly qualifies as an entirely voluntary leisure activity (e.g., playing tennis for fun), the entitlements comprising the right to work would not attach. That does not mean, however, that work of this latter type is not entitled to societal support. Article 24 of the Universal Declaration recognizes that everyone also has a right to leisure which includes a right to the material support ("holidays with pay") required to allow them to stop working long enough both to rest and to engage in leisure activities.

6. Author's estimate using data from the US Department of Labor Employment and Training Administration.

7. Author's estimate using data from Harvey (2011a, 11).

References

Center of Full Employment and Equity. (n.d.). "Learn about the Job Guarantee, Question 1: What Is the Job Guarantee?" In *Centre of Full Employment and Equity*. http://e1.newcastle.edu.au/coffee/job_guarantee/JobGuaranteeAnswer.cfm?question_id=1. Accessed February 19, 2012.

Committee on Economic Security. 1935. Report of the Committee on Economic Security. http://www.ssa.gov/history/reports/ces.html.

Glendon, M. A. 2001. *A World Made New: Eleanor Roosevelt and the Universal Declaration of Human Rights*. New York: Random House.

Goldberg, G. S., P. L. Harvey, and H. L. Ginsburg. 2007. "A Survey of Full Employment Advocates." *Journal of Economic Issues* 41(1): 1161–1168.

Gulick, L. H. 1941. "Memorandum on Conference With FDR Concerning Social Security Taxation, Summer, 1941." Social Security History On-Line Research Note 23. http://www.ssa.gov/history/Gulick.html. Accessed March 3, 2012.

Harvey, P. L. 1989. *Securing the Right to Employment: Social Welfare Policy and the Unemployed in the United States*. Princeton, NJ: Princeton University Press.

———. 1995. Paying for Full Employment: A Hard-Nosed Look at Finances. *Social Policy* 25(3): 21–30.

———. 1998. "The History of Right to Work Claims." Rutgers-Camden Series of Occasional Papers 1. http://www.camlaw.rutgers.edu/faculty/occasional/1-harvey.html. Accessed March 1, 2012.

———. 2006. "Funding A Job Guarantee." *International Journal of the Environment, Workplace and Employment* 2(1):114–132.

———. 2007. "Benchmarking the Right to Work." In *Economic Rights: Conceptual, Measurement and Policy Issues*. Edited by Alanson Minkler and Shareen Hartel. New York: Cambridge University Press, 115–141.

———. 2011a. *Back to Work: A Public Jobs Proposal for Economic Recovery*. New York: Demos. http://www.demos.org/sites/default/files/publications/Back_To_Work_Demos.pdf. Accessed March 1, 2012.

———. 2011b. *Securing the Right to Work at the State or Local Level with a Direct Job-Creation Program*. Berkeley, CA: Institute for Research on Labor and Employment. http://www.bigideasforjobs.org/wp-content/uploads/2011/09/Harvey-Full-Report-2-PDF.pdf. Accessed March 1, 2012.

Hogler, R. L. 2006. "The Historical Misconception of Right to Work Laws in the United States: Senator Robert Wagner, Legal Policy, and the Decline of American Unions." *Hofstra Labor and Employment Law Journal* 23(1): 101–152.

Minsky, H. P. 1986. *Stabilizing and Unstable Economy: A Twentieth Century Fund Report*. New Haven, CT: Yale University Press.

Mitchell, W. F. and M. J. Watts. 1997. "The Path to Full Employment." *The Australian Economic Review* 30(4): 436–443.

———. 2005. "A Comparison of the Macroeconomic Consequences of Basic Income and Job Guarantee Schemes." *Rutgers Journal of Law and Urban Policy* 2(1): 64–90.

Mitchell, W. F. and L. R. Wray. 2005. "In Defense of Employer of Last Resort: A Response to Malcolm Sawyer." *Journal of Economic Issues* 39(1): 235–244.

Morsink, J. 1999. *The Universal Declaration of Human Rights: Origins, Drafting, and Intent*. Philadelphia: Penn Press.

Mosler, W. 1997–1998. "Full Employment and Price Stability." *Journal of Post Keynesian Economics* 20(2): 167–182.

National Resources Planning Board. 1942a. "Our Freedoms and Rights." Quoted in Marion Clauson, *New Deal Planning: The National Resources Planning Board* 183–184. (1981). Baltimore: Johns Hopkins Press.

———. 1942b. *Security, Work and Relief Policies*. Washington, DC: US Government Printing House.

Roosevelt, F. D. 1934. Executive Order No. 6757, June 29, 1934. http://www.presidency.ucsb.edu/ws/index.php?pid=14707#axzz1o3uZbqe8. Accessed on March 4, 2012.

———. 1938. *The Public Papers and Addresses of Franklin D. Roosevelt*. Vols. 1–5 (1928–1936). Compiled by Samuel I. Rosenman. New York: Random House

———. 1941. *The Public Papers and Addresses of Franklin D. Roosevelt*. Vols. 6–9 (1937–1940). Compiled by Samuel I. Rosenman. New York: MacMillan.

———. 1950. *The Public Papers and Addresses of Franklin D. Roosevelt*. Vols. 10–13 (1941–1945). Compiled by Samuel I. Rosenman. New York: Harper and Brothers.

Schwartz, B. F. 1984. *The Civil Works Administration, 1933–1934*. Princeton, NJ: Princeton University Press.

Siegel, R. L. 1994. *Employment and Human Rights: The International Dimension*. Philadelphia: Penn Press.

Social Security Administration. 1997. *Social Security Programs in the United States* (SSA Publication 13–11758). Washington, DC: Social Security Administration Office of Research, Evaluation and Statistics. http://www.ssa.gov/policy/docs/progdesc/sspus/sspus.pdf. Accessed on March 3, 2012.

Tcherneva, P. 2011. "Permanent On-The-Spot Job Creation—The Missing Keynes Plan for Full Employment and Economic Transformation." *Review of Social Economy*, forthcoming.

United Nations. 1945. *Charter of the United Nations*, 1 UNTS XVI.

———. 1948. *Universal Declaration of Human Rights*, G.A. Res. 217A (III), U.N. GAOR, 3d Sess., Resolutions, Part I, U.N. Doc. A/810.

US Bureau of the Census. 1975. *Historical Statistics of the United States, Colonial Times to 1970, Bicentennial Edition*. Washington, DC: US Government Printing Office.

Wooldridge, J. and J. Micklethwait. 2004. *The Right Nation: Conservative Power in America*. New York: Penguin Press.

Wray, L. R. (1998). Zero Unemployment and Stable Prices, *Journal of Economic Issues* 32(2): 539–545.

———. 1999. *Understanding Modern Money: The Key to Full Employment and Price Stability*. Aldershot: Edward Elgar.

Wray, L. R. 2001. "Buckaroos: The Community Service Hours Program at the University of Missouri—Kansas City." *The Economic and Labour Relations Review*, Special Supplement: Achieving Full Employment (12): 46–61.

———. 2012. "The Euro Crisis and the Job Guarantee: A Proposal for Ireland" Levy Economics Institute Working Paper 707. Annandale-on-Hudson, NJ: Levy Economics Institute. http://www.levyinstitute.org/pubs/wp_707.pdf. Accessed March 1, 2012.

CHAPTER 3

THE LOW COST OF FULL EMPLOYMENT IN THE UNITED STATES

FADHEL KABOUB

THE US CENSUS BUREAU REPORTS THAT 46.2 MILLION PEOPLE, THAT IS about one in seven Americans (including 16.4 million children), lived below the official poverty level of $22,000 for a family of four in 2010. The 2010 official poverty rate of 15.1 percent was the highest since 1993. According to the 2010 data, 8.9 million people fell below the poverty line in the United States since the beginning of the Great Recession in 2007. Between 2007 and 2010, the poverty rate for non-Hispanic Whites increased from 8.2 percent to 9.9 percent, and for Asians the poverty rate went from 10.2 percent to 12.1 percent. Blacks and Hispanics have experienced the largest percentage point increases from 24.5 percent to 27.4 percent and from 21.5 percent to 26.6 percent respectively. Economists have officially declared the recession over in June 2009 despite the major woes that continue to drain the US and the global economy. The economy has registered nearly 15 million foreclosure filings since 2007. The unemployment rate continues to hover around 9 percent and other labor market indicators continue to alarm the most optimistic observers, despite quarterly GDP growth averaging 3.1 percent in 2010 and 1.5 percent in 2011.

This chapter does not claim that addressing the unemployment problem will eradicate poverty, inequality, and homelessness in the United States; but rather argues that guaranteeing a job opportunity for anyone ready, willing, and able to work at a living wage, establishes the necessary (but not sufficient) conditions for moving toward a broad-based social and economic justice. Following the tradition of Hyman P. Minsky's Employer of Last Resort (ELR) program, this chapter demonstrates that a true full employment program is not only feasible from a logistical standpoint, desirable from a social justice perspective, but also financially cheaper than the so-called stimulus spending plans put forward by the Bush and Obama administrations since 2008. The analysis will proceed as follows. First, we present a critical assessment of the labor market situation in the United States and the so-called economic recovery efforts. Second, we briefly acquaint the readers with the logistical implementation of the ELR program, its financing mechanism, and its macroeconomic stabilization effects. Next, the paper estimates the cost of implementing ELR in the United States. Unlike most ELR studies, this paper will use a multitier ELR wage scale based on occupation, prior experience, length of service, and performance on the job. Our estimates will show that whether ELR is implemented as a shock therapy treatment or is phased in over a three-year period, its total net cost amounts to a small fraction of what the government has spent on Wall Street bailouts since 2007. Finally, the chapter closes with summary and concluding remarks.

The Persistence of Unemployment and the Failure of Neoliberalism

The 1980s Reagan-Thatcher era has ushered in a devastating set of macroeconomic reforms to undo the structural foundations of the post–World War II welfare state. The economic program that was put in place aimed at promoting private enterprise, market deregulations, and the privatization of state-owned enterprises, in addition to undermining labor unions and social welfare programs. This economic policy approach was initially referred to as "supply side economics," "Reaganomics," or "trickledown economics," but it was George Soros (1998) who later coined the term "market fundamentalism" to refer to this quasi-religious belief in the capability of unregulated markets to deliver the best possible outcomes not only for individuals but also for society as a whole. One of the most important aspects of market fundamentalism is the belief that government deficits are inherently destabilizing and that the accumulation of a large national debt is financially unsustainable. As a result, governments have gone into a wild cycle of budget cuts across the United States and the Eurozone. Needless to say, it is developing countries that have suffered the most under the Washington consensus budget cuts mania that was introduced during the 1980s debt crisis through the standard structural adjustment programs. The overall result has been high unemployment and socioeconomic exclusion for a large portion of the population.

After the 2007 subprime financial crisis, the United States has experienced its worst employment performance in decades. The official unemployment rate peaked at 10 percent in October 2009 but has since declined to about 8.5 percent by the end of 2011 thanks to moderately aggressive fiscal and monetary policy interventions that have prevented the Great Recession from turning into a Great Depression. More than 8 million jobs were lost since the beginning of the Great Recession in December 2007. The official unemployment rate has remained above 8 percent for 40 consecutive months. By the beginning of 2012, nearly 13 million people were officially unemployed, with 5.5 million of them being considered long-term unemployed; meaning that they have been actively seeking work for 27 weeks or more. Long-term unemployment is now the highest it has been since the 1930s, representing 43 percent of the unemployed population in 2012, compared with less than 20 percent before the 2007 crisis. Unfortunately, these grim statistics tend to underestimate the extent of the unemployment problem. These numbers do not take into account the fact that more than 6 percent of the employed population, or 9.5 million people, are involuntary part-time workers, and that nearly 2.5 million people are marginally attached to the labor force. These individuals are not in the labor force; they wanted and were available for work, and had looked for a job sometime in the prior 12 months. In addition, more than 5.5 million people, nearly 4 percent of the labor force, are not counted in the labor force despite the fact that they want a job and are ready to work now. They were *not* counted as unemployed because they had not actively searched for work in the 4 weeks preceding the unemployment survey. In short, the official unemployment statistics underestimate the extent of the crisis, which is why we rely on the underemployment rate, which includes involuntary part-time workers and the marginally attached to the labor force, in addition to the officially unemployed. This rate has now reached 16.7 percent, nearly double its level in December 2007.

THE FULL EMPLOYMENT SOLUTION

One cannot even begin to think of social justice when nearly 24 million people are jobless (Wray, Randall, and Forstater 2004). Can we even speak of social justice when so many people and their families have no stable source of income (Harvey 1989)? If the answer to social injustice is job creation, the question then is how can we reach full employment? Free market mechanisms can, under the right circumstances, create jobs, but not nearly enough to guarantee jobs for all. The very nature of capitalism ensures a certain amount of unemployment. Therefore, what social and political activism should aim for is a government policy that guarantees a useful and productive job opportunity at a socially established living wage for everyone who is ready, willing, and able to work. Well-designed full employment programs are automatic stabilizers for the violent fluctuations of free markets. ELR will also produce considerable cost savings as it would make several unemployment-related government assistance programs redundant. ELR is not a silver bullet program to end all socioeconomic malaise, but it can lay out the cornerstone for social justice and economic prosperity for millions of people suffering from socioeconomic exclusion under the current system.

A true full employment program is one in which the government would "take workers as they are" and provide "on the job training" when required (Minsky 1986). This proposal is known in economics literature as the ELR program, also often referred to as the "Job Guarantee" or "Public Service Employment" program. ELR theory was developed by Hyman P. Minsky in the 1960s in the context of the war on poverty (Minsky 1965; 1966). His work was further developed and refined by Wray (1998), Mosler (1997–1998), Papadimitriou, Forstater, and Wray (1998), Mitchell (1998), Forstater (2006), Kaboub (2007; 2008), and Tcherneva (2012). The government would establish a decentralized job-creation system whereby it would offer to hire anyone who is ready, willing, and able to work at a socially established living wage. Jobs would be selected by local community groups and nonprofit organizations based on the social benefits to the community. The implementation and management of ELR projects will be locally based, whereas funding would be provided by the federal government. ELR projects would be selected to match the skills of the local unemployment pool and would not compete with projects already undertaken by the private sector (or the traditional government sector). This program would stabilize economic activity at full employment by operating as a countercyclical buffer-stock for labor. So, when the private sector slows down, the ELR administration would hire more ELR workers, and as the private sector recovers, it can hire ELR workers away from the government at a premium above the ELR wage.

Minsky argued that once ELR is put in place, it would create an infinitely elastic demand for labor and establish a positive effective minimum wage. According to Minsky (1986), when there is unemployment, the effective minimum wage is zero. In the private sector, the market determines the quantity of labor it can absorb and allows wages to fluctuate to meet that quota under competitive conditions; whereas in the ELR system, the basic ELR wage is fixed, while the quantity of labor fluctuates with the business cycle. Private sector employers will have the advantage of hiring workers who have a proven current employment record, as opposed to hiring from the unemployment pool. This allows employers to recruit more productive workers, and serves as a check on productivity because employees may be replaced by productive labor from the ELR pool (instead of the unemployed or the unemployable). Therefore, despite the "job guarantee" nature of ELR, it still provides incentives for productivity both in the private sector as well as in the ELR sector, since ELR workers will be subjected to performance evaluations.

Private sector employers do, however, have to offer their employees a tangible markup over the ELR wage and benefits package. The markup may be in the form of monetary compensation, retirement benefits, health benefits, college fund for dependents, paid vacation time, better workplace environment, and so on. Therefore, the ELR system will establish a floor for compensation, benefits, and workplace conditions that all private sector employers have to meet or exceed in order to attract workers. This does not imply a wage-price inflation spiral, but rather a onetime upward movement in wages and prices. To put it in Kaleckian terms, since workers spend what they get and capitalists get what they spend; the ELR system will result in an economy-wide macroeconomic adjustment that will lead to an overall increase in aggregate demand, revenues, and profits.

Fiscally speaking, the ELR program is inexpensive. Several earlier studies have shown that the cost of implementing ELR in the United States is around 1 percent of GDP (Gordon 1997; Majewski 2004; and Fullwiler 2007). The next section will present an up-to-date estimate for the creation of 23.4 million new jobs and will demonstrate that ELR is much more cost effective than the trillions of dollars spent so far on the bank bailouts and so-called stimulus fiscal policies of tax cuts and tax incentives. However, it is important to note that as long as ELR is providing useful and productive services to the community, its financial cost can never be a burden on a financially sovereign government with a floating exchange rate. With proper fiscal and monetary policy coordination, the US federal government can afford to finance an ELR program without any concerns over inflation, deficits, or national debt.

The fiscal policy foundations of ELR stem from functional finance theory (Lerner 1943; 1947), endogenous money theory (Minsky 1986; Wray 1998; and Moore 1988), and modern money theory (Wray 2012). As the monopoly issuer of the currency, the federal government injects money into the economy by printing dollars and spending them on goods and services that it wants to purchase. The tax liability imposed on the population is what creates a demand for the unbacked currency. Tax revenues do not and cannot logically finance government expenditures. Furthermore, bond sales provide the private sector with a safe interest-bearing alternative to cash and allow the government to withdraw excess reserves from the system (Bell 2000; 2001). Therefore, money enters the system when the government either spends or buys bonds, and it exits the system when the government collects taxes or sells bonds. As a result, the government can pay for anything it wants (including hiring 23.4 million people in the ELR program) as long as it retains its financial sovereignty status, which entails its monopoly over the printing US dollars, its taxation authority, and a floating exchange rate. A systematic policy coordination between the treasury and the Fed will, therefore, ensure full employment and price stability.

Community organizations can play a crucial role in getting true full employment back on the policy radar screen through community organizing at the grassroots level. All that is needed from the federal government is financing, not management and control. Community organizations know the needs of their local community; they have better knowledge about the pool of available skills and resources, and they have a vested interest in the economic success of their community projects. Financing full employment must be centralized, but the selection, implementation, management, and assessment of full employment projects must be community-based. This kind of full employment is democratic, inclusive, and just.

A well-designed full employment program will benefit the most marginalized groups in society, those who tend to be the first to be fired during a recession, and the last to be hired during an economic boom. Those groups include women, single mothers, ethnic minorities, individuals with disabilities, and individuals with a criminal record. They tend to have a very modest work experience, education, and training. Historically, these individuals rely on support from family, the government, and charitable organizations. In the best case scenarios, they can manage to find low-paid part-time employment on a sporadic basis. Private sector employers consider them unemployable because they are viewed as being unreliable, inexperienced, and unskilled. The federal government must, therefore, act as the employer of last resort in the same way that it did during the 1930s under the New Deal programs. Today, however, we need to rethink the concept of "public works" to accommodate the contemporary needs of society. Public work projects must include not only the traditional infrastructure projects such as roads, bridges, dams, airports, ports, and railroads, but also projects that are consistent with the current environmental challenges that we face.

Green jobs must be at the heart of a full employment program (Forstater 2006). For instance, the manufacturing, installation, and maintenance of photovoltaic cell solar panels can lead the way for a new energy-efficient green economy.

ELR Cost Estimation

Critics of the ELR program and other government-led employment programs often claim that such programs are very expensive and unaffordable. The aim of this section is to demonstrate that, on the contrary, the ELR program is not only financially inexpensive for the United States, but also productive in terms of its contribution to GDP growth. Let us consider a very generous ELR program that would target the heart of the unemployment problem rather than just the official unemployment rate of 8.3 percent. Hence, the unemployment population targeted in this study will amount to 23.4 million people, which includes the 12.7 million who are officially unemployed, the 2.6 million marginally attached to the labor force, and the 8.1 million involuntary part-time workers. Let us assume a three-tier ELR wage structure whereby skilled workers earn $21/hour, semiskilled workers earn $18/hour, and unskilled workers earn $15/hour. All ELR workers will also receive an annual benefits package of $10,000. Even though not all ELR workers will opt for full time employment, we will assume that the 23.4 million people in the ELR program are working 40 hours/week. This will tend to overestimate the actual cost of the program, but we will ignore this for the sake of argument. Let us further assume that the annual material cost of running the ELR program is $50 billion. Finally, we will assume that the unemployment pool is evenly divided between skilled, semiskilled, and unskilled workers.

The ELR program can be implemented either as a "shock therapy" measure or as a "gradual" policy phased in over a certain number of years. The only difference between the two approaches would be the management of the logistical challenges of the program rather than the financial affordability for the government. We will begin the analysis with the assumption that we can implement a "shock therapy" ELR program in one year to employ 23.4 million people. This implies that we have a reserve shelf of "shovel ready" ELR projects across the country. If we also assume a modest Keynesian multiplier of 1.5, an average income tax rate of 15 percent, and an average sales tax of 6.5 percent, then the total annual wage bill of the ELR program would be $808 billion. Furthermore, if we add 50 billion for material cost and the benefits package for all the ELR workers, the total cost of the program will amount to $1.09 trillion.

On the tax revenue side, the ELR program will generate $52.5 billion in sales tax revenues annually for state and local governments and $121.3 billion in income tax for the federal government. Additionally, we must take into account a variety of cost reduction benefits that will be derived from ELR. Those would include a $150 billion in savings from unemployment benefits, $100 billion from food and nutrition assistance programs, and $75 billion from incarceration costs. There is a variety of other cost saving benefits, but we will limit our analysis to these three items only. Therefore, the net annual cost of employing 23.4 million workers in the ELR program is only $593.8 billion or 3.93 percent of GDP. Compare this to Bush's $700 billion Troubled Assets Relief Program (TARP) money and Obama's $787 billion Recovery Act spending, with stubbornly high unemployment rates for the last five years. Furthermore, the multiplier effect of the annual net wage bill of the ELR program will amount to $1.03 trillion or 6.83 percent of GDP.

It is worth noting that this analysis tends to overestimate the costs and underestimate the benefits of the ELR program. For instance, the achievement of higher levels of employment, income, and spending will automatically stimulate the private sector and will lead to an increase in private sector employment and consequently to a decrease in the size of the ELR labor pool. Figure 3.1 shows that by 2020 the ELR program will not only maintain continuous full employment, but will also add more than $1.4 trillion to GDP; needless to mention all the noneconomic benefits that full employment will bring to those who are currently excluded from participating in socioeconomic provisioning.

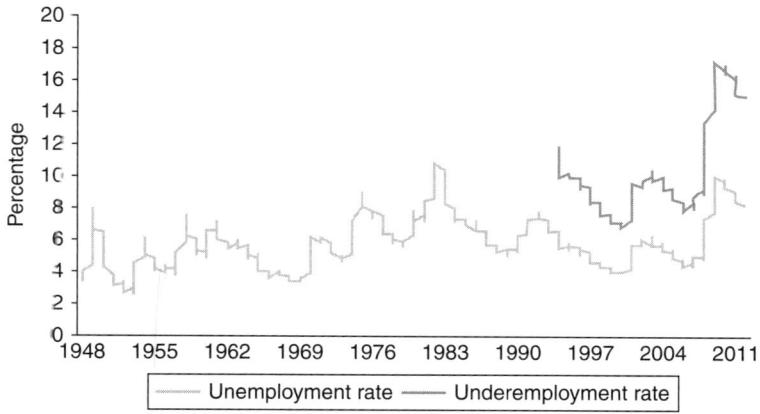

Figure 3.1   US GDP with and without the ELR program ($ trillions).
Source: Bureau of Labor Statistics.

Now, let us consider a more realistic scenario in which the federal government would gradually implement the ELR program over a three-year period. Therefore, instead of hiring 23.4 million workers at once, the government would hire the 5.5 million long-term unemployed in year 1, followed by 9.8 million workers in year 2 (2.6 million marginally attached to the labor force and the remaining 7.2 million from the official unemployment pool), and finally in year 3, the ELR program will employ the remaining 8.1 million involuntary part-time workers. Using the same assumptions applied in the case of "shock therapy" ELR, and assuming a proportional annual material cost, we estimate the total annual ELR wage bill, the total annual cost, the annual net cost of the program, as well as its impact on GDP growth. The results are summarized in table 3.1.

In short, whether ELR is implemented as a shock therapy treatment or gradually over a three-year period, its annual net cost does not exceed $600 billion. This is merely a fraction of the $29 trillion that the Federal Reserve Bank and US Treasury have spent to bailout Wall Street since 2007 (Felkerson 2011). The difference, however, is that the ELR program ensures full employment, price stability, stable economic growth, and social justice; whereas the current economic policies have not only failed to create enough jobs, but also produced more poverty, inequality, and economic uncertainty. The lesson we must draw from the $29 trillion experiment is that the Fed does have the legal and technical capacity to create money without congressional approval, and that it does have the tools to inject money in the economy without fearing the inflationary consequences. What needs to be done is for the US Congress to explicitly give the Fed a mandate to finance full employment and abandon the fiction of central bank independence.

Table 3.1 Three-year ELR Plan

	Year 1	Year 2	Year 3
Number of ELR workers (millions)	5.5	15.3	23.4
Total wage bill	189.7	528.7	808.7
Total benefits	55	153	234
Material cost	11.7	32.7	50
Income tax revenues	28.4	79.3	121.3
Multiplier effect	241.9 (1.6% of GDP)	674.2 (4.3% of GDP)	1,031 (6.33% of GDP)
Unemployment-related savings	76.3	212.5	325
Total net cost	139.2 (0.92% of GDP)	388.3 (2.48% of GDP)	593.8 (3.65% of GDP)

Source: Author's calculations (all figures are in billions of dollars, except where indicated).

Summary and Concluding Remarks

This chapter has underlined the unprecedented nature of the Great Recession and its brutal impact on the unemployed population. One has to go back to the Great Depression to find a comparable historical precedent. Today, however, we have the advantage of having learned the lessons from the Great Depression and from the Keynesian revolution. We do have the technical tools to make long-term involuntary unemployment a thing of the past. Attaining and maintaining full employment today is more urgent than ever. The only obstacles preventing the United States from implementing ELR are the obsession over balanced budgets and national debt reduction. The ELR work developed by Minsky and other post-Keynesians has provided ample support for the pursuit of the right to a job for everyone as a civil right. The analysis in this chapter has also demonstrated that the idea of the government as an employer of last resort is the only effective way to achieve social justice, reduce poverty, and put an end to involuntary unemployment. The US experience with the New Deal policies serves as a good illustration of creating and maintaining full employment and price stability (Ginsburg 1983).

This chapter did not intend to cover all the important logistical details of ELR implementation, nor did it claim to answer all the macroeconomic questions that are often raised by the critics of the ELR program. This chapter did, however, address two important questions; how much does ELR cost, and can the United States afford it? The analysis proceeded to establish the low cost of implementing a very aggressive and generous ELR program to employ 23.4 million people for less than $600 billion annually, or less than 4 percent of GDP, with the added benefit of increasing GDP by nearly one trillion dollar per year. This is a real policy solution that is far superior and more effective than the fiscal stimulus and bailout policies that we have seen since the onset of the Great Recession in 2007.

Even though the ELR literature does not claim that the program will be a silver bullet to solve all socioeconomic problems, one cannot deny the many opportunities that it offers us to restructure the fabric of the US economy. The traditional engine of US economic growth has been consumer spending, which, by the early 1980s, began to shift from being primarily financed out of earned income to being increasingly financed by consumer debt. Average US household-debt-to-income ratio reached world records exceeding 136 percent in 2007 and has been driven by very risky financial innovations, high leverage ratios, and predatory lending behavior, all of which contributed to several episodes of financial instability leading up to the 2007 subprime financial crisis. ELR has the potential to restore stability to household balance sheets, especially for those at the bottom of the income ladder (Kaboub 2011). Furthermore, the global climate crisis calls for urgent and aggressive structural changes to the way we produce and consume goods and services in the twenty-first century. ELR can be the catalyst for structural transformation to steer the economy away from fossil fuel and into renewable sources of energy. As the leading economic power in the world and the number one energy consumer, the United States has the responsibility to lead the way not only in research and innovation, but also in public spending on green infrastructure (Forstater 2006).

A new government administration must be created to direct the financing of full employment from the federal government to local and state governments. There are thousands of useful and productive tasks that are currently not supplied by the private sector and that can be financed through a true full employment program. Local government agencies and nonprofit organizations are better equipped to identify the urgent needs of the community and can match them with the skills of the unemployed individuals in those communities. They can, therefore, do the hiring, the project implementation, supervision, and assessment in a decentralized manner if the federal government provides the financing. What this chapter has demonstrated is that the low cost of full employment calls for urgent action to reorient the public policy debate towards direct job creation and active labor market policies. The alternatives are very expensive and ineffective; whereas full employment is socially desirable, logistically possible, and financially affordable.

NOTE

The author would like to thank Mathew Forstater, Mike Murray, Erika Johnson, Dave Locke, Patrick Humes, and Rana Odeh for their thoughtful comments and suggestions. The usual disclaimer applies.

REFERENCES

Bell, Stephanie. 2000. "Do Taxes and Bonds Finance Government Spending?" *Journal of Economic Issues* 34(3): 603–620.

———. 2001. "The Role of the State in the Hierarchy of Money." *Cambridge Journal of Economics* (2): 149–163.

Bureau of Labor Statistics. 2012. *Labor Market Statistics (Historical Data)*. Washington, DC: US Department of Labor.

Felkerson, James. December 2011. "$29,000,000,000,000: A Detailed Look at the Fed's Bailout by Funding Facility and Recipient," Working Paper No. 698. *Levy Economics Institute of Bard College.*

Forstater, Mathew. 2006. "Green Jobs: Public Service Employment and Environmental Sustainability." *Challenge* 49(4): 58–72.
Fullwiler, Scott. 2007 "Macroeconomic Stabilization and the Employer of Last Resort." *Journal of Economic Issues* 16(1): 93–134.
Ginsburg, Helen. 1983. *Full Employment and Public Policy: The United States and Sweden.* Lexington, MA: Lexington Books.
Gordon, Wendell. 1997. Job Assurance: The Job Guarantee Revisited. *Journal of Economic Issues* 31(3): 826e834.
Harvey, Philip. 1989. *Securing the Right to Employment.* Princeton, NJ: Princeton University Press.
Kaboub, Fadhel. 2011. "Understanding and Preventing Financial Instability: Post Keynesian Institutionalism and Government as Employer of Last Resort." In *Financial Instability and Economic Security after the Great Recession.* Edited by Charles Whalen. Northampton, MA: Edward Elgar Publishing, 77–92.

———. 2008. "Elements of a Radical Counter-Movement to Neoliberalism: Employment-Led Development." *Review of Radical Political Economics* 40(3): 220–227.

Kaboub, Fadhel. 2007. "Institutional Adjustment for Full Employment." *Journal of Economic Issues* 41(2): 495–502.
Lerner, Abba P. 1947. "Money as a Creature of the State." *American Economic Review* 37(3): 312–317.

———. 1943. "Functional Finance and the Federal Debt." *Social Research* 10(1): 38–51.

Majewski, Raymond. 2004. "Simulating an Employer of Last Resort Program." In *Growth, Distribution, and Effective Demand: Alternatives to Economic Orthodoxy, Essays in Honor of Edward J. Nell* (163–180). Edited by G. Argyrous, M. Forstater, and G. Mongiovi. Armonk, NY: M. E. Sharpe.
Minsky, Hyman P. 1966. "Tight Full Employment: Let's Heat up the Economy." In *Poverty American Style* (294–300). Edited by H. P. Miller. Belmont, CA: Wadsworth.

———. 1965. "The Role of Employment Policy." In *Poverty in America* (175–200). Edited by M. S. Gordon. San Francisco, CA: Chandler.

Minsky, Hyman P. 1986. *Stabilizing an Unstable Economy.* New Haven: Yale University Press.
Mitchell, William F. 1998. "The Buffer Stock Employment Model and the NAIRU: The Path to Full Employment." *Journal of Economic Issues* 32(2): 547–556.
Moore, Basil. 1988. *Horizontalists and Verticalists: The Macroeconomics of Credit Money.* Cambridge and New York: Cambridge University Press.
Mosler, Warren B. 1997–1998. "Full Employment and Price Stability." *Journal of Post Keynesian Economics* 20(4): 167–182.
Papadimitriou, Dimitri B., Mathew Forstater, and L. Randall Wray. 1998. "Toward Full Employment without Inflation: The Job Opportunity Program." *Levy Economics Institute of Bard College* 8(3): 5–8.
Soros, George. 1998. *The Crisis of Global Capitalism: Open Society Endangered.* New York: PublicAffairs.

Tcherneva, Pavlina R. 2012. "Permanent On-The-Spot Job Creation: The Missing Keynes Plan for Full Employment and Economic Transformation." *Review of Social Economy* 70(1): 57–80.

United States Census Bureau. 2010. *Income, Poverty and Health Insurance in the United States: 2009*. Washington, DC: US Department of Commerce.

Wray, L. Randall. 2012. *Modern Money Theory: A Premier for Sovereign Money Systems*. New York: Palgrave Macmillan.

———. 1998. *Understanding Modern Money: The Key to Full Employment and Price Stability*. Northampton, MA: Edward Elgar Publishing.

Wray, L. Randall and Mathew Forstater. 2004. "Full Employment and Social Justice." In *The Institutionalist Tradition in Labor Economics* (253–272). Edited by D. P. Champlin and J. T. Knoedler. Armonk, NY: M. E. Sharpe.

CHAPTER 4

THE COSTS AND BENEFITS OF A JOB GUARANTEE: ESTIMATES FROM A MULTICOUNTRY ECONOMETRIC MODEL

SCOTT T. FULLWILER

THE JOB GUARANTEE (MOSLER 1997–1998; MITCHELL AND MUYSKEN 2008; Wray 1998; hereafter JG) is a policy proposal designed as an alternative to the neoclassical natural rate of unemployment or Nonaccelerating Inflation Rate of Unemployment (NAIRU). Whereas that approach presumes that some positive percentage of the total labor force must be sustained as involuntarily unemployed in order to avoid accelerating inflation, the JG literature argues instead that a buffer stock of the *employed* can enable true full employment without compromising price stability, with the additional benefit of mitigating the economic and social costs of involuntary unemployment.

The core of the proposal is for the government to offer a job at a base wage to anyone willing and able to work (i.e., the JG would ideally not be means tested). Proponents argue that a JG should be financed by a national government that spends in its own currency under flexible exchange rates, since such a government can always afford to provide an inelastic demand for labor at a base wage. This does not mean, however, that the program should be necessarily run by a federal government; indeed, jobs programs in India and Argentina have been quite decentralized in their operations. Further, jobs do not necessarily have to be provided by the government sector; for instance the nonprofit sector will generally have intimate knowledge regarding community needs while often being short of available workers (or funds to hire workers) to meet these needs (Tcherneva 2012). The JG is a specific application of Abba Lerner's (1943) theory of functional finance, whereby government deficits are to be judged on their effects upon the economy rather than the more typical criteria of "sound finance" (Nell and Forstater 2003). Consistent with the functional finance view, proponents argue that for a currency-issuing government that can always afford a JG program it is the macroeconomic costs and benefits of the program that must serve as the criteria for judging the policy, not the deficits that might (or might not) result, *per se*.

Consequently, analysts and proponents of policy proposals must be able to provide an indication of the effects, costs, and benefits of their preferred policies if they expect that policy makers will advocate and ultimately implement them. One way to obtain such information is via simulation using a large macroeconometric model of the economy. Any estimate of a policy proposal not already in place necessarily relies on counterfactuals—that is, comparing the macroeconomic outcomes of the program relative to not having the program—even when there are similar or at least related programs in place elsewhere (such as programs in India, Argentina, and South Africa, for instance, or Great Depression–era programs). A related reason for simulating a policy proposal is that it illustrates the logic of how a proposal is supposed to actually work. This is useful both for proponents and critics of a policy, as it provides a test of sorts with respect to one's understanding of a proposed policy within the context of an accepted understanding of how the macroeconomy functions.

The purpose of this chapter is to provide such estimates derived for the first time from a model that places the US economy in a global context with dozens of other countries. To do this, the JG is simulated within the multicountry version of the Fairmodel (Fair 2004).

A Brief Overview of the Fairmodel

The Fairmodel is a large macroeconometric model developed in the 1970s by Ray Fair. The model is dynamic, nonlinear, and simultaneous and it incorporates household, firm, financial, federal government, state and local government, and foreign sectors of the economy. The US portion of the model combines 28 stochastic equations that are estimated using the Two Stage Least Squares (2SLS) method with another 100 identity equations. National Income and Product Account (NIPA) and Flow of Funds data are completely integrated into the model within the identity equations; balance sheet and flow of funds constraints are thus fully accounted for. There are 128 endogenous variables and over 100 exogenous variables.

This paper uses the multicountry (MC) or MCF version of the model that adds 59 other countries and thereby places the US part of the model into an endogenously functioning global economy. The non-US portion of the MC model is referred to as the ROW or Rest of the World part. Of the 59 countries, there are a total of 279 stochastic equations estimated for 37 of these (up to 13 stochastic equations and 16 identities for each); the remaining 22 have only trade share equations that estimate to which countries exports and imports for a given country are distributed (trade shares are estimated for the main 37 countries, as well). The total number of equations in the MC model (including the US portion) is around 1,600.

The main source on the Fairmodel is Fair (2004). The model's overarching intellectual tradition is the Cowles Commission approach to econometric modeling, which is strongly empirical but nonetheless relies heavily on theory—and in the case of the Fairmodel, particularly on an acceptance of the possibility of market disequilibrium—in specifying the stochastic equations that are the model's core (see Fair 1994, Chapter 1, for further discussion). Fair contrasts this approach with the Dynamic Stochastic General Equilibrium (DSGE) models that rely heavily on calibration. Fair (2007) shows that the predictive abilities of the MC model dominate New Keynesian and Real Business Cycle Models; this is likely a result of the Fairmodel's far more detailed treatment of household, firm, and international sectors (Fair 2007, 18).

Beyond the fact that the Fairmodel presents an opportunity to simulate a policy proposal within an empirically estimated setting, there are many similarities between the model and post-Keynesian models, including the following:

- The model makes significant use of expectations—though these are of the adaptive variety, not the Rational Expectations Hypothesis version of expectations.
- Nominal interest rates drive household spending, not real interest rates.
- Firm sector production is driven by sales and inventories, not a neoclassical production function.
- Investment spending by firms is driven by expected production relative to existing capital stock.
- Monetary policy is carried out through an interest rate target reaction function that is fit to historical data.
- There are no NAIRU dynamics in the model; unemployment drives the price level, not inflation, which is consistent with Fair's empirical analysis as well as post-Keynesian research.

- Long-term interest rates are driven by monetary policy and markups, not a loanable funds market.

Fullwiler (2007) describes these characteristics as well as the foundations of the model overall in more detail, focusing on the relationship between it and heterodox macroeconomics.

THE JOB GUARANTEE IN THE FAIRMODEL

The JG simulated in this paper is largely the same as that in Fullwiler (2007), the difference here being that the international sector is now completely incorporated given use here of the MC version instead of only the US version; thus the trade balance and exchange rate effects of the program are endogenized. The simulation here also adds five years of data that include the global financial crisis and "Great Recession" that has followed. This section provides a brief overview of the JG's incorporation into the Fairmodel for the simulations in this paper.

The point of the simulation here is not necessarily to consider how a JG would look in the United States. Rather, it is to consider how a well-functioning JG would look *given* historical correlations between macroeconomic variables as suggested by the stochastic equations in the Fairmodel. In other words, the simulations here describe the *logic* of the JG and its macroeconomic effects along with providing some information on magnitudes of these effects (again, according to historical correlations among macroeconomic variables). As such, the simulations here will assume a JG that functions as it would be hoped to be functioning.

To accomplish this, it is assumed that workers in the JG program are equal in number to the total unemployed. This does not necessarily mean that everyone who is unemployed would take a position in the JG. Instead, it could be that there are others from outside the labor force entering the JG program in similar numbers to those that are becoming unemployed but not joining. Regardless, the stabilization effects of the program—the primary focus of these simulations—do not rely on the size of the program *per se* as much as on changes in the number of JG workers. Since the purpose here is to simulate a well-functioning buffer stock, the assumption is that the changes in the number of JG workers match changes in the ranks of the unemployed.

For the Fairmodel, the number of unemployed (U) thus equals the job guarantee jobs (JJG), as in (1):

(1) JJG = U × PHASE

The PHASE variable is designed to phase the program in over a period of three years, or 8.33 percent per quarter. The start of the JG is set to the first quarter of 1983 (hereafter, 1983q1) with the program fully implemented by 1985q4.

The wage of JG workers is a policy variable. This ensures that the JG doesn't contribute to private sector wage increases related to the business cycle; indeed, private sector employers always have the option of hiring out of the JG "pool" of workers at just above the JG wage (assuming comparable skill level needed), which provides more credible competition to private sector workers (again, at comparable skill levels) than those that are traditionally unemployed or out of the labor force. At the same time, where the JG wage is set will become the economy's effective minimum wage, and therefore the least disruptive approach (assuming one desires this) is to at least begin with the wage at or near the existing minimum wage. The approach here is to begin the JG wage at $3.80/hour in 1983 and grow it 2.5 percent per year (there is a one-time increase in the first quarter each year, as with other government spending). The starting level is to be consistent with the going minimum wage at the time ($3.35/hour) and also be able to achieve the 2000s the minimum wage of $7.25 via 2.5 percent annual growth. The 2.5 percent growth rate is consistent with an inflation target of 2 percent plus modest increase beyond that to enable JG workers to share in national productivity gains at least modestly. There are many alternatives that could be employed here, but as a general rule it is more stabilizing to tie increases to a fixed percentage, with the inflation target being a logical choice that would enhance the countercyclical nature of the program.

For the Fairmodel, the JG wage (WJG) is thereby set equal to the previous year's JG wage (WJG[–1], where [–1] signifies a lag of one year) plus 2.5 percent growth, as in (2):

(2) $WJG = WJG(-1) \times 1.025$

JG workers are assumed to work on average 34 hours per week. The total income earned by JG workers (YJG) is then set as follows, with HJG denoting the hours worked by JG workers:

(3) $YJG = JJG \times WJG \times HJG$

It is assumed that nonwage spending on the program (COJG—since the Fairmodel uses CO to represent consumption spending, as in COG to represent general consumption spending by the federal government—which represents materials, supervision where necessary, etc.) will be 15 percent of YJG. Total spending (SPENDJG) on the program is thus set by (4):

(4) SPENDJG = YJG + COJG

Variables in equations 1 through 4 are added to the following identity equations in the Fairmodel in order to incorporate the JG's effects on income, spending, and so forth into National Income and Product Accounts (NIPA) and Flow of Funds accounting:

> *Equation 43:* Average hourly wage of all workers excluding overtime.
>
> *Equation 53:* Employee payroll taxes paid to the federal government (JG workers are assumed to have roughly the same after-tax income as minimum wage earners in the private sector).
>
> *Equation 60:* Total inflation-adjusted sales of the firm sector (nonwage spending in the JG program is assumed to be for materials and so forth purchased from the private sector).
>
> *Equation 61:* Total nominal sales of the firm sector (same reason as equation 60, which is simply equation 61 divided by a price index).
>
> *Equation 65:* Total nominal saving of the household sector (income for JG employees can affect their saving).
>
> *Equation 76:* Nominal saving of the federal government (expenditures on the JG program can affect the government's deficit).
>
> *Equation 82:* Nominal GDP (spending by JG employees is included in GDP).
>
> *Equation 83:* Real GDP (same as previous equation but adjusted for inflation).
>
> *Equation 95:* Total hours worked divided by population over 16 years of age.
>
> *Equation 104:* Nominal spending of goods and services by the federal government (spending on nonlabor costs for the JG program are federal government spending on goods and services).
>
> *Equation 115:* Nominal disposable income of the household sector (income for JG program workers is part of household sector income).

Parenthetical descriptions of the above equations are obviously presuming *ceteris paribus*. There will clearly be feedback effects within the model that can offset or even completely reverse initial effects.

Some adjustments are made for cost-push effects of WJG versus the minimum wage that prevailed during the simulation period. If WJG is set above the minimum wage—as is the case here, modestly—then it would be reasonable to expect that there would be some pass-through effect to average wages and prices given that WJG becomes the effective minimum wage. At the same time, the actual effect on the overall wage structure could be far less than the rise in the effective minimum wage since WJG affects primarily the low end of the wage structure. While there is no mechanism within the Fairmodel to account for such a pass-through effect, the simulations here follow Appendix B of Fullwiler (2007), which uses the Federal Reserve's FRB/US model's approach to incorporate such an effect in its dynamic wage-adjustment equation. By integrating this into the simulation here, the effect on the Firm-sector Wage (WF) in the Fairmodel is such that at least 33 percent of the difference between the actual minimum wage and WJG is passed through to WF.

Finally, JG employees are assumed to be unproductive. That is, their work adds nothing to national productivity or national output directly. (Fullwiler (2007) relaxes this assumption in some of the stochastic simulations.)

To conclude this section, the stabilizing properties of the JG program are intentionally understated in the simulations, aside from the assumption of an efficiently functioning buffer stock of workers. Relaxing the assumptions that JG workers are unproductive, or incorporating the JG literature's suggestion that JG workers are a more competitive alternative to low-skilled workers in the private sector than involuntarily unemployed workers, would enhance any results below that suggest the program is functions as the JG literature predicts.

MACROECONOMIC EFFECTS

The JG program is simulated for the period 1983–2010. The base data that the effects of the program are compared to are the actual data for the period. Errors from the stochastic equations are added into the simulation. This means that absent the JG program there would be no change—simulated variables would be equal to actual data for the period. It more significantly means that the simulated JG program is being subjected to the same shocks as to all the stochastic equations that occurred during this period. As such, the logic of the JG program is demonstrated within business cycles of actual historical magnitude. Throughout the simulation, the Federal Reserve's reaction function is turned off; the effects of the JG program in the simulation are then entirely the result of the JG program, not a reaction to the program by monetary policy makers. Instead, the Federal Reserve's interest rate target remains at the levels set during 1983–2010.

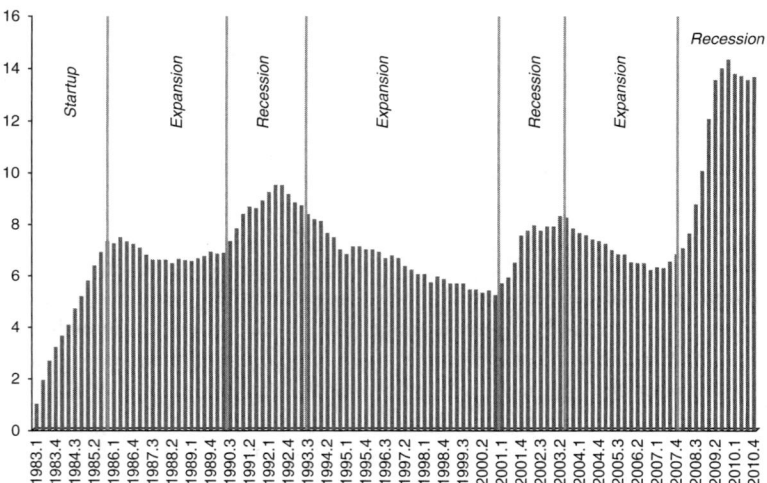

Figure 4.1 Job guarantee employees (millions).

Figure 4.1 shows the number of JG employees as set via equation 1 above. As each figure hereafter will do, periods of economic expansion and recession are presented as determined by the National Bureau of Economic Research. As desired for purposes of the simulation, JG employees increase and decrease countercyclically in order to illustrate the effects of a program that has a buffer stock of employed workers as the JG literature says it should. (Fullwiler (2007) shows that a JG program with a less well-functioning buffer stock still has stabilization properties that are macroeconomically significant.)

Figure 4.2 shows how the program affects nominal GDP relative to the base data, which is increased throughout but also demonstrates countercyclical properties as the difference between simulated and base GDP rises in recessions and levels out in expansions. Figure 4.3 shows simulated real GDP relative to the base data. Here again there are countercyclical effects, with the inflation-adjusted measure of GDP suggesting that the real effects are significantly more countercyclical. Note how in both figures the period of implementation (1983–1985) shows a slow increase in the program's effects. Shortly thereafter, the already strong economic expansion causes the rise in program employees to halt and then reverse as shown in figure 4.1. This causes a strong reversal in the program's effects on real GDP in figure 4.2 throughout the rest of the 1980s as employees leave the program and take private sector jobs. As the economy slips into recession in the early 1990s, the number of JG employees rises again and the effects in figures 4.2 and 4.3 reverse again. This pattern is repeated and continues through 2010q4.

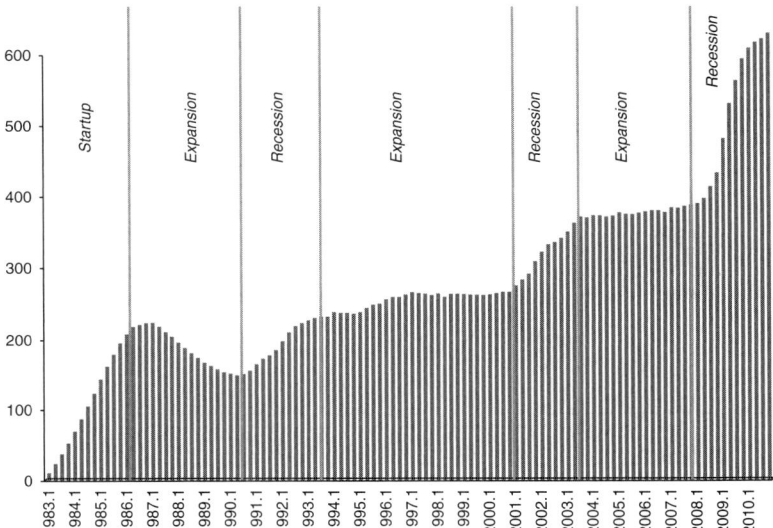

Figure 4.2 Annualized nominal GDP for JG program less base data ($ billions).

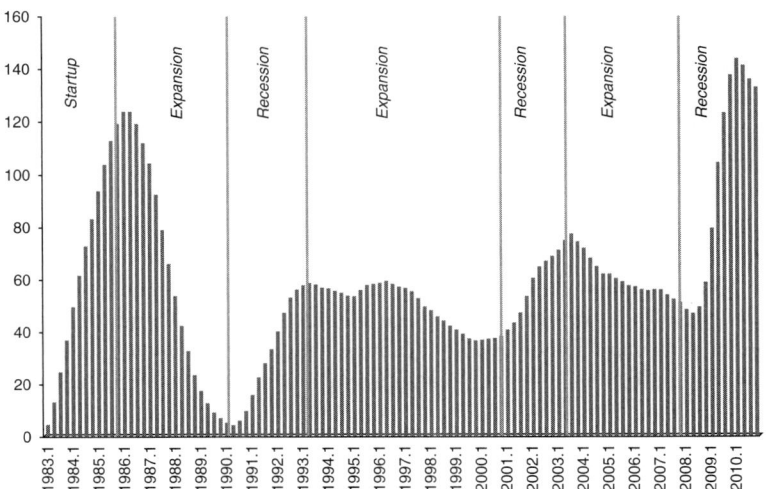

Figure 4.3 Annualized real GDP for JG program less base data ($ billions).

Figure 4.4 shows the program's effects on inflation relative to the base data. As with figures 4.2 and 4.3, there is an increase during the implementation period; that is, consistent with JG literature, the program appears to create a one-time increase in the price level that temporarily raises inflation,

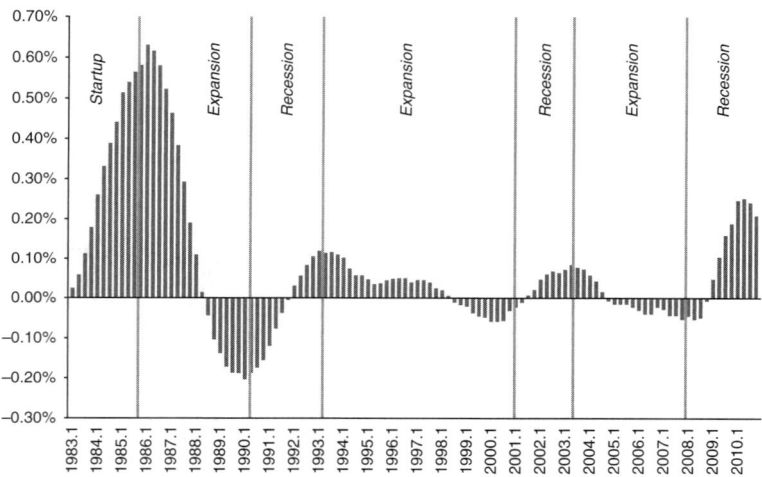

Figure 4.4 Quarterly annualized inflation for JG program less base data.

though modestly as the effect peaks at about a 0.6 percent increase over the base level of inflation. Thereafter the effects of the program on inflation are countercyclical—very modest increases in inflation relative to the base level during recessions and similarly modest decreases in inflation relative to the base level toward the peak of expansions. Figure 4.4 thereby shows that the JG program does not itself create inflation and very modestly contributes to price stability across business cycles.

(Note that it is not necessarily the case in the JG literature that a JG program will permanently raise nominal or real GDP. This is more inherent in the particular "plain vanilla" version of the program simulated here. JG programs could be designed that do not do this, and in general the JG should be considered an automatic stabilizer, not a stimulus, aside from a potential "one-time only" increase related to the startup phase, again depending on program design and timing relative to the business cycle.)

Figure 4.5 shows the effect on the firm sector's capacity utilization for the JG program relative to the base data. This measure is unique to the Fairmodel and is not the same as official government statistics on capacity utilization. The measure is designed by dividing actual firm production (Y in the Fairmodel) by potential firm production (YP). It is thereby a measure more similar to an output gap as used by macroeconomists (and, like that measure, Y/YP has been greater than 1.0 at times) except that it

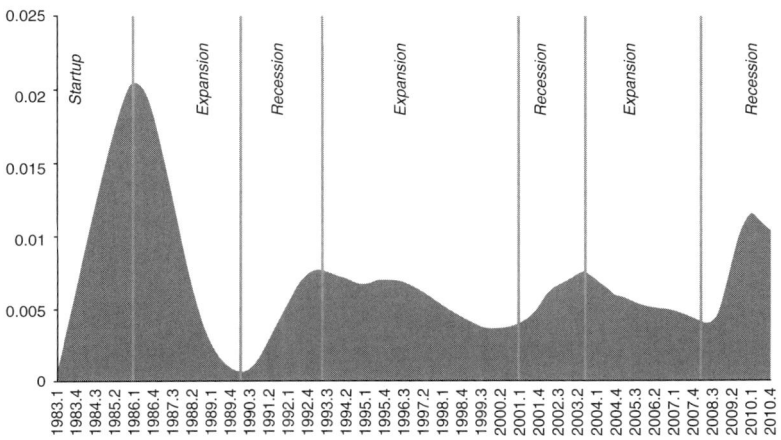

Figure 4.5 Capacity use (Fairmodel-specific measure) for JG program less base data.

applies specifically to the firm sector of the economy, not to GDP relative to potential GDP. The percentages in figure 4.5 appear small—with the peak difference from base data being 2 percent during the startup phase—but they are macroeconomically significant when one considers that in recessions it is rare for real GDP to fall by more than a few percentage points.

Figure 4.6 shows the effects of the program on the exchange rate value of the US dollar against the Canadian dollar, yen, and euro (deutschemark prior to 1999). During the startup phase the US dollar falls about 2.5 percent against the other currencies, and thereafter largely stabilizes to remain about this much below the yen and the euro throughout, though it improves to about 1 percent below base level relative to the Canadian dollar. Against all three, the US dollar falls modestly following the 2008 recession; this is largely due to the fact that the JG program is having its strongest effect on inflation—aside from the startup phase—due to the rather quick increase in the program's size. This one-time decrease in the exchange rate—itself largely due to the increase in the price level during the startup phase—and then relative stabilization is smaller in magnitude though qualitatively similar to the experience of Argentina following its implementation of the *Jefes de Hogar* program (Tcherneva and Wray 2005).

Taken together, figures 4.1 through 4.5 show that an efficiently functioning JG buffer stock is able to move counter to fluctuations in the

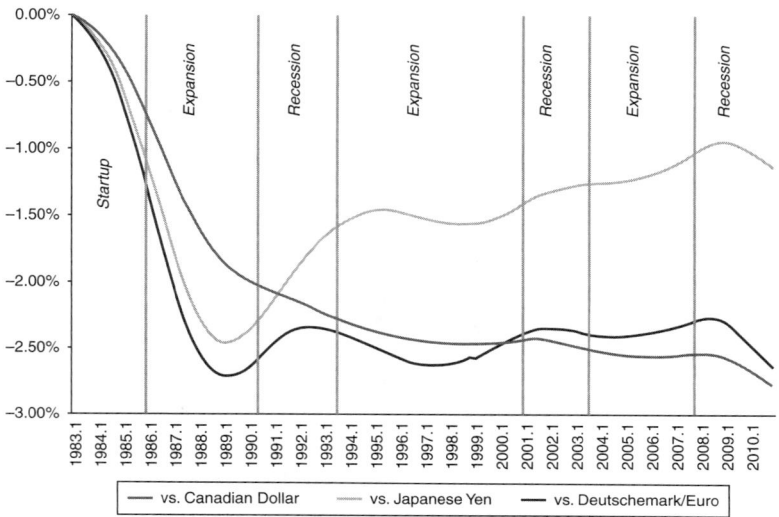

Figure 4.6   Value of US$ for JG program less base data (percent difference).

economy relative to its "potential" or full capacity utilization. Thus, as the JG literature argues, at least in Fairmodel simulations here, a buffer stock of the employed can create true full employment without compromising price stability. This is obviously contrary to the NAIRU view that a buffer stock of the involuntarily unemployed is necessary for this purpose. Figure 4.6 complements this by suggesting that an employed buffer stock does not adversely affect the exchange rate either, in an economically significant way. Finally, the fact that the simulations presume that the program begins near the end of a recession and then is at full strength just as economic expansion is in full force does not hinder the stabilization effects; indeed, once completely implemented, the program begins to slow the 1980s expansion rather strongly, partially as an offset to the effects of the startup period.

BUDGETARY EFFECTS

The budgetary effects of the JG program at the federal level are shown in figures 4.7 and 4.8, which consider the total spending on the program and the effect of the program on the federal government's budget position, respectively. All data are shown as a percent of GDP.

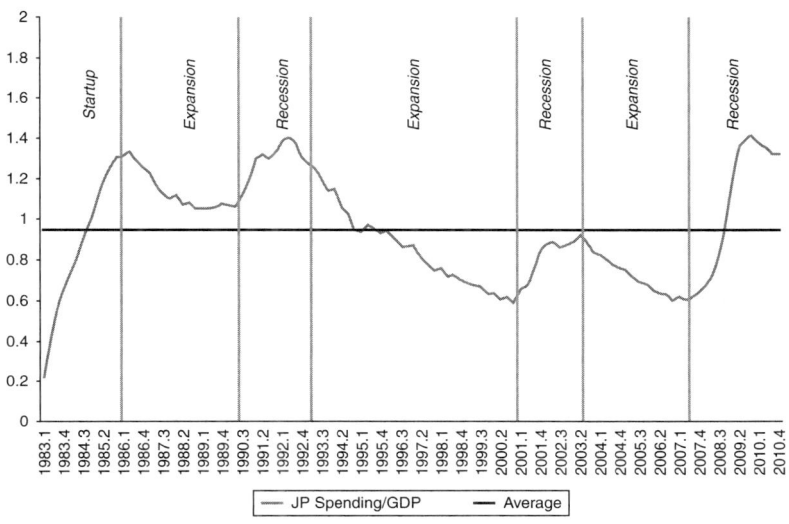

Figure 4.7 Total spending on JG program as a percent of GDP.

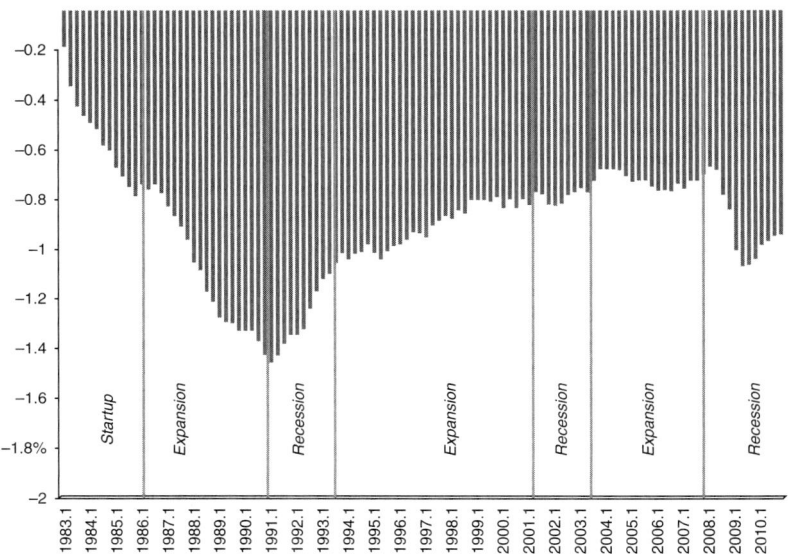

Figure 4.8 Federal government deficit/surplus as a percent of GDP for JG program less base data.

Total spending on the program—figure 4.7—peaks in 2009q4 when it reaches 1.41 percent of GDP. It reaches nearly the same level in 1992q2 and shortly after the startup phase in 1986q1. Throughout, spending on the program averages 0.95 percent of GDP with a median of 0.91 percent and standard deviation of 0.27 percent. The program is at its minimum level at the end of the 1990s expansion in 2000q4 at 0.59 percent of GDP.

While one can see rather clearly the countercyclical movements in JG program spending in figure 4.7, the effects on the federal government's budget deficit in figure 4.8 are less intuitive and require one to consider both spending on the program and feedback effects on the budget from the state of the economy. During the startup phase, the effect on the deficit reaches 0.79 percent of GDP; recall from figure 4.7 that JG program spending reaches 1.33 percent of GDP at the same time. This suggests rather strong feedback effects from the program to the government's budget position, though the rise in the program's spending is obviously the driving force in the rise in the deficit relative to base data. Thereafter, the effect on the budget deficit continues to increase, reaching 1.22 percent of GDP at the end of 1988q4 when spending on the program bottoms at 1.05 percent of GDP. Here, then, the effect of the fall in program spending by 0.28 percent of GDP has *raised* the deficit by 0.43 percent of GDP; clearly this increase was driven this time instead by the fact that the JG program slowed the economy and, through it, tax collections. The effect on the deficit peaks in 1991q1 at 1.46 percent of GDP and thereafter moves downward to apparently settle into a bit more countercyclical trend that averages around 0.8 percent of GDP through 2010.

As there are numerous different ways to design a JG program, one must be careful with using any particular estimate of the budgetary effects as a representative case. These effects can rather easily be altered by raising the wage paid JG workers, creating most JG jobs through the nonprofit sector (which would minimize nonwage spending on the program), or altering the social safety net significantly in either direction, for instance. Further, the number of people outside the official labor force that would enter the program is difficult to estimate (though the Fairmodel does have three labor force equations that are fit to historical data, which together could provide some idea how at least the economy's performance would influence labor force participation). Nevertheless, the results here are consistent with estimates discussed in the JG literature and also with experience in Argentina's *Jefes* program (Tcherneva and Wray 2005), which suggests that a JG program would have very modest budgetary effects for the federal government.

The Costs and Benefits 87

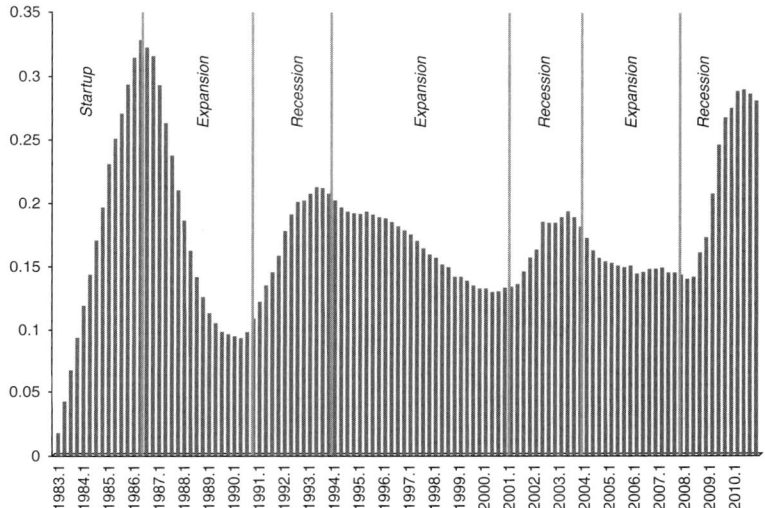

Figure 4.9   State/local government surplus/deficit as a percent of GDP for JG program less base data.

Side Effects

Beyond considering traditional benefits of macroeconomic stabilization and traditional costs or budgetary effects of the JG program, there are side effects that are also important. This section considers the JG program's effects on state and local government budgets, the sector financial balances, private sector hiring, and private sector capital stock accumulation within the simulation.

The effect on the budgets of the aggregated state and local government sector in figure 4.9 is more clearly countercyclical in nature than the effects on the federal government budget. Here the JG program time adds to budget positions given the countercyclical effect of the program on the economy. As such, the JG program appears to have the ability to modestly offset repeated moves toward cutting spending and raising taxes during recession in order to balance budgets. This in itself is a stabilizing force for the economy given that these moves to austerity at the state and local level work obviously make the recession worse while offsetting any stimulus coming from the federal government.

The financial sector balances are based upon the simple national accounting fact that financial flows in the economy are a closed system. Just as it is impossible for every country in the world to simultaneously run a trade surplus, it is similarly impossible for all sectors of the economy to have

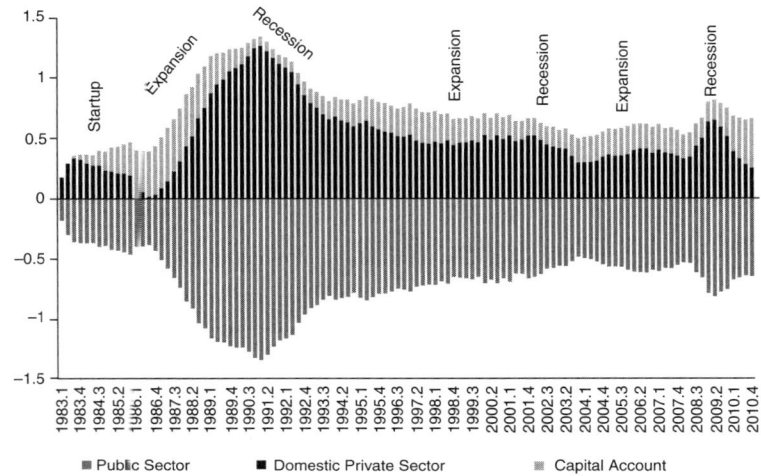

Figure 4.10   Sector financial balances as a percent of GDP for JG program less base data.

surpluses with each other. In general, it has been rare for nations to run budget surpluses without relatively strong trade surpluses; that is, the international sector's net position with the country is in deficit, which shows up in the national accounts as a capital account deficit for the nation running a trade surplus (Kelton and Baranes 2012). This is because, by and large, the domestic private sector attempts to maintain a net surplus position over the longer run vis-a-vis the other two sectors; net deficit positions in the domestic private sector (or within its subsectors, discussed next) are consistent with a Minskyan interpretation of financial fragility leading to financial instability (Minsky 1986). In the United States, the domestic private sector traditionally ran positive balances that were around 2 percent of GDP on average; the stock market and housing market bubbles of the late 1990s and 2000s were not coincidentally accompanied by the only significant periods in the post–World War II era in which the domestic private sector ran net deficit positions with the other two sectors (see Fullwiler and Wray 2010, figure 1). Figure 4.10 shows the effects of the JG program on the financial sector balances, which is to generate around a 0.5 percent increase in the domestic private sector's balance on average following a peak of about 1 percent in the early 1990s. Given that the program raises GDP, it is understandable that there is also a modest permanent increase in the US capital account (the equivalent with a decrease in the current account). These are both necessarily offset by increased deficits in the government sector throughout, largely as described in figure 4.8. (Note here that "surplus" and "deficit" for the domestic private sector is not

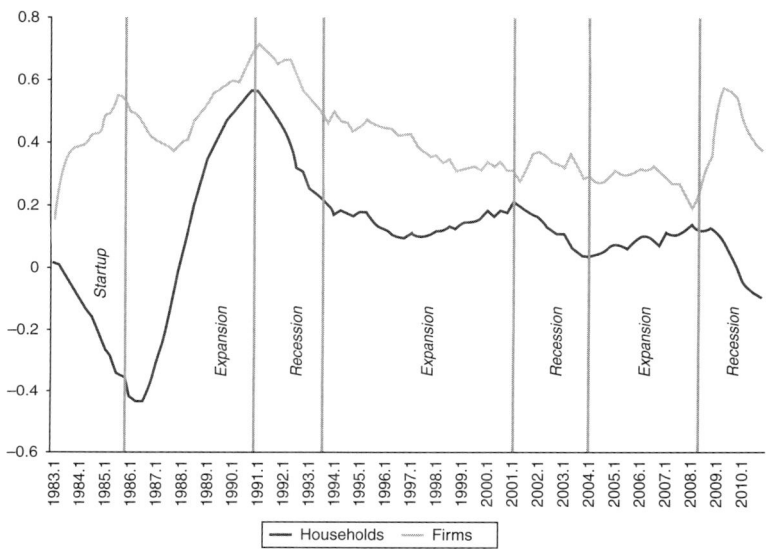

Figure 4.11 Financial balances for household and firm sectors as a percent of GDP for JG program less base data.

intended to imply profits or losses, but rather refer to net flows of funds to/from the sector.)

Figure 4.11 breaks down the domestic private sector balance into household and firm sectors (financial sector effects were economically significant and thus omitted) to see the program's effects on these. Historically, the household sector runs net surpluses throughout—aside from the housing bubble in the 2000s—while the firm sector balance moves cyclically between deficit (during expansion) and surplus (during recession), which is again consistent with Minsky's explanation of cyclical patterns of financial fragility (see Fullwiler and Wray 2010, figure 4.3). During the startup phase, the effects diverge, as the household sector's position improves as a result of income received from the JG program while the firm sector's position worsens as it spends to expand production to meet increased demand in the economy. The expansion following the startup phase sees the household sector continue to improve its position, while the firm sector now does the same relative to base data due to the fact that the JG program is contracting and thus modestly slowing the economy. The early 1990s recession that follows sees both sectors reducing their positions, consistent with the stimulus added by the JG program. Later in the 1990s expansion, the firm sector again improves its position relative to base and repeats this pattern of improving its position during expansions and doing the opposite during recessions, again relative to base data. In the recession beginning in 2008, the two positions diverge significantly again, as the JG program enables households to earn more income relative to base data while firms spend more—both are consistent with the stimulative effect of the JG program during a deep recession.

Overall, the effects of the JG program on the domestic sector balance and the household and firm sectors that comprise it are modest in terms of economic significance but nonetheless consistent with improved macroeconomic and financial stability in the Minskyan sense. The domestic private sector's balance improves throughout. The household sector's balance also improves throughout and the sector's ability to weather the early 1990s and late 2000s recessions is improved in terms of the sector's net financial position. The firm sector's tendencies to move to improve its position in a recession—which by and large *is* the recession—and to reduce its balance during an expansion—again, related to an increase in Minskyan fragility—are both tempered, if modestly.

Beyond hiring workers directly, the JG program should be expected to influence private sector hiring, particularly if it enhances macroeconomic stability. Figure 4.12 shows the additional jobs created by the *private* sector in the simulation relative to base data. Following an increase of around 1.8 million jobs during the startup phase relative to base, the program's quick turnaround to temper the 1980s expansion reduces this to around

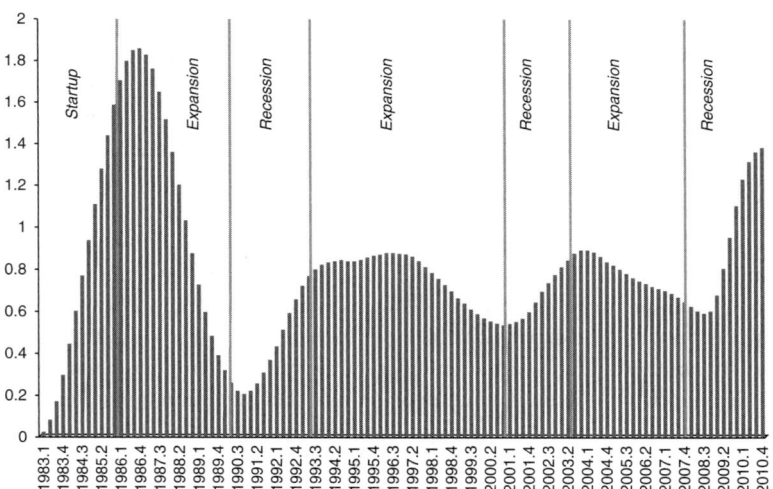

Figure 4.12 Private sector employment (millions) for JG program less base data.

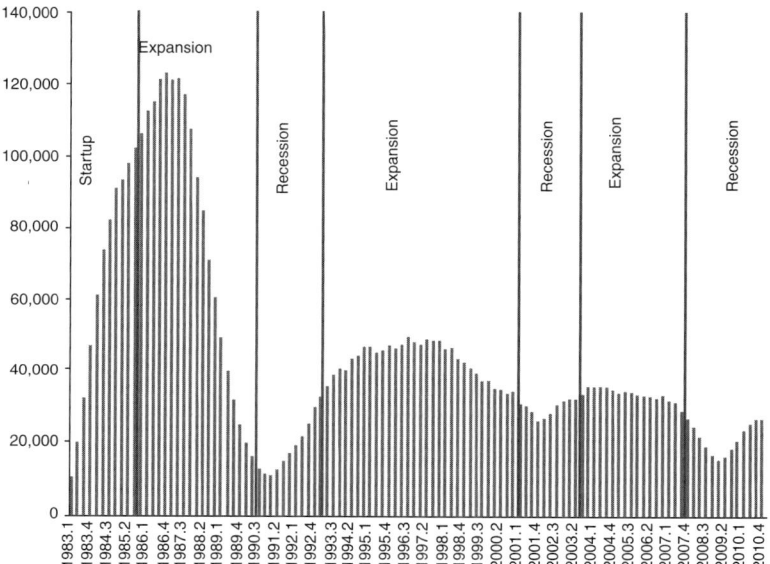

Figure 4.13 Private sector jobs created per $1 billion in JG program spending.

200,000 more jobs by the end of the decade (again, relative to the strong expansion and hiring in the base data). Thereafter, the program's effects are countercyclical while averaging around 600,000 additional private sector jobs. Figure 4.13 shows additional private sector jobs created per $1 billion in JG spending. Here again the startup phase sees private sector job creation that rises to around 120,000 per $1 billion and then falls to about 10,000 per $1 billion by the peak of the 1980s expansion. Job creation thereafter settles into a countercyclical pattern that peaks in after the 1990s recession at around 50,000 jobs created per $1 billion and trends modestly downward from there to around 25,000 per $1 billion by 2010. This downward trend is due to the modest inflation during the period since, over time, $1 billion in nominal terms provides less and less purchasing power.

Figure 4.14 shows the private sector's additional nominal capital stock relative to base data, which follows a similar pattern to additional jobs created by the private sector. Following the peak during the startup phase, the additional capital stock shows a counter cyclical pattern that is slightly lagged— smaller additional capital stock purchases during expansions are reversed during recessions. This is closely tied to figure 4.11, in which businesses are spending more to expand and reduce their financial position in recessions

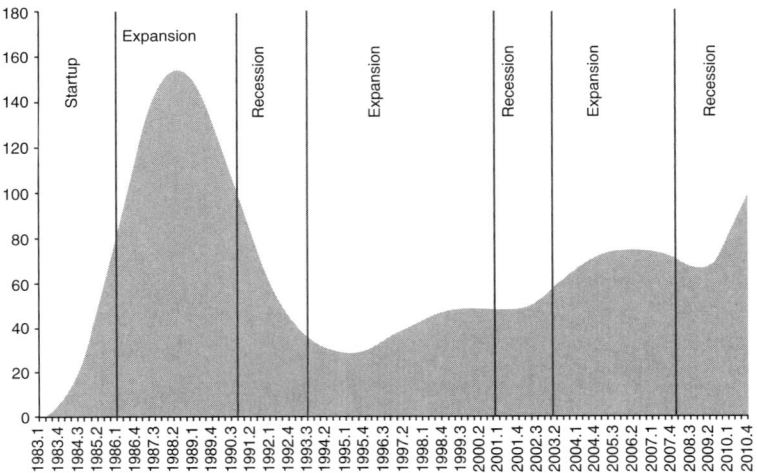

Figure 4.14 Real private sector capital stock ($ billions) for JG program less base data.

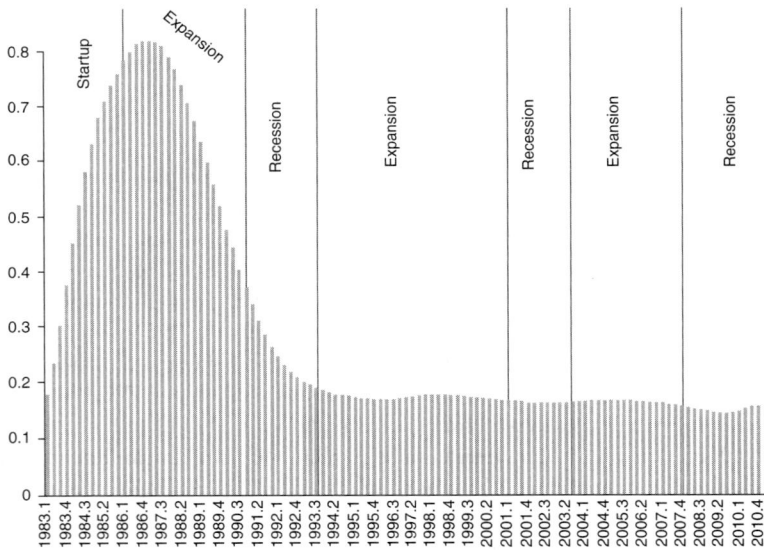

Figure 4.15 Increase in nominal private sector capital stock per $1 in JG program spending.

relative to base, and then improve their financial positions during expansions relative to base data. The upward trend in figure 4.14 is due to the nominal measure of capital stock. Figure 4.15 presents additional real private sector capital per dollar of JG spending relative to base data, and ultimately suggests that the JG program leads the private sector to add 15 cents of additional inflation-adjusted capital for every $1 spent in the program.

Any serious analysis of costs and benefits always recognizes side effects. For the JG program simulated here, figures 4.9 through 4.15 suggest these are economically significant and enhance macroeconomic stability, financial stability, private sector job creation, and private sector investments in productive capacity. This is in addition to the numerous social benefits of eliminating involuntary unemployment, which numerous studies show to have statistically significant correlations with many social and economic problems (Cook et al. 2008). It is also in addition to the likelihood that eliminating involuntary unemployment can reduce skills depreciation through continued work and the potential for additional training or education depending upon the design of a JG program. None of these latter side effects can be reasonably represented in a quantitative simulation of this sort even though they may have large economic significance.

Conclusion

This paper provides the first simulation of the JG within a multicountry macroeconometric model. According to the simulations that presume a well-functioning employed buffer stock, the JG provides significant benefits in terms of (1) macroeconomic stabilization, eliminating involuntary unemployment without sacrificing price stability, (2) actual modest benefits in terms of price stability, (3) modest added protection in terms of financial fragility, (4) increased job creation in the private sector, and (5) additional capital accumulation in the private sector. Further, while it is generally the case in the real world that large-scale employment programs are implemented in times of significant recession, the simulation shows that implementing the JG program in a time of rather brisk economic expansion does not lead to macroeconomic instability—following the startup period, the program quickly begins to promote macroeconomic stabilization. And while the functional finance view argues that the financial costs of such a program should not be a deterrent if it is beneficial in terms of its effects, the simulation also suggests that the financial expenditures and deficit impacts of the program are quite modest.

References

Cook, Beth, William Mitchell, Victor Quirk, and Martin Watts. 2008. *Creating Effective Local Labor Markets—A New Framework for Regional Employment Policy*. Newcastle, Australia: Centre of Full Employment and Equity. http://e1.newcastle.edu.au/coffee/pubs/reports/2008/CofFEE_JA/CofFEE_JA_final_report_November_2008.pdf

Fair, Ray. 1994. *Testing of Macroeconometric Models*. Cambridge: Harvard University Press.
———. 2004. *Estimating How the Macroeconomy Works*. Cambridge, MA: Harvard University Press.
———. 2007. "Evaluating Inflation Targeting Using a Macroeconometric Model." *Economics—The Open Access, Open Assessment E-journal*, June. http://fairmodel.econ.yale.edu/rayfair/pdf/2006A.PDF
Fullwiler, Scott T. 2007. "Macroeconomic Stabilization through an Employer of Last Resort." *Journal of Economic Issues* 41(1) March: 93–134.
Fullwiler, Scott T. and L. Randall Wray. 2010. "Quantitative Easing and Proposals for Reform of Monetary Policy Operations." Working Paper No. 645 Jerome Levy Economics Institute (December).
Kelton, Stephanie and Avraham Baranes. 2012. "Adding the Domestic Private Sector Balance." Unpublished presentation. http://www.slideshare.net/MitchGreen/adding-the-domestic-private-sector-financial-balance
Lerner, Abba. 1943. "Functional Finance and the Federal Debt." *Social Research* 10 (February): 38–51.
Minsky, Hyman P. 1986. *Stabilizing an Unstable Economy*. New Haven, CT: Yale University Press.
Mitchell, William, and Joan Muysken. 2008. *Full Employment Abandoned: Shifting Sands and Policy Failures*. Northampton, MA: Edward Elgar.
Mosler, Warren B. 1997–1998. "Full Employment and Price Stability." *Journal of Post Keynesian Economics* 20(4) (Winter): 167–182.
Nell, Edward J. and Mathew Forstater (eds). 2003. *Reinventing Functional Finance: Transformational Growth and Full Employment*. Northampton: Edward Elgar.
Tcherneva, Pavlina. 2012. "Full Employment through Social Entrepreneurship." Policy Note 2012/2. Jerome Levy Economics Institute (March).
Tcherneva, Pavlina and L. Randall Wray. 2005. "Is Argentina's *Jefes de Hogar* Program an Employer of Last Resort?" Working Paper No. 43. Center for Full Employment and Price Stability (August).
Wray, L. Randall. 1998. *Understanding Modern Money—The Key to Full Employment and Price Stability*. Northampton: Edward Elgar.

CHAPTER 5

EFFECTIVE DEMAND, TECHNOLOGICAL CHANGE, AND THE JOB GUARANTEE PROGRAM

MICHAEL J. MURRAY

THE GOAL OF THIS CHAPTER IS TO STUDY THE CONDITIONS REQUIRED FOR the maintenance of full employment within a growing economy comprised of ongoing structural change. Two conditions are considered: an effective demand condition and a structural change condition (Pasinetti 1981). The effective demand condition is mostly associated with the work of John Maynard Keynes and has become a central focus in post-Keynesian economic analysis. As in Keynes (1964), post-Keynesians have rejected the notion that self-regulating markets bring about conditions to attain full employment, whereby full employment becomes only a special case scenario and unlikely to occur in a laissez faire economy. "Pump priming" stimulus may not be sufficient to bring the economy to full employment as different public policies have different effects on private sector employment. Rather, post-Keynesians have favored a targeted demand approach (Tcherneva 2011). Absent of direct federal job creation, fiscal policy must target job creating sectors, which will be much more effective than traditional aggregate demand stimulus.

The employment effects of technological and structural change have for the most part become a separate line of research for heterodox economists.[1] The negative effects of technological progress on the working class are seen as early as the third edition of Ricardo's *Principles* by the inclusion of his chapter "On Machinery." Ricardo retracted his earlier position that the application of labor-saving machinery was beneficial to both capitalists and laborers. In the third edition, Ricardo opened up the possibility of the adverse effects of technological advancement:

> There is one other case that should be noticed of the possibility of an increase in the amount of the net revenue of a country, and even of its gross revenue, with a diminution of demand for labour, and that is, when the labour of horses is substituted for that of man. If I employed one hundred men on my farm, and if I found that the food bestowed on fifty of those men, could be diverted to the support of horses, and afford me a greater return of raw produce, after allowing for the interest of the capital which the purchase of the horses would absorb, it would be advantageous to me to substitute the horses for the men, and I should accordingly do so; but this would not be for the interest of the men, and unless the income I obtained, was so much increased as to enable me to employ the men as well as the horses, it is evident that the population would become redundant, and the labourers' condition would sink in the general scale. (Ricardo 1817)

The second inclusion of note is Karl Marx's analysis of the "laws of motion" of capitalist development, which centers on capital accumulation. Fierce competition drives capitalists towards labor-saving innovations. Existing laborers become the "lever" of capitalist accumulation, producing new, innovative capital goods to be used in forthcoming production (Lowe 1976). By doing so, the class of laborers becomes obsolete; essentially, they are working themselves out of a job, creating a "mass of human material" (technological unemployment) that is always ready for exploitation.

Ricardo and Marx's analysis set the foundation for the structural and technological unemployment debates to follow, known as the "compensation controversies" (Hagemann 1995). On one side, there were followers of Ricardo and Marx who were *pro-displacement* and on the other were political economists who were *pro-compensation*. The pro-compensation camp argued that wage reduction caused by reduced demand would reabsorb those who became technologically unemployed. This list included economists such as John Stuart Mill, Knut Wicksell and later Joseph Schumpeter.

The pro-displacement camp included Hans Neisser (1942) who concluded that technological progress results in permanent technological unemployment. Neisser's conclusion resulted from the realization that the demand for commodities is not the demand for labor. Technological advancement requires the utilization of less labor per unit of output, thus even when labor productivity couples with the growth in the demand for commodities, by definition less labor would be required for its production than was initially expelled. Expansion of output involves a continuous race between capital accumulation and the demand for workers; capital accumulation always wins out leaving a portion of the labor supply permanently redundant.

John R. Hicks also favored Ricardo's assertion, and concluded (at least for the short run) that technological innovation would be detrimental to the class of workers. Hicks (1973) later refined his analysis extending his contribution in his last book *Capital and Time*. Here Hicks developed the theory of "traverse analysis" or the study of the employment effects of technological progress in historical time. Adolph Lowe (1976) resumed Hick's traverse analysis in *The Path of Economic Growth,* in which, among other objectives, Lowe set out to delineate the compensation requirements for workers expelled by technological progress. An intriguing conclusion arising from Lowe's (1965; 1976) analysis is that full compensation of expelled workers in the shortest possible time requires some form of government intervention in the workings of the economy.

Structural and technological unemployment is a consequence of growing, competitive economies, as evidenced by recent US experience. The 1990s experienced the expansion of the Information-Communication-Technologies (ICT) sector, which created a surge in labor productivity throughout the decade. However, the 1990s also witnessed wage stagnation and growing inequality and deterioration of the standards of living of people in the United States and abroad (Pollin 2003) and followed by unemployment and recession in the 2000s. In the present day, global economies are suffering the effects of the financial crisis. The crisis not only brought US unemployment rates to post–World War highs, but the duration of unemployment is at a historic high. Deficient demand is certainly one reason for the stagnation. However, the current period is also experiencing structural unemployment—which is harder to address with Keynesian stimulus policies.

The financial crisis has had unequal effects. Minorities, youth, and low-skilled individuals have been disproportionately affected. Some productive sectors have been harder hit than others; these include manufacturing, construction, and parts of the financial industry (Estevão and Tsounta 2011). More striking is that for some of the unemployed, their job is not coming back. Over half of the layoffs during the Great Recession have been permanent layoffs (7).

The Great Recession has created a skills mismatch in the United States—there has been a wedge created between the available pool of skills and the demand for labor. The unemployment rate for low-skilled workers (in terms of years of schooling) has increased disproportionately during the current crisis, while demand for high-skilled labor (which comprises a third of the US civilian labor force) is already on the rise (8–10). Moreover, moving forward, this mismatch might intensify further as manufacturing dwindles as a share of total output while the ICT sector and the "knowledge economy" become critical components to US production (Gualerzi and Nell 2010).

The agenda for government needs retooling given continuous structural change in the US economy. It is a myth that governing officials can stand idly aside and let markets resolves these issues. Markets are ill-equipped to deal with unemployment given the complexities of modern-day production. The maintenance of full employment must be an active policy pursued by federal governments. A federal direct job creation strategy such as the Employer of Last Resort (ELR) program has the potential to provide the economy with "flexible full employment" in the face of structural rigidities (Forstater 1998) and structural change (Forstater 2002) that is illustrative of modern day economies. By maintaining full employment, the ELR program accounts for the effective demand condition by stabilizing consumption demand and accounts for the structural and technological change condition by creating employment programs and offers retraining and education to those whose skills become obsolete.

The ELR program as a job creation strategy maintains full employment while benefiting consumers with higher aggregate wages and consumption levels, and benefiting private sector businesses with higher aggregate profits and investment. The stimulus generated by ELR employment leads to higher levels of Gross Domestic Product (GDP) as compared to a non-ELR economy. The current chapter studies these outcomes.

To make the argument of the effectiveness of the ELR program for private businesses and consumers, a simplified economy with three market participants "capitalists," "workers," and "government" operating in a closed economy is considered. Then simulations are conducted to decipher the dual consequences of consumer demand growth generated by a growth in the labor force coupled with labor productivity in a free-market economy (base-model); and comparing these results with identical simulations for an economy in which the government operates an ELR program (ELR-model). Comparisons between the base-model simulations and the ELR-model simulations allow conclusions to be drawn of the ELR programs effectiveness over laissez-faire policies. To begin, some initial assumptions regarding the behavior of our market participants are in order.

THE INITIAL CONDITIONS OF THE ECONOMIC MODEL

Let N represent the aggregate population and let w represent wages and W the wage bill; thus aggregate consumption (C) becomes equal to the whole of workers' wages plus an autonomous component (a) to satisfy basic needs. Let aggregate investment (I) equal capitalists' profits (π). Governments spend on roads, bridges, hospitals, military, and a variety of additional public services so as a first pass assume government spending is autonomous. We get the following identities:

Y = C + I + G	(aggregate income)
W = wN	(wage income)
C = a + W	(aggregate consumption)
I = Π	(aggregate investment = aggregate profits)
G = G	(autonomous government spending)

We will consider a five-sector capitalist economy with fixed production coefficients under constant returns to scale[2] operating initially at full employment. The statement of full employment is *not* an assumption that the model economy tends to full employment. By taking the extreme case that the model economy is initially at full employment, if it is demonstrated that the model economy cannot maintain this level of production over time, then by no means can "normal economies" attain full employment for any significant period without direct government involvement (Forstater 2002; Pasinetti 1993; 2007).

Table 5.1 displays the initial economy described in an input-output model. The columns of final demand are disaggregated into their consumption and investment components as this separation highlights the effects that labor-displacing technological process has on the distribution of the social surplus between capitalists' profits and workers' wages.

Traditional notation (a_{ij}, l_i) is used to represent the coefficient matrix calculated from table 5.1 where:

$$a_{ij} = \frac{A_{ij}}{Q_i} \quad \text{(capital inputs per unit of output)} \tag{1}$$

$$l_i = \frac{L_i}{Q_i} \quad \text{(labor requirement per unit of output)} \tag{2}$$

$$\pi = \frac{\Pi}{Q_i} \quad \text{(profits per unit of output)} \tag{3}$$

where a_{ij} represents the amount of commodity i used by industry j; l_i represents the labor requirement per units of output in sector i; π represents

Table 5.1 Hypothetical base-model input output table; initial period

Industry/Commodity	A	B	C	D	E	Intermediate Output	Consumption	Investment	GDP	Total Output
A	100	20	50	350	200	720	250	200	450	1170
B	80	40	20	140	150	430	150	150	300	730
C	300	10	60	410	300	1080	270	120	390	1470
D	200	50	60	80	150	540	290	220	510	1050
E	90	35	40	200	120	485	220	170	390	875
Intermediate Purchases	770	155	230	1180	920	3255	–	–	–	–
Wages	236	236	236	236	236	–	1180	–	–	–
Profits	200	150	120	220	170	–	–	860	–	–
Total VA	436	386	356	456	406	–	–	–	2040	–
Total Income	1206	541	586	1636	1326	–	–	–	–	5295

Table 5.2 Base-model coefficient matrix; initial period

Industry/Commodity	A	B	C	D	E
A	0.085	0.027	0.034	0.333	0.229
B	0.068	0.055	0.0136	0.134	0.171
C	0.256	0.014	0.041	0.286	0.343
D	0.171	0.068	0.041	0.076	0.171
E	0.076	0.048	0.027	0.19	0.137

profits per unit of output in the initial period. Table 5.2 details the coefficient matrix.

With this information, the quantity model for our hypothetical economy equates:

$$AQ + Y = Q \tag{4}$$

Solving for Q:

$$(1-A)^{-1}Y = \begin{bmatrix} 1170 \\ 730 \\ 1470 \\ 1050 \\ 875 \end{bmatrix} \tag{5}$$

In the simulations to follow, allow prices to remain stable over time. This assumption is a matter of convenience but this assumption is also consistent with historical experience (Lee 1998; Blinder 1994; Small and Yates 1999) and is consistent with economic impact analysis utilizing Regional Impact Multipliers of Bureau of Labor Statistics (RIMS II multipliers),[3] and REMI forecasts.[4] The pricing model is given in equations 6 and 7. Wages and profits (expressed in terms of per unit of output, denoted π and w respectively) are paid post factum. The product Ap equates to the material cost of producing one unit of output; added onto this product is the value added component divided between wages per unit of output (w) and the markup per unit of output (π).

$$Ap + (\pi + w) = p \tag{6}$$

Solving for p:

$$(1-A)^{-1}(\pi+w) = \begin{bmatrix} 2.13 \\ 1.67 \\ 2.89 \\ 1.79 \\ 1.63 \end{bmatrix} \tag{7}$$

Table 5.3   Base-model distribution of the social surplus; initial period

Sector	A	B	C	D	E
Wages	0.202	0.323	0.161	0.225	0.27
Profits	0.171	0.205	0.082	0.209	0.194

Table 5.3 displays the initial labor requirements and profits per unit of output for each sector; this table also represents the distribution of the social surplus between wages and profits.

The numeraire is $1.00. The wage rate will also be given a value of $1.00. This wage rate creates equality between the wage bill and the physical quantity of hours and remedies the problem that an input-output matrix measures economic activity in monetary dollars rather than in physical units. When $w = \$1.00$ the inter-industry matrix depicts both physical requirements of production and the distribution of the surplus between wages and profits. (For example, table 5.1 depicts wages per sector equal to $236. Aggregate wages in all sectors (W) = $1,180 which is equal to aggregate consumption. Aggregate profits are equal to aggregate investment which is equal to $860. Aggregate employment is equal to 1,180 workers, which under the initial assumption of full employment is equal to the initial size of our population.)

BASE-MODEL SIMULATIONS

From this initial setup, base-model simulations are conducted. Two structural dynamics are considered: an exogenous rate of population growth (g) and an exogenous rate of labor productivity (ρ), which serves as a proxy for technological progress.[5] These magnitudes affect the movement of both labor coefficients and consumption coefficients over time.

The first dynamic to be considered is a growing population. From table 5.1 the initial population is 1,180. Let the population grow at constant positive rate g. For matters of convenience, let the total population at time t be equal to the labor force at time t. From the initial conditions the population at any time ($N[t]$) can be expressed as:

$$N(t) = 1180 e^{gt} \qquad (8)$$

Similarly, the labor force at any time ($L[t]$) is:

$$L(t) = 1180 e^{gt} \qquad (9)$$

The next dynamic to consider is technological progress. Labor becomes more productive with the passage of time due to labor operating alongside faster and more efficient capital goods, which is consistent with US historical experience.[6] The rate of diffusion of new technology is dependent upon the physical life of capital goods. Worn out capital goods get replaced with new capital goods which are the most efficient and embody the latest inventions. Innovations which speed up production and utilize less labor are more rapidly diffused.

Diffusion becomes continuous. With durable capital equipment, there is a continual game of "leap-frog" being played (Robinson 1965, 86). If ten years is the profitable life of capital equipment, a nine-year-old plant will have the highest costs and yield the lowest profits. When this equipment is replaced the following year, the plant enjoys the lowest costs and highest profits. Every successive year new entrants produce with the latest capital equipment causing plants utilizing older equipment to lose their competitive advantage over time (Robinson 1965, 85–85). The diffusion of capital equipment becomes very rapid as each plant is exposed to pressure of existing competitors and new entrants (Robinson 1965, 87).

To simulate these phenomena, allow the labor requirement per unit of output in sector i at time t to be a continual function of the rate of technical progress as expressed in equation 10.

$$li(t) = li(0)e^{-\rho t} \tag{10}$$

We can now see that population growth and technological progress are opposing forces. Depending upon the relative degree of the population growth rate *vis-a-vis* the rate of technological progress, employment may increase, decrease, or remain unchanged. Technological unemployment becomes a natural occurrence in a laissez-faire economy when the rate of labor productivity exceeds the rate of consumer demand growth, leaving workers unabsorbed into the workforce. Economists call this "jobless growth" and it is characteristic of the stagnation seen in global economies following the financial crisis.

To have jobless growth, then, "no jobs" must be coupled with "economic growth." At the outset, this seems like a paradox. Typically, economic growth means more demand and hence more jobs; but when technological advancement makes labor superfluous both technological and Keynesian unemployment are the natural outcome, even in the face of economic growth.

Nevertheless, for there to be economic growth there must be a source of spending and demand. Consumption is a function of wage income, wage income is lost because of lost work; and workers decrease their consumption expenditures considerably. Thus, the source of economic growth in a jobless recovery is found in the capitalist class. Capitalist's savings from a smaller wage bill due to implementing advanced technologies are held over into profits to further investment spending in even newer technologies.[7] This shift in spending compensates for the reduction in consumption demand.

Jobless growth can be simulated in the model. To do this, assume a rate of technological progress (say 4%) just above that of the growth of the labor force (say 3%)[8] (which is a proxy for the growth rate of consumption demand) and simulate the results through seven periods. This situation is characteristic of the current stagnation during the Great Recession (2007–present) and the results are similar to the US economic situation in the early 2000s when labor productivity grew faster (3%) than output (1%) which resulted in a rise in unemployment (Stiglitz 2003, 182).

The results of the simulation are displayed in figures 5.1 and 5.2. Figure 5.1 illustrates the reductions in labor (wages), per unit of output for each sector over seven periods (indicated graphically by a reduction in the width of the l_i coefficients). Essentially, what this graph is demonstrating is that there is a continual replacement of workers by machines, creating a reduction in average variable cost, an increase in surplus value for capitalists, and exploitation of laborers. Figure 5.2 illustrates the redistribution of income from the working class to the capitalist class depicted by an increase in profit per unit of output for each sector (indicated graphically by an increase in the respective width of the ρ_i coefficients).

An ever-increasing portion of the total output shifts from worker consumption to capitalist earnings. This dynamic constitutes a shift in the composition of the social surplus away from wage earners to capitalists. Nevertheless, the whole of the social product is always purchased, but this

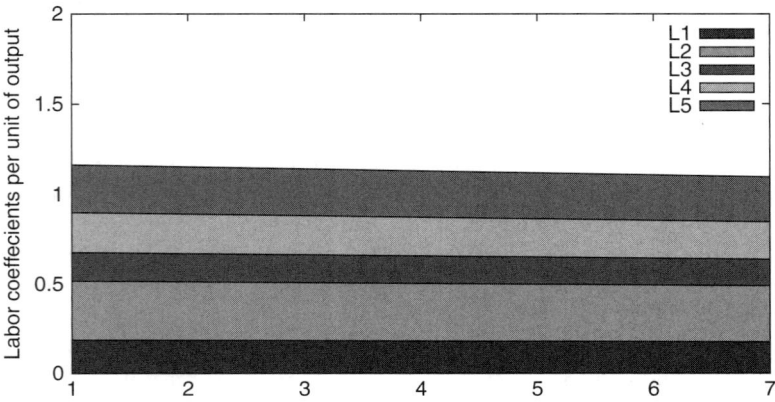

Figure 5.1 Reduction in labor coefficients over seven simulated periods.
Source: Author's *calculations*.

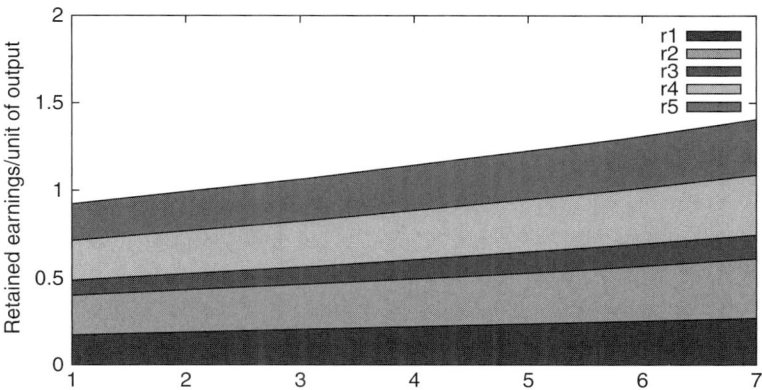

Figure 5.2 Retained earnings through simulated time.
Source: Author's calculations.

does not generate full employment. Labor productivity through technological progress makes labor redundant and the earnings saved through the expulsion of labor are transferred to profits for accumulating additional capital (which further creates conditions for labor to become obsolete in the future!) The change in the technical composition of capital towards the production of profits becomes the "formative element" of accumulation and economic growth. As in Marx:

> This change in the technical composition of capital, this growth in the of the mass of the means of production, as compared with the mass of the labour-power that vivifies them, is reflected in its value-composition by the increase of the constant constituent of capital at the expense of the variable constituent.... This law of the progressive growth of the constant part of capital in comparison to the variable part.... [A]ll methods of raising the social productivity of labor...are at the same time methods for increased production of surplus value or surplus product, which is in turn the formative element of accumulation. (Marx 1990, 773–775)

Such being the case, the simulations illustrate changes to the technical composition of capital and the creation of surplus value in the form of higher profits. This redistribution allows for economic growth, depicted by higher rates of GDP and total output, but creates a detrimental effect on wage laborers reflected by a fall in aggregate wage income and aggregate consumption and higher rates of unemployment as illustrated in figure 5.3.

Table 5.4 details the full simulation results over seven periods for all economic sectors and the economy as a whole. Aggregate wages and aggregate

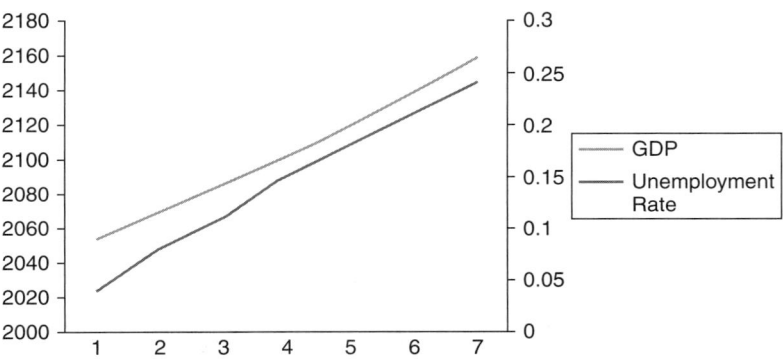

Figure 5.3 GDP and unemployment rates.
Source: United States Bureau of Labor Statistics.

consumption fall as time progresses; this corresponds to an increase in profits, which furthers investment. Investment expenditure becomes the driver of economic growth. GDP and total output increase over all seven periods. On the other hand, consumption as a share of GDP steadily declines over time. At the initial period, the consumption-GDP ratio stood at 56.8 percent. After technological advancement, the share of consumption spending relative to total GDP fell to 50.6 percent.

US consumption rates as a percentage of GDP are much higher than what are simulated here. However, it is not the absolute data that are important, but rather the patterns of movement in the data over time. The drop in consumption as a share of GDP in the simulations is representative of the drop in US consumption spending as a share of total GDP since the onset of the Great Recession. This fact is evidenced by figure 5.4, which displays the drop in Real Personal Disposable Income (PDI) for the United States. In 2009 when the US recession "officially ended," real PDI slightly rebounded and is now stagnating up to the present day. These results are consistent with the drop in wage income depicted by the base-model simulations in figure 5.1.

In addition, the base-model simulations predict that the savings in the wage bill are retained in the form of corporate profits to be used for financing investment activity. As figure 5.2 demonstrates, profits per unit of output steadily rise for every sector over the course of time. This behavior is consistent with recent US experience. Coming out of the recession in 2009, as real PDI stagnates, US corporate profits have been on the rise. As predicted from the simulations, corporate profits have been the driving force behind the current growth in US GDP. Figure 8.5 illustrates

Table 5.4 Input-output base-model simulations; periods one–seven

Input/Output	A	B	C	D	E	Intermediate Output	Consumption	Investment	GDP	Total Output
Period One										
A	103	20.6	51.5	360.5	206	741.6	247.5	206	453.5	1195
B	82.4	41.2	20.6	144.2	154.5	442.9	148.5	154.5	303	754
C	309	10.3	61.8	422.3	309	1112.4	267.3	123.6	390.9	1503.3
D	206	51.5	61.8	82.4	154.5	556.2	287.1	226.6	513.7	1069
E	92.7	36.05	41.2	206	123.6	499.55	217.8	175.1	392.9	892.45
Intermediate Purchases	793.1	159.65	236.9	1215.4	947.6	3352.65	–	–	–	–
Wages	233.64	233.64	233.64	233.64	233.64	–	1168.2	–	–	–
Retained Earnings	206	154.5	123.6	226.6	175.1	–	–	885.8	–	–
Total Value Added	439.64	388.14	357.24	460.24	408.74	–	–	–	2054	–
Total Income	1232.74	547.79	594.14	1675.64	1356.34	–	–	–	–	5406.65
Period Two										
A	106.09	21.22	53.05	371.32	212.18	763.85	245.03	212.18	457.21	1221.05
B	84.87	42.44	21.22	148.53	159.14	456.19	147.02	159.14	306.15	762.34
C	318.27	10.61	63.65	434.97	318.27	1145.77	264.63	127.31	391.94	1537.71
D	212.18	53.05	63.65	84.87	159.14	572.89	284.23	233.4	517.63	1090.51
E	95.48	37.13	42.44	212.18	127.31	514.54	215.62	180.35	395.98	910.51
Intermediate Purchases	816.89	164.44	244.01	1251.86	976.03	3453.23	–	–	–	–
Wages	231.3	231.3	231.3	231.3	231.3	–	1156.52	–	–	–
Retained Earnings	212.18	159.14	127.31	233.4	180.35	–	–	912.37	–	–
Total Value Added	443.48	390.44	358.61	464.7	411.66	–	–	–	2068.91	–
Total Income	1260.38	554.88	602.62	1716.56	1387.68	–	–	–	–	5522.12

continued

Table 5.4 Continued

Input/Output	A	B	C	D	E	Intermediate Output	Consumption	Investment	GDP	Total Output
Period Three										
A	109.27	21.85	54.64	382.45	218.55	786.76	242.57	218.55	461.12	1247.88
B	87.42	43.71	21.85	152.98	163.91	469.87	145.54	163.91	309.45	779.33
C	327.82	10.93	65.56	448	327.82	1180.15	261.98	131.13	393.11	1573.25
D	218.55	54.64	65.56	87.42	163.91	590.07	281.39	240.4	521.79	1111.86
E	98.35	38.25	43.71	218.55	131.13	529.97	213.47	185.76	399.23	929.2
Intermediate Purchases	841.4	169.37	251.33	1289.42	1005.31	3556.83	–	–	–	–
Wages	228.99	228.99	228.99	228.99	228.99	–	1144.95	–	–	–
Retained Earnings	218.55	163.91	131.13	240.4	185.76	–	–	939.75	–	–
Total Value Added	447.54	392.9	360.12	469.39	414.75	–	–	–	2084.7	–
Total Income	1288.94	562.27	611.45	1758.81	1420.06	–	–	–	–	5641.52
Period Four										
A	112.55	22.51	56.28	393.93	225.1	810.37	240.15	225.1	465.25	1275.62
B	90.04	45.02	22.51	157.57	168.83	483.97	144.09	168.83	312.92	796.88
C	337.65	11.26	67.53	461.46	337.65	1215.55	259.36	135.06	394.42	1609.97
D	225.1	56.28	67.53	90.04	168.83	607.77	278.57	247.61	526.18	1133.96
E	101.3	39.39	45.02	225.1	135.06	545.87	211.33	191.34	402.67	948.5
Intermediate Purchases	866.64	174.45	258.87	1328.1	1035.47	3663	–	–	–	–
Wages	226.7	226.7	226.7	226.7	226.77	–	1133.5	–	–	–
Retained Earnings	225.1	168.83	135.06	247.61	191.34	–	–	967.94	–	–
Total Value Added	451.8	395.53	361.76	474.31	418.04	–	–	–	2101.44	–
Total Income	1318.44	569.98	620.63	1802.41	1453.51	–	–	–	–	5764.97
Period Five										
A	115.93	23.19	57.96	405.75	231.85	834.68	237.75	231.85	469.6	1304.28
B	92.74	46.37	23.19	162.3	173.89	498.49	142.65	173.89	316.54	815.03
C	347.78	11.59	69.56	475.3	347.78	1252.02	256.77	139.11	395.88	1647.9

	1	2	3	4	5	6	7	8	9	10
D	231.85	57.96	69.56	92.74	173.89	626.01	275.79	255.04	530.83	1156.84
E	104.33	40.57	46.37	231.85	139.11	562.25	209.22	197.08	406.29	968.54
Intermediate Purchases	892.64	179.69	266.63	1367.94	1066.53	3773.44	–	–	–	–
Wages	224.43	224.43	224.43	224.43	224.43		1122.17			
Retained Earnings	231.85	173.89	139.11	255.04	197.08	–	–	996.98	–	–
Total Value Added	456.29	398.32	363.55	479.47	421.51	–	–	–	2119.14	–
Total Income	1348.93	578.01	630.18	1847.42	1488.04	–	–	–	–	5892.58
Period Six										
A	119.41	23.88	59.7	417.92	238.81	859.72	235.37	238.81	474.18	1333.9
B	95.52	47.76	23.88	167.17	179.11	513.44	141.22	179.11	320.33	833.77
C	358.22	11.94	71.64	489.56	358.22	1289.58	254.2	143.29	397.49	1687.06
D	238.81	59.7	71.64	95.52	179.11	64.79	273.03	262.69	535.72	1180.51
E	107.46	41.79	47.76	238.81	143.29	579.12	207.13	202.99	410.11	989.23
Intermediate Purchases	919.42	185.08	274.63	1408.98	1098.53	3886.64	–	–	–	–
Wages	222.19	222.19	222.19	222.19	222.19		1110.95			
Retained Earnings	238.81	179.11	143.29	262.69	202.99	–	–	1026.88	–	–
Total Value Added	461	401.3	365.48	484.88	425.18	–	–	–	2137.83	–
Total Income	1380.42	586.38	640.11	1893.86	1523.71	–	–	–	–	6024.47
Period Seven										
A	122.99	24.6	61.49	430.46	245.97	885.51	233.02	245.97	478.99	1364.5
B	98.39	49.19	24.6	172.18	184.48	528.85	139.81	184.48	324.29	853.14
C	368.96	12.3	73.79	504.25	368.96	1328.26	251.66	147.58	399.24	1727.51
D	245.97	61.49	73.79	98.39	184.48	664.13	270.3	270.57	540.87	1205
E	110.69	43.05	49.19	245.97	147.58	596.49	205.05	209.08	414.13	1010.62
Intermediate Purchases	947	190.63	282.87	1451.25	1131.48	4003.24	–	–	–	–
Wages	219.97	219.97	219.97	219.97	219.97		1099.84			
Retained Earnings	245.97	184.48	147.58	270.57	209.08	–	–	1057.69	–	–
Total Value Added	465.94	404.45	367.55	490.54	429.05	–	–	–	2157.52	–
Total Income	1412.95	595.08	650.42	1941.79	1560.53	–	–	–	–	6160.77

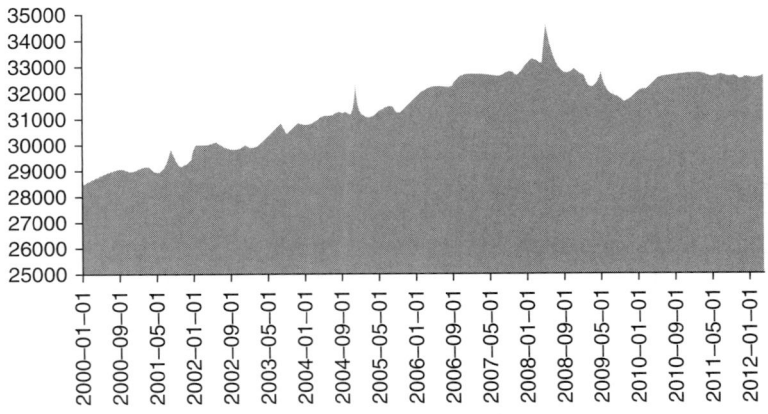

Figure 5.4 Real personal disposable income (2005 chained dollars).
Source: United States Bureau of Labor Statistics.

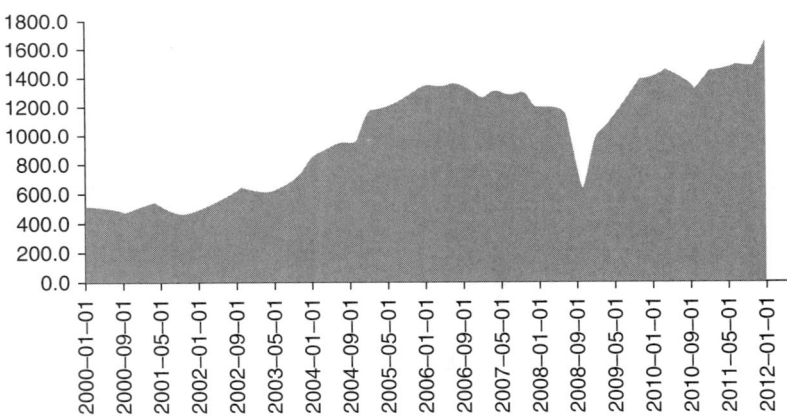

Figure 5.5 US corporate profits (2000–2012).
Source: US Census Bureau, Statistical Abstract of the United States.

the rise in US corporate profits following the recession. Together, the empirical data presented in figures 5.4 and 5.5 are consistent with the base-model simulations and the full input-output simulations presented in table 5.4.

To gain a better understanding of what is being presented in the simulations; specifically the interacting effects of Keynesian unemployment with structural unemployment, let us isolate the effects of a growing population coupled with technological progress just after one period of time and analyze the results step by step.

In our model, at period (t+1) the population (and the labor force) grew at 3 percent and equates to a population of 1,216 people. Now of those 1,216 there were 1,180 people previously employed at the initial period. This leaves 36 new workers looking for employment after the first year, who cannot find employment because the current level of activity meets current demand expectations. This is the traditional Keynesian aggregate demand problem. However, over time demand expectations change as the additional population begins demanding products first to meet their basic needs, and then on their wants and conspicuous products. This change in business expectations causes a change in the behaviors of the capitalist class.

To meet this demand requires additional investments from capitalists in sectors A–E. Members of the capitalist class (the corporate CEOs in sectors A through E) are in heated competition with each other for both market share and profits. Thereby, capitalists are compelled to innovate, and are driven by such motivations. As such, capitalists do innovate and labor becomes more productive. Labor productivity increases by 4 percent, and the new machines expel a portion of the workforce. The total addition to the workforce becomes the difference between the growth rate and labor productivity, or, in the current simulation, minus 1 percent. Consumption falls by 1 percent and employment falls to 1,169.

The labor force added 36 workers because of population growth. However there were no job opportunities in the private sector. The unemployment problem became magnified when twelve additional employees were expelled from the labor force because of increased mechanization. After the first period a total of 48 workers were unemployed.

Over time continued technological progress potentially leads to the occurrence where labor makes up such a small component of production that it can be envisioned that production entails commodities producing commodities. The working class becomes marginalized. As Marx put it:

> In proportion as the bourgeoisie, i.e., capital, is developed, in the same proportion is the proletariat, the modern working class, developed—a class of labourers, who live only so long as they find work, and who find work only so long as their labour increases capital. (Marx 1965, 68)

The laboring class becomes worse off with technological advancement; however, capitalists become better off with a smaller wage bill. In the simulations, capitalists' profits increased to $885.80. Aggregate demand rises as the savings in the wage bill is turned over to profits and then towards investment spending which also stands at $885.80. Increased profits validate business investment in newer technologies, which will stimulate another round of investment activity over the next period (Minsky 1986). GDP rises from $2,040 to $2,054, and total output rises from $5,295 to $5,406.65. The simulations clearly depict economic growth, but GDP is still well below potential GDP because of both Keynesian and technological unemployment, which is reflective of jobless growth or a jobless recovery.

Employer of Last Resort in a Leontief Input-Output Model

The simulations from the base-model conclude that a free market economy exhibiting population growth and technological advancements is incompatible with maintaining full employment.

> [T]he fulfillment of [the effective demand condition] at any given time, no longer automatically entails that it will remain fulfilled through time... [E]ven if full employment of the labour force and full capacity utilisation are realised at a given point in time... the structural dynamics of the economic system cause that position to change and therefore make it impossible in general to maintain full employment through time. (Pasinetti. 1981, 87)

If full employment is to be maintained through time, it must be a direct agenda for government policy. The ELR program is one solution that allows competitive economies to maintain full employment, without hindering private sector advancement and ingenuity. The key is that goods and services produced by ELR employment do not compete with the private sector.[9] The government's role as a sector in the economy is for the welfare of its citizens. This role is left unchanged with the implementation of an ELR program.

The government is the only sector in a capitalist economy that can divorce itself from the profit motive and engage in production whose only outcome is that it benefits the welfare of the public. This standard is how an ELR project is measured. The private sector does not have this privilege which is why a self-regulating market can never achieve full employment. Private sector businesses must have pecuniary objectives, which is a natural consequence of doing business in a competitive society. Full employment must be an actively pursued policy agenda.

> The policy problem is to develop a strategy for full employment that does not lead to instability, inflation, and unemployment. The main instrument of such a policy is the creation of an infinitely elastic demand for labor... that

does not depend upon long- and short-run profit expectations of business. Since only government can divorce the offerings of employment from the profitability of hiring workers, the infinitely elastic demand for labor must be created by government. (Minsky 1986, 308)

An ELR program further allows for variability in the technique of production while maintaining full employment. The government operates with its own set of rules. Their objective are toward the macro goals of societal welfare, the profitability of individual ELR projects is of no concern. Further, the government itself is not concerned about final demand of ELR services, because "they themselves determine the purpose of investment and what its final output is to serve" (Lowe 1987b, 107).

Unlike private businesses, public sector employment is not dependent upon the prior construction of real capital goods (Lowe 1987a, 1976). This statement is not to mean that an ELR sector will not utilize intermediate inputs. In fact, they most likely will, and the inputs that the ELR sector requires will be specific toward specific types of public sector projects. Nevertheless, public sector employment can forego automation and be as labor intensive as required, a luxury that is not available for private businesses (Forstater 2006; Wray 1998). The utilization of technology would be employed to complement the labor force, not replace it. Such circumstances for the utilization of capital equipment would be for training and for certification which are marketable in the private sector. There is also a vast array of pure services in the fields of health, education, community services, environmental cleanup, construction of public infrastructure, green jobs, and many more (Wray 1998).

ELR-MODEL SIMULATIONS

To illustrate the effectiveness of the ELR program, the same simulations will be conducted for the ELR-model as was conducted upon the base-model. The key difference between the simulations is that the ELR-model replicates the base-model and then implements the ELR program. The first step is to add in the government and ELR sector into the original base-model input-output table from table 5.1.

The ELR sector will utilize no intermediate inputs and will require only labor. The ELR sector will typically use both intermediate capital inputs and labor for production of goods and services. Capital inputs are strictly dependent upon the work performed by a specific ELR project and the needs of the regional community (Murray 2012). Given the capital specificity of ELR projects, as a first pass we assume that the ELR sector uses labor as its

Table 5.5 Hypothetical ELR-model input output table; initial period

Industry/Commodity	A	B	C	D	E	ELR	Intermediate Output	Consumption	Investment	Government Purchases	GDP	Total Output
A	100	20	50	350	200	0	720	250	200	0	450	1170
B	80	40	20	140	150	0	430	150	150	0	300	730
C	300	10	60	410	300	0	1080	270	120	0	390	1470
D	200	50	60	80	150	0	540	290	220	0	510	1050
E	90	35	40	200	120	0	485	220	170	0	390	875
ELR	0	0	0	0	0	0	0	0	0	0	–	–
Intermediate Purchases	770	155	230	1180	920	0	3255	–	–	–	–	–
Wages	236	236	236	236	236	0	–	1180	–	–	–	–
Profits	200	150	120	220	170	0	–	–	860	–	–	–
Total VA	436	386	356	456	406	0	–	–	–	–	2040	–
Total Income	1206	541	586	1636	1326	0	–	–	–	–	–	5295

only input and produces pure services (Wray 1998). For the analysis, assume the ELR sector pays workers a wage equal to that of the private sector to eliminate a one-time cost-push inflation.[10]

Table 5.5 illustrates the ELR-model at the initial period. Initially there are no workers employed in the ELR sector and no ELR output produced (because of our assumption of initial full employment). Column and row vectors of zero for the ELR sector, and a column of zeros for government purchases represent this scenario.

SIMULATIONS OF TECHNICAL PROGRESS AND AGGREGATE DEMAND IN AN ELR-MODEL ECONOMY

Simulations of the effects of continual structural and technological change are performed for the ELR-model so a comparison may be made with the base-model. As with the base-model, allow for a growth rate of 3 percent and a rate of labor productivity at 4 percent. Table 5.6 depicts the simulation results for the ELR-model after one period.

From table 5.6, the ELR workers provide services that enhance public welfare; so unlike the other industrial sectors in the economy, there is no private sector demand for ELR services. The ELR produces "free goods and services," much like the New Deal programs of the Great Depression era. The purpose of the ELR program is not to make a profit but to provide employment to those who are unemployed while simultaneously retraining laborers and providing public works. Therefore, it follows that there are also no profits earned for the ELR program. This does not mean that specific ELR projects cannot be profitable; it simply means that the profit motive is not the primary objective of ELR projects. Here the extreme case is taken and it is assumed that the ELR program earns absolutely no revenue.

After one period, additional wage income of newly hired ELR workers is $31.96 and expended on consumer goods. Here we assumed an equal division of consumer expenditures across sectors A through E. This is certainly only one of many possible scenarios.

For instance, Lavoie (1994) would most likely contend with this oversimplification, as consumption is based upon a hierarchy of needs. There are primary needs that are necessary for survival. Once these needs are satisfied, consumers move to another bundle of needs. In that sense all needs are not equal. By contrast, wants evolve from needs. Social norms and customs, and individual behaviors and desires determine people's wants. Wants are dynamic and evolve over time with new product innovations and societal changes. Thorstein Veblen describes the evolution of wants from the framework of conspicuous consumption and pecuniary emulation, in a

Table 5.6 Hypothetical ELR-model input output table; period = 1

Industry/Commodity	A	B	C	D	E	ELR	Intermediate Output	Consumption	Investment	Government Purchases	GDP	Total Output
A	103.81	20.86	51.82	362.67	208.17	0	747.33	256.94	207.63	0	464.57	1211.9
B	83.05	41.72	20.73	145.07	156.13	0	446.7	157.94	156.46	0	314.4	761.1
C	311.44	10.43	62.19	434.84	312.27	0	1131.17	276.74	124.37	0	401.11	1532.28
D	207.63	52.15	62.19	82.9	156.13	0	561	296.54	227.96	0	524.5	1085.5
E	93.43	35.5	41.46	207.23	124.91	0	502.53	227.24	176.95	0	409.19	911.72
ELR	0	0	0	0	0	0	0	0	0	–	–	–
Intermediate Purchases	863.73	160.66	238.39	1232.71	957.61	0	3388.73	–	–	–	–	–
Wages	235.49	236.6	235.11	235.05	236.11	31.9	–	1215.4	–	–	–	–
Profits	207.63	156.46	124.37	227.96	176.95	0	–	–	893.37	–	–	–
Total VA	443.12	393.06	359.49	464.07	413.02	31.9	–	–	–	–	2105	–
Total Income	1306.85	553.72	597.88	1675.64	1370.63	31.9	–	–	–	–	–	5453.85

way "keeping up with the Joneses." Consumers desire goods because others have them.

Both the hierarchy of needs and the evolution of wants suggest that ELR wage income will most likely be skewed to those sectors that produce necessities and service basic needs and have a minimal effect on those sectors that satisfy higher end wants. Thus the assumption made here is an over simplification, but analyzing consumption behavior out of ELR income is beyond the scope of this chapter. So, as a first pass the assumption is made that ELR wages are expended evenly across sectors.

For the ELR-model, consumption expenditures per sector increased by $9.44 and aggregate consumption increased to $12,515.40. This result contrasts the results for the base-model, which resulted in a drop of consumption to $1,168.20 after one period. The growth in private sector consumption is in stark contrast to the reduction of private sector spending in the base-model.

Consumption generated by ELR income means additional inputs are needed in the private sector, including labor inputs, than prior to the implementation of the ELR program. It is seen from the base-model compared to the ELR-model that after one period, all inputs, including labor inputs, have increased in the ELR-model.

The jobs generated by additional consumption demand from ELR workers results in the demand for 16 additional private sector workers.[11] Businesses pull employees from the ELR sector and the aggregate wage bill rises with the ELR program (compare the "wages column" of table 5.6 to the wages column of table 5.4, period one). Average variable costs still fall at the same rate in the ELR-model as with the base-model, and the profit per unit is the same in both the ELR-model and the base-model. After the implementation of the ELR, private sector employment still falls short of full employment leaving a proportion of the labor force remaining in ELR employment.

Intermediate output increased in the ELR-model to $3,383.73 from $3,352.65 in the base-model. The newer, more profitable technology is still in place in the private sector, even after the introduction of the ELR. Thus additional demand for private sector products means additional profit for capitalists. After the introduction of the ELR, business profits increased from $885.80 to $893.37, reflecting the additional output sold. The additional profit is a modest increase, but nevertheless the conclusion remains the same—the ELR program does not compete with the private sector, but rather allows private sector businesses to reach their full potential and achieve maximum earnings.

GDP has grown significantly after the introduction of the ELR program. The government was not assumed to be a component to final demand in either simulation. The federal government simply employed ELR workers, paying their wages, and the ELR wage income was spent on additional consumption goods and services throughout the private sector. As consumption demand grew, so did businesses profits, and in turn the level of investment across sectors increased. This additional investment demand set off a further increase in the demand for intermediate inputs, which further increased the demand for labor in the private sector.

However, in this model, the increase in the demand for laborers does not spur another round of stimulus from consumption expenditure. Additional workers demanded by businesses have come from the ELR sector; and these workers are already consuming. There is simply a shift in employment from the ELR sector to the private sector and from expending ELR wage income to expending private sector wage income.

The conclusion from the ELR-model simulations is that actual ELR employment, after multiplier effects have set it in, is less than initial ELR employment. However, it should be noted that the multiplier effects in these simulations are conservative estimates and the actual multiplier effect would be greater. Here we considered only the multiplier effects created by an increase in the final demand for consumer goods. In reality, the ELR program would set off both demand and supply side multipliers. This would crate a greater multiplier effect than what was generated here, and would allow for more workers to be shifted over to private sector employment.

The reason for omitting supply-side effects in these simulations is that these effects would be unique to specific ELR jobs. For example, one of the most popular ELR-type New Deal programs was the Civilian Conservation Corp (CCC). Part of the projects of the CCC was the construction of service buildings, fire lookout stations, roads, bridges, and other structural improvements. ELR employment in structural development and improvement generates demand for lumber, steel, iron, cement, glass, heavy machinery, hand tools, and many other inputs. The demand by the ELR sector for capital inputs induces investment in these sectors in addition to the induced investment in the consumer goods sectors set off by the increase in wage income by ELR workers.

One more point of note regarding the ELR wage. The ELR exogenously sets the marginal price of labor by setting the Basic Public Sector Wage (BPSW) (Wray 2002), a uniform wage for all ELR workers. The ELR wage may be the existing statutory minimum wage, or it may pay living wages. Either way, by doing so the ELR creates a wage anchor. The private sector would likely pay a wage incrementally above the ELR wage to attract workers out of the ELR program.

When the BPSW was set at the minimum wage, the shift of workers from private sector employment to ELR employment would create a drop in aggregate consumption and a possible shift in the composition of consumption demand. For example, consistent with current US experience, the employment in the construction and equipment sector has lagged behind other sectors during the fragile recovery. It would be likely that these workers would be employed in the ELR sector, perhaps doing structural improvements similar to the CCC programs (without the age limitations) of the New Deal. The 2010 median annual salary for those in construction industry is estimated as: construction and equipment operators $38,490; electricians $48,250; drywall and ceiling tile installers and tapers $38,290; construction building and inspectors, $52,360; cement masons $35,530.

If the BPSW is equal to the federal minimum wage and it was set for all ELR workers, then all ELR workers, regardless of occupation would earn only $14,500 annually (based on $7.25 per hour and 2,000-hour work year). Thus, those in the construction industry would earn less than half of their previous income. Certainly, any wage is better than no wage; but what will likely happen is that there would be a change in the composition in the demand for consumer goods and services toward necessary goods and services. Surely, the federal government can control the extent of this drop by setting the ELR wage. If the ELR wage were only marginally lower than private sector wages these effects will diminish and could potentially be insignificant.

A uniform basic public sector wage has the additional advantage of maintaining price stability. Think of a buffer stock scheme in which the government sets a price floor for a good, and the federal government stands ready and willing to purchase that good when the price reaches that mark. Further, the government stands ready and willing to sell that good at a specified price ceiling. By doing so, the federal government creates macroeconomic stability by preventing prices from falling below a floor or rising above a ceiling. In the ELR-model, by creating a price floor (set at $1.00) the ELR anchors the wage. The simulations reflect the BPSW proposals.

The simulations also reflect the wage proposal favored by Harvey (1989, and this volume). Harvey argues that ELR workers should be paid market wages for similar skills. In the model, all sectors of the economy, including the ELR sector, are paid the uniform wage of $1.00. (The market wage is the ELR wage. Of course this is unrealistic, however the simulations detail the effects of tying the ELR to the market wage for similar occupations.) In this scenario, the effects seen are that a shift in employment from the private sector to the ELR sector completely stabilizes personal disposable income. The shift over to the ELR sector would not result in a lower standard of living, and will not result in a change in the composition of consumption. If the ELR sector were to pay market wages, the simulations reflect Harvey's scenario. The ELR program still provides a wage anchor by setting a price floor on wages, and achieves price stability (see Harvey, this volume, chapter 2).

Conclusion

The ELR approach to full employment is more effective than current policy approaches to the problem of unemployment. The simulations, albeit simple, produced results that mirror the outcomes suggested by the ELR literature. The macroeconomic effects to the ELR-model over the base-model are increased aggregate wages in the ELR-model; increased consumption in the ELR-model; increased private sector profits in the ELR-model; and an inducement of private sector investment in the ELR-model leading to a shift of workers away from the ELR program into the private sector, all leading to higher total output and higher levels of GDP for economies operating and ELR program. From this initial setup, a more complete study could be accomplished utilizing historical input-output data, and employment data, with estimates of labor productivity and factoring in forecasted growth in the labor force.

These are purely quantitative results. Omitted here are the economic and noneconomic benefits to employment, such as increased morale, reduction in crime, increased education and training, rebuilding infrastructure (green infrastructure), building better communities, reducing social and racial antagonism, and other many more positive social benefits (Wray and Forstater 2004).

The ELR program becomes important in maintaining skills and retraining the workforce given technological and structural change. As technology improves, and improves more rapidly, the skills of the workforce need to be just as dynamic. The unemployed suffer the dual problem of losing previously acquired skills, but also do not develop new skills for new techniques. Thus, the duration of unemployment matters. The ELR sector can counteract this by offering continual training to help maintain a skilled workforce.

The primary objective of the chapter was to demonstrate how the ELR approach to full employment contemporaneously addresses both structural unemployment and Keynesian unemployment while coordinating with private sector in response to the market rather than competing with the private sector. There are certain limitations to the simulations provided in the chapter. As with all attempts to model economic behavior, the conclusions followed from the assumptions made. The assumptions attempted to model the economic reality for our current period.

NOTES

1. A notable exception is Luigi Pasinetti 1981. See also Forstater 1998; 2002.
2. Constant return to scale is a simplifying assumption as a first pass. The effects of increasing returns to scale easily are simulated.
3. For a handbook on conducting economic impact studies with regional multipliers see www.bea.gov/scb/pdf/regional/perinc/meth/rims2.pdf.
4. For further information of REMI forecasts see the webpage for *Regional Economic Modeling Incorporated*: www.remi.com.
5. This assumption follows the structural dynamic modeling of Pasinetti's approach (1993; 2007). Harald Hagemann would disagree arguing that technical progress should be an endogenous variable as the diffusion of new technologies is dependent upon inputs of interrelated industries (Hagemann 1992, 44–48). *It is not the purpose of the current essay to model technical progress so as a first pass will be treated as exogenous.*
6. For a nice summary of the effects of technological progress for U.S., see Heilbroner and Milberg 2012.
7. Investment is for the most part financed out of retained earnings. In nonrecession years, retained earnings finance over 90 percent of total investment see, Albert M. Teplin 2001. "U.S. Flow of Funds Accounts and Their Uses," 87 *Federal Reserve Bulletin*, no. 43, and also see Harcourt and Kenyon (1976).
8. These assumptions are very similar to Marx's analysis of capital accumulation. Capital accumulation "comes to fruition through a progressive qualitative change in its composition, i.e. through a continuing increase of its constant component at the expense of its variable component (Marx 1990, 781). In Marx's analysis of the capitalist process capital accumulation and technological progress go hand in hand. Therefore, capital accumulation also causes technological unemployment. Laborers are the source of technical progress, so they create conditions which make themselves superfluous, they become part of the "surplus population" (Marx 1990, 784).
9. For this issue, and a nice overview of the key ingredients of an ELR program see Pavlina Tcherneva (2003), also see Pavlina Tcherneva's chapter in this volume.
10. More on ELR wages and wage effects in the final section.
11. This multiplier effect is generated from an increase in consumption demand. In reality this is only the partial effect, once capital goods for ELR production are introduced there would be supply-side and demand-side multipliers. For an economic impact study of the effectiveness of the ELR program for a regional economy see Murray 2012.

References

Blinder, A. 1994. "On Sticky Prices: Academic Theories Meet the Real World." In *Monetary Policy* NBER Studies in Business Cycles vol. 29. Edited by N. G. Mankiw. Chicago and London: The University of Chicago Press.

Courvisanos, J. and C. Richardson. 2008. "Invention, Innovation, Investment: Heterodox Simulation Modeling of Capital Accumulation." In *Future Directions for Heterodox Economics*. Edited by J. Harvey and R. Garnett. Ann Arbor: The University of Michigan Press, 185–224.

Estevão, M. M. and E. Tsounta. May 2011."Has the Great Recession Raised U.S. Structural Unemployment?" *IMF Working Papers*, 1–46.

Forstater, M. 1998. "Flexible Full Employment: Structural Implications of Discretionary Public Sector Employment." *Journal of Economic Issues* 32(2): 557–564.

———. 2002. "Full Employment Policies Must Consider Effective Demand and Structural and Technological Change." In *A Post Keynesian Perspective on Twenty-First Century Economic Problems*. Edited by Paul Davidson. Cheltenham: Edward Elgar.

———. 2006. "Green Jobs: Public Service Employment and Environmental Sustainability." *Challenge* 49(4): 58–72.

Gualerzi, D. and E. J. Nell. 2010. "Transformational Growth in the 1990s: Government, Finance and High-tech." *Review of Political Economy* 22(1): 97–117.

Hagemann, H. 1992. "Traverse Analysis in a Post-classical Model. In *Beyond the Steady-State: A Revival of Growth Theory*. Edited by J. Halevi, D. Laibman, and E. Nell. London: Macmillan, 235–263.

———. 1995. " Employment and Machinery." In *The Legacy of Hicks*. Edited by H. Hagemann, and O. Hamouda. New Brunswick: Routledge, 200–224.

Harcourt G. C. and P. Kenyon. 1976. "Pricing and the Investment Decisions." *Kyklos* 29(3): 449–477.

Harvey, Philip. 1989. *Securing the Right to Employment: Social Welfare Policy and the Unemployed in the United States*. Princeton: Princeton University Press.

———. 2006. "Funding a Job Guarantee." *International Journal of Environment, Workplace & Employment* 2(1): 114–132.

———. 2012. "Wage Policies and Funding Strategies for Job Guarantee Programs." In *The Job Guarantee: Toward True Full Employment*. Edited by M. J. Murray and M. Forstater. New York: Palgrave.

Heilbroner, R. and W. Milberg. 2012. *The Making of Economic Society,* 13th ed. Upper Saddle River, NJ: Pearson Education.

Hicks, J. 1973. *Capital and Time*. Oxford: Clarendon.

Kalecki, M. 1943. "Political Aspects of Full Employment." *Political Quarterly* 14(4): 322–331.

Keynes, J. 1964 (1936). *The General Theory of Employment Interest and Money*. New York: Harcourt Brace.

Laibman, D. 1992. "Optimal Choices of Technique and Biased Technical Change." In *Beyond the Steady State: A Revival of Growth Theory*. Edited by J. Halevi, D. Laibman, and E. Nell. New York: St. Martin's Press, 175–197.

Lavoie, M. 1994. "A Post Keynesian Theory of Consumer Choice." *Journal of Post Keynesian Economics* 16(4) (Summer): 539–562

Lee. F. S. 1998. *Post Keynesian Price Theory*. Cambridge: Cambridge University Press.

Lee, J., R. Pau, and D. Sandri. 2010. "U.S. Consumption Rates after the 2008 Crisis." *International Monetary Fund* SPN 10/01.

Lowe, A. 1965. *On Economic Knowledge*. New York: Harper and Row.

———. 1976. *The Path of Economic Growth* Cambridge: Cambridge University Press.

———. 1987a (1955). "Structural Analysis of Real Capital Formation." In *Essays in Political Economics: Public Control in a Democratic Society*. Edited by A. Oakley. New York: New York University Press, 60–106.

———. 1987b. *Has Freedom a Future?* New York: Praeger.

Luxemburg, R. 1951. *The Accumulation of Capital*. London: Routledge.

Marx, K. 1965. *The Communist Manifesto*. New York: Washington Square Press.

———. 1990. *Capital: A Critique of Political Economy*. Volume One. London: Penguin Classics.

———. 1991. *Capital: A Critique of Political Economy*. Volume Two. London: Penguin Classics.

Minsky, H. 1986. *Stabilizing an Unstable Economy*. New Haven, CT: Yale University Press.

Murray, M. J. 2012. "The Regional Benefits of the Employer of Last Resort Program." *Review of Radical Political Economics* 44(3) (September): 327–336.

Neisser, H. 1942. "'Permanent' Technological Unemployment: Demand for Commodities Is Not Demand for Labor." *American Economic Review* 32(1): 50–71.

Okishio, N. 1961. "Technical Change and the Rate of Profit." *Kobe University Economic Review* 7(1): 87–89.

Pasinetti, L. 1981. *Structural Change and Economic Growth*. Cambridge: Cambridge University Press.

———. 1993. *Structural Economic Dynamics*. Cambridge: Cambridge University Press.

———. 2007. *Keynes and the Cambridge Keynesians, A Revolution to Be Accomplished*. Cambridge: Cambridge University Press.

Pollin, R. 2003. *Contours of Descent: U.S. Economic Fractures and the Landscape of Global Austerity*. Brooklyn: Verso.

Ricardo, D. [1817] (edited by Piero Sraffa) 2004. *The Works and Correspondence of David Ricardo: On the Principles of Political Economy and Taxation*. Indianapolis, IN: Liberty Fund Press, Volume 1.

Ricardo, D. 2004. *On the Principles of Political Economy and Taxation*. Indianapolis, IN: Liberty Fund Press.

Robinson, J. 1965. *The Accumulation of Capital*. 2nd Edition. New York: St. Martin's Press.

Small I. and T. Yates. 1999. "What Makes Price Sticky? Some Survey Evidence for the United Kingdom." *Bank of England Quarterly Bulletin* (August): 262–270.

Stiglitz, J. 2003. *The Roaring Nineties*, New York: W. W. Norton.

Tcherneva, P. R. 2003. "Job or Income Guarantee." Working Paper 29, Center for Full Employment and Price Stability, Kansas City, MO.

———. "The Case for Labor Demand Targeting." *Journal of Economic Issues* 0(2): 401–410.

Wray, L. R. 1998. *Understanding Modern Money: The Key to Full Employment and Price Stability,* Cheltenham: Edward Elgar.

———. 2002. "Public Service Employment without Inflation." *Problemas del Desarrollo, Revisita Latinoamericana de Economica* 33(128).

Wray, L. R. and M. Forstater. 2004. "Full Employment and Social Justice." In *The Institutionalist Tradition in Labor Economics.* Edited by D. P. Champlin and J. T. Knoedler. Armonk, NY: M. E. Sharpe, 253–272.

CHAPTER 6

Transformational Growth, Endogenous Demand, and a Developmental ELR Program

Edward J. Nell and George Argyrous

Both neoclassical and post-Keynesian growth theory fails to explain the determinants of the growth of demand. Historically, the growth of demand has depended on the changing structure of social classes, which in turn is also a key to the growth of productivity. Understanding this makes it possible to develop a simple theory in which the growth of demand is endogenous, and interacts with capital intensity, productivity, and relative shares. By defining a distinction between "collective" goods and "personal" goods, this model can be extended further to include the growth of government. Moreover, the Employer of Last Resort (ELR), which has hitherto been considered a countercyclical policy, can now be extended to questions of development, in economies in which there is a shortage of capital. The paper closes with comments on the limitations of theories of endogenous demand growth.

Understanding the Growth of Demand

At present, neither conventional nor alternative approaches to economic theory provide much help in understanding the growth of demand, either in the aggregate, or for specific markets and sectors. "Growth of demand" refers here to repeated, continuing expansion of demand (either at a steady rate or at a fluctuating rate with a persistent average), where the expansion is not offset by contraction elsewhere. Such growth of markets, and expected growth of markets, will be important in making business decisions, and will be an object of study by marketing divisions.

Yet explaining such growth has not been an objective of theorists. Indeed, from a "real-economy," or barter exchange perspective it might seem that any growth of demand has to be based on a corresponding growth of supply. For if a new demand for a certain set of goods is to be effective in real terms, there must be an expanded supply of some other goods with which to pay for the newly demanded set. Explaining the growth of supply has therefore seemed adequate.

But this is a way of thinking that overlooks the role of finance. Finance breaks the link between demanding one set of goods and paying for them with another; once finance is in the picture, goods can be demanded even if the other goods needed to pay for them have not yet been produced. Finance makes possible the familiar pattern, "buy now, pay later." For business, this becomes: build factories and capacity now for markets that will emerge later—if development has been accurately foreseen. With finance, growth of demand is not only separable from the growth of supply, the two can, and indeed must, be coordinated over time.

Yet for the most part, growth models have been held in thrall by the "real-economy" perspective, and so have tended to focus on the supply side, assuming implicitly or explicitly that the growth of supply will generate an equivalent growth of demand, a sort of long-run Say's Law. Both Solow and Kaldor, for example, assumed that in the long run investment would reflect the "natural rate of growth." Their models differed in that Solow assumed that the warranted rate would adjust to the natural through a process of substitution between capital and labor, whereas Kaldor assumed that the adjustment would come about through changes in income distribution resulting from variations in demand pressure. In both, however, the natural rate—a supply side variable—determines the long run course of investment, a Keynesian expenditure variable.

However, this has to be considered implausible. Surely, plans to spend on the expansion of productive capacity will not be developed without a prior expectation of an appropriate growth in demand. For the Keynesian separation of investment from savings to hold, there has to be finance available. So the growth of demand will not be constrained by the growth of supply and cannot be inferred from supply-side considerations. A demand-side account is required. We can start from the beginning.

Malthus and Ricardo

The debate between Malthus and Ricardo over the role of effective demand has rightly been seen as an early controversy over Say's Law, that is, over whether the effective demand would be sufficient to purchase full employment output. Malthus worried that increased saving would reduce demand. Both agreed that, in such a case, prices would fall, raising real wages and therefore consumption demand. The total output would be purchased. But the higher real wages tended to reduce profits, leading accumulation to fall. Ricardo replied that, generally, saving will only be increased if needed for additional investment. So the rise in saving would normally be matched by increased demand for capital goods, so that accumulation will tend to rise, rather than fall. What happens then, he contends, depends on whether accumulation is proceeding faster, slower or at the same rate as the growth in the labor force. For that will determine whether wages rise, fall, or remain steady. A rise in wages will reduce profits, and therefore reduce the rate of accumulation; a decline in wages will raise profits, and so raise the rate of accumulation. The system is stable around a rate of growth of capital equal to the rate of growth of labor.

But another, more subtle thread can be detected, running through the argument. Malthus repeatedly claims that an excessive urge to save will hinder rather than promote accumulation, that is to say, growth. He sometimes phrases this dynamically, claiming that an increase in saving will reduce the rate of accumulation, or conversely, that an increase in spending would raise the rate of accumulation. Ricardo, in reply, denies that saving can be "excessive." If there is a shortfall of investment, prices fall. So real wages rise, and workers consume more. All goods produced will be sold. If too much is invested in relation to the growth of the labor force, wages will rise and profits fall. Therefore, investment will be cut back.

What is implicit here, especially in Malthus, though perhaps not clearly spelled out, is an instability argument: once the rate of accumulation declines, there may be no reliable forces that will tend to raise it again. Suppose efforts to save increase, reducing the employment of servants and retainers paid for out of profits (this is Malthus's case of reducing "unproductive consumption"), there will be a shortage of effective demand and prices will fall. So real wages will rise, profits will decline, investment will fall or fall further and consumption will increase. Now growth is slower. If before it was just keeping pace with the growth of the labor force, now it no longer will. Hence, wages will be driven down.[1] For simplicity, assume that the decline in wages is proportional to the rise in the labor force. The wage bill and so consumption will now be unchanged. *There is no need for further investment in the consumer goods industries.* Existing capacity will be sufficient. Next period investment will again be low, prices will tend to fall, so real wages and consumption will tend to rise, but again labor will be increasing faster than capital, so wages will also fall. The system will become locked into a pattern of falling prices and wages, with labor regularly growing faster than capital, so that unemployment rises.

Ricardo replies in effect that so long as whatever is saved is accumulated (invested) no commodities will fail to find purchasers; but he does not seem to see the possibility of low-level trap. Malthus may never have articulated his concerns adequately, but he does have an answer—a market for consumption goods, independent of wage-earners, is needed. He calls this "a class of unproductive consumers," and he notes that they are supported by wealth (he also discusses support by taxation). Their consumption must stand in the "right proportion" to the "value of the whole produce"—a proportion that can be expected to differ between different countries. The unproductive classes must therefore grow at the rate of accumulation, and, in particular, this growth of consumption will provide the basic motive for accumulation.[2] However, though suggested in passing, this last point, the crucial one for our purposes, is never developed (Malthus 1836, Section IX, 421–436).

HARROD-DOMAR AND MULTIPLIER-ACCELERATOR MODELS

It is often thought that, at the macro level, the growth of demand is explained by the Harrod-Domar model. The "warranted rate of growth" is that rate at which the growth of demand just equals the growth of capacity; but in fact this model equates the current level of expenditure, as determined by the multiplier, with the current capacity output of the capital stock, in accordance with the productivity of capital (inverse of the capital-output ratio). There is no necessary connection with growth.

To see this consider an example that substitutes government spending for investment (Nell 1998a, 599–600). Let G be government spending, K be the capital stock, v the capital-output ratio, K/Y; assume all profits, P, are saved and all wages consumed. Then $z = 1-wn = P/Y$, where w is the wage rate, and $n = N/Y$. $G/z = K/v$ tells us that aggregate demand equals capacity output, and this implies $G/K = z/v = r$.

The formula, analogous to the Harrod-Domar condition, states that the ratio of government spending to capital must equal the ratio of profits' share to the capital-output ratio in order for capacity to be fully utilized; but the latter ratio reduces to the rate of profit; the condition is analogous to the Golden Rule.

Now let the productivity of capital depend on the level of G. Suppose that higher levels of G lead to higher productivity (lower v.) Then if $G/z > K/v$, it would appear that capacity is too low, so $1/v$ should be increased, and the way to do this is to increase G. Similarly, if $G/z < K/v$ it would appear that the appropriate move would be to reduce G. The Harrod-Domar "knife-edge" results are reproduced—there is only one level of G at which there will be equilibrium, and it is unstable.[3] Any movement away from it will be reinforced. Although the model is static, the Harrod-Domar results have been reproduced. Growth does not figure into it at all. The Harrod-Domar relationships do not necessarily offer an account of the growth of demand.

The multiplier-accelerator model suffers from a related disability.[4] The accelerator comes into play because output, responding to demand, is pressing on capacity. So more capacity should be built; but the multiplier only works if there is some flexibility in employment; then additional workers can be hired, and their spending will increase demand. If there is flexibility in employment, there is unused capacity. So why should more capacity be built? The answer that is usually given is that there is a "normal" or "desired" level of capacity, which can be exceeded, but only at higher cost. As it is exceeded, demand will increase, but so will costs. To keep the latter down, additional capacity will be built. But this just pushes the problem back one step—how is desired or normal capacity set?[5] It is still the case that when the multiplier works best, the accelerator will not be in play, and when accelerator effects are most obviously called for, the multiplier is questionable, because capacity is limited and costs are rising. In short, the multiplier-accelerator may have a role to play at points in the business cycle, but it is difficult to see how this relationship can give a reliable and long-term account of the growth of demand.

Cambridge Growth Models

The problems of the Harrod-Domar account of the growth of demand surely cannot be found in the "Cambridge" growth model in the form developed by Robinson (Robinson 1956; 1963; also cf. Kaldor 1960; 1961). But a related difficulty emerges. This approach determines growth by balancing the saving and investment respectively induced by the rate of profits.[6] A simple version (modifying the treatment in Chapter 10 of Foley and Michl 1999) can be illustrated on a diagram with the growth rate on the vertical axis and the profit rate on the horizontal. Two functions are then defined: The first shows the growth rate made possible by the saving out of various levels of the profit rate. This starts from the origin and rises with a slope that represents the propensity to save out of profits. The second shows the growth rate determined by the investment called forth by the expectation of a rate of profit. This will normally have a positive intercept, indicating that some investment, and therefore growth, would take place even if profits were expected to be zero (due to competition, especially for innovations). Higher expected profit rates stimulate investment, but not excessively, so this line will rise with a flatter slope than that of the saving function. The first relationship is based on the Classical saving function. While this has limitations, they are well understood and it is surely a reasonable first approximation. The second relationship is more problematic. Profits, business earnings, are a withdrawal.[7] How can investment depend on a "withdrawal" variable? (That is akin to saying that saving determines investment. The Keynesian insight was that spending responds to spending; business will invest more when spending rises, not when savings rise.)

Looking at it another way: why should we build more capital for tomorrow's markets in proportion to the rate of earnings of today's capital? The current rate of profit tells us how well capital is doing today; but today's investment spending will not come on line until tomorrow. Today's profit helps to finance today's investment (as accounted for in the first equation). It provides no reason to build more capacity. Even interpreting the variable as an expected future rate of profits does not help, (quite apart from the fact that the rates in the two equations would refer to different time periods).[8] Suppose the rate of profits is expected to rise; why should that lead to building more capacity? The rate of profit on current capital will have risen without doing anything. On the other hand, if the rate in question is the expected rate of profit on the newly built capacity after it comes into operation, then it is a marginal rate, and is not comparable to the rate which figures in the Classical savings equation. If it is the expected future rate on all capital—present plus new investment—the question still arises, why does a higher rate induce more investment now?

The correct answer, it will be argued here, requires first making an important distinction—between investment decisions and investment spending (to carry out those decisions). Then what induces decisions to invest, to build more capacity, is the anticipated growth of markets. If markets are growing strongly, decisions to invest will be made readily, even if expected profitability is low. If markets are sluggish, however, even though profitable, there will be little reason to build more capacity, and decisions to invest will be few. Capacity is planned to service demand. Spending on capacity construction, however, requires considering another variable—the cost and availability of funds. This affects the timing of capital construction, not the decision whether the capacity should be built.[9]

Pricing

Neither equilibrium—determinateness—nor stability can be established for prices (in mass production markets) unless the growth of demand equals the growth of supply. Suppose current supply and demand are equal, but while new markets are opening up, firms are not building new capacity (for whatever reason). Future prices will start to rise, and this will lead to an increase in current demand for stockpiling, upsetting the current equilibrium. (Even if future prices were sluggish, or the futures market undeveloped, stockpiling in the light of anticipated shortages would be a good idea.) The same results follow in reverse if supply is expanding with no growth of markets in sight.[10]

By contrast, suppose current demand lies below current normal capacity, but new markets are opening up at the same rate that new capacity is being built. Current demand and supply can be brought into line by raising the scrapping or lowering the replacement rate. The same holds if current demand is above current normal capacity—scrapping can be postponed, or replacements enhanced. These are one-shot adjustments. However, when current demand and supply are equal but the growth rates are out of line, no one-shot adjustment can restore the balance. If the growth of demand and supply are not equal, the market cannot reach equilibrium, but if growth is in balance, and current levels are not, capacity is easily adjusted to bring them into line.

The significance for theory lies in the fact that prices are important long-term factors influencing the growth of supply on the one hand, and the growth of demand on the other. Given unit costs, higher prices—relative to money wages—increase profit margins, and thus provide both internal finance and borrowing power, making it possible to underwrite the construction of additional capacity. On the other hand, higher prices (relative to money wages) make it harder, lower prices make it easier, to break into and develop new markets (Nell 1992; 1998a, Chapter 10). So we can define a positive or rising relationship between long-term or "target" prices and the planned growth of capacity, and an inverse or falling relationship between such prices and the growth of demand.[11]

However, while this approach will help in understanding the practice of modern corporations in managing their markups, it sheds little light on why new markets are opening up in the first place. Corporations can lower their prices, and attract more business; that is simply static demand. It becomes dynamic only in a limited sense, when conjoined to the income distribution. In a class society with a hierarchical income distribution, as price falls relative to the wage, new groups can progressively incorporate the good into their budgets. Such "incorporation effects" are fully accounted for in the "Lfestyle" approach to the household, discussed below. A function can be derived showing the expansion of markets with each lowering of the price. This is an important step. Yet it is no more than the expansion of an already existing good into new areas; innovation and social change are not involved, suggesting that more fundamental forces remain to be explored.

CHOICE

Utility theory and the principal versions of the mainstream theory of consumer behavior seek to determine choices in static terms. Not only are preferences given, agents are also assumed to know their preferences without having to learn or experiment. Skills and information are likewise given without regard to learning and, of course, endowments of resources, including labor, are assumed known and available. The theory then determines current levels of household expenditure, but it contributes nothing to explaining how this level might change or grow in a systematic way.

Household budgets do present serious choice problems, but these must be considered in a programming format, as, for example, in the work of Lancaster, where consumers are understood not to want goods for their own sake, but for what they offer—their "characteristics." That is, we want apples for taste, nutrition, or to complement other foods. Bananas also offer taste, nutrition, and (different) complementarities. We choose the bundle of goods, apples and bananas that offers us the best deal for the desired characteristics, taste, nutrition, and so on—the minimum cost bundle that provides a given level of the characteristics, or the highest fulfillment of desire for a given cost. Lancaster leaves his "characteristics" floating free. They need to be fitted into a larger picture, in which certain "characteristics" will be desired because they are part of a "lifestyle," which in turn reflects class and social pressures (Nell 1998a, 470–473). This then will allow for choices of goods and services to achieve the standards imposed by a lifestyle (Nell 1998, Chapter 10). Demand functions can be developed; they will show stretches of unresponsiveness to price changes alternating with large rapid responses. "Composition" effects—changing the proportions of categories of goods in the budget—and "incorporation" effects—including new goods, dropping others—can be distinguished and their causes studied (Nell 1998a, 474–475).

Certain lifestyles will call for self-improvement, and for competition to rise to in social status. Self-improvement and rising in status will also tend to increase productivity. The social pressures generating this kind of competitive career and social climbing are likely to be class-related. Responding to such pressures will tend to lead to setting aside part of the household budget for investment in education, training, and other efforts directed to achieving promotions and rise in social status. It will also call for labor-saving innovation in household tasks, since more time will be needed for household members to engage in the new activities. This will open the door for new products.

Setting out on such a path might be associated with reaching a certain level of real wages, a level associated with lifestyles in which achievement is measured in terms of income and status. That is, a certain level of real wages might be associated with investment in self-improvement, and so with increases in productivity and growth in incomes. Investment in self-improvement is likely to lead to changes in the composition of demand. Growth of productivity and income, of course, will tend to lead to growth of demand.

These issues are discussed in the following sections. We will examine the qualitative, historical process of the growth of markets. This discussion can then inform the modeling of the growth process to take account of the problems raised above in the models we considered. The analysis will also lead us to question whether demand from government spending should be seen as exogenous, as is commonly assumed in post-Keynesian models, or whether it should be considered a partially endogenous variable, both affecting and affected by the evolution of consumption demand.

THE EMERGENCE OF WAGE LABOR AND THE ORIGINS OF MASS MARKETS

The theory of Transformational Growth (TG) emphasizes the role of mass production technology in altering the fundamental operations of a capitalist economy (Nell 1998b). Of equal importance, though, is the rise of mass markets that make such a technology viable. TG therefore also seeks to explain the rise of mass markets and the consumer behavior that underpins them. Mass markets arise in a historical process involving complex changes in the way household activities are related to industrial production.

In fact, three distinct processes are involved in the rise of mass markets, each of varying importance at different stages of development. The first is the formation of an industrial working class that purchases subsistence goods in the market rather than producing them within a largely self-sufficient household. The second process by which mass markets form is the productivity effects of mass production technology on the aggregate incomes of workers, once this technology becomes established as a result of the formation of an industrial working class. The third is the changes in the composition of demand resulting from income growth.

The theory of TG draws a distinction between preindustrial, predominantly agrarian, societies and modern mass production economies. The family unit in traditional society produced for itself the goods its members consumed. Each family had access to the raw materials it needed such as cotton, wool, and grains, and applied domestic labor to transform these raw inputs into useable goods, often drawing on the extended family when labor was required for major tasks such as homebuilding. "Our forefathers in colonial America lived on their own farms, built their own houses, raised their own food, and made their own clothes. Each family was a little world in itself, capable of meeting most of the needs of its existence. Today, an individual produces few of the commodities he consumes" (Andrews and Michels 1938, 44). For the bulk of the population, consumption was satisfied through direct production by the consuming household.

Alongside this system of household production, there existed commercial producers who sold commodities in a market. These markets were based largely on the discretionary needs of aristocratic households or the occasional needs of village households for specialized goods they could not make for themselves. Thus, these firms were characterized by craft technology that could be adapted to meet the discretionary needs of such expenditure. The need to literally tailor goods to the specific demands of individual consumers restricted production technology to a small-scale craft technology using very simple equipment. Producers knew who would consume their product and were geared toward adapting production to the particular needs of these consumers.

The basis of this system was the access of the peasantry to land upon which they could obtain the raw materials as inputs to domestic production, and the availability to the household of the labor time of its members. The breakdown of this system can therefore be found in the alienation of the peasantry from land, or the removal of members of the household so that their labor time was no longer available (as when male members were conscripted into the army). Without access to land and the raw materials it provided, or the domestic labor to produce subsistence goods, previously self-sufficient peasants were forced to purchase the inputs to domestic production on the market. Their only means for doing this was to offer their labor power for sale in return for wages that could be used to purchase these inputs.

This process, in other words, of alienating the peasantry from the material inputs to domestic production, as in the enclosure system in the United Kingdom, creates alongside it the markets for goods that were previously produced by the household. As Marx cogently summarized, "in fact, the events that transformed the small peasants into wage-labourers, and their means of subsistence and of labour into material elements of capital, created, at the same time, a home market for capital" (1886, 910).

As workers are created out of this breakdown of the traditional system, they have to spend their wages on the materials or finished goods that they once produced for themselves. With the market for such goods expanding, more labor is drawn away from the countryside in order to meet the demand. These additional workers, in turn, can no longer devote their time to domestic production and therefore add to the demand for industrially produced goods. When a critical mass of wage laborers forms, the process becomes cumulative and draws more of the peasantry into its orbit.

It is important to note that the rise in money income as a means for satisfying demand is not necessarily equated with an improvement in the living standards of the working class. Indeed, it is sometimes the impoverishment of households brought about by their alienation from the means of household production that forces them to seek wage labor, thereby simultaneously creating and expanding consumer markets. In periods of recession, for example, the decline in wage income coming into the household upsets the balance between labor supplied to the market and labor devoted to domestic production. With less money income from wage labor, the inputs needed for domestic production will be more difficult to purchase. Without their own land to cultivate, the family will not be able to maintain its standard of living by opting out of industrial production. More members of the family will have to offer their labor power in the market, or existing workers will put in overtime in order to maintain the flow of money income. This means that there is less labor available for household production. Households will thereby use their income to purchase final commodities, or labor-saving inputs to domestic production that embody a higher degree of industrial production. In other words, these changes imply a rearrangement of the entire lifestyle of the household and its operation. Bernstein (1987), for example, has argued that the mass unemployment of the 1930s in the United States lowered the money wage level of many working classes' households. In order to maintain the money income of the family, other members of the household, especially housewives, had to seek employment. With less time available to devote to household production, activities such as the preparation and storage of food could no longer be undertaken domestically. This created a market for consumer durables and for packaged food, which in turn fostered expansion of the canning and bottling industries. Bernstein argues that with sufficient time, these processes may have allowed the economy to move out of depression, albeit very slowly.

The Demand Effects of Productivity Growth

With the formation of an industrial working class, the market can continue to grow by cheapening the commodities that make up their consumption basket, thereby raising the real incomes of consumers. This has been a focal point of the cumulative causation literature, particularly that of Allyn Young (1926) and Nicholas Kaldor (1966). The division of labor raises productivity and allows a cheapening of commodities, which leads to an expansion of the market for that commodity, which then induces further division of labor and the extension of the mass production system. This mutually reinforcing feedback between technology and market demand led Young (1928) to amend Adam Smith's famous dictum such that "the division of labor is limited by the division of labor." He could alternatively have stated this apparent tautology by arguing that the extent of the market is limited by the extent of the market. In fact, neither statement is a tautology, since they are backed by a theory which explains the self-reinforcing feedbacks between productivity growth and market demand.

It is important to identify the precise ways in which productivity growth induces an expansion of demand. The first and most obvious channel is the way in which new consumers are able to enter the market for the commodity whose production is undergoing transformational growth. As a commodity cheapens, more consumers are able to include it into their consumption bundle; the emergence of the mass market for home computers and the constant reduction in price is a classic example of this process. A cost-cutting innovation may allow a drop in price that will bring the product into the affordable region for a whole new class of customers. This will set off a new competitive sales drive and expansion for the firms in the industry. Indeed, this suggests a regular relationship between price and the expansion of a market.

A second channel through which productivity growth expands demand in such a way as to induce further productivity growth is the increase in the real income of those people who already purchase the commodity whose relative price is declining. No longer needing to devote as much of their real income to purchasing a given commodity, these consumers redirect their demand to other commodities that they could previously not afford. This extends the division of labor in these other industries, which raises the real of income of their consumers, and so on.

A third channel that is especially important in the early stages of capitalism is the way in which the cheaper (and sometimes better) goods produced in the factories destroy small-scale production of similar goods. This forces more people to enter the wage labor class, who add to demand for a variety of other goods as they spend their money wages. The fall in the price of a commodity means that small-scale producers are competed out of the market. An example of this process is the rapid decline of domestic spinning in the face of the mechanization of the cotton industry in England in the late 1700s. "The mechanical advantage of even the earliest jennies and water frames over hand-spinning was enormous: anywhere from six up to twenty-four to one for the jenny; several hundred to one for the frame. The spinning wheel, which had taken some centuries to displace the rock, became an antique in the space of a decade" (Landes 1972, 85).

Growth through Changes in the Composition of Demand

We have noted that households begin as production units, with the inputs to production consisting largely of homegrown raw materials to which domestic labor is applied to transform them into consumption goods. As industrialization takes hold and mass production spreads from industry to industry, drawing workers into its orbit, less labor can be devoted to domestic production. The household remains a production unit (usually through a sexual division of labor), but the inputs are no longer raw; they have already been transformed in the industrial sphere, and are transformed further in the household sphere with the aid of labor saving devices such as washing machines and microwave ovens. Eventually, very little production is undertaken in the household, which becomes almost a pure consumption unit.

The history of the sewing machine illustrates this evolution. No longer having access to raw materials nor having the time to spin cotton and wool into yarn to make cloth, households purchase the cloth ready-made and produce clothing with the aid of sewing machine. This creates a mass market for sewing machines, the production of which requires a large labor force, which adds to overall effective demand and the growth of markets for consumption goods in general. Eventually, though, households purchase industrially produced finished clothing, rather than transforming semifinished inputs through domestic labor. In the process, the entire manufacture of finished clothing is eventually transferred to industry.

When households come to purchase an increasing proportion of finished goods as part of their consumption bundle, the determination of consumption norms becomes a central issue to market creation. Since households now purchase goods that are identically available to other households, the composition of consumption takes on an increasingly cultural and social significance. Purchases become a signal of one's station in life. This sets up new pressures that drive consumption, particularly the need to express self-improvement in terms of the composition of demand. The reasons for this are complex, and grounded in the changes in culture as the social system develops from a one of tradition and "natural order" to one of "regular progress" (Nell 1998b, 9–19). Households seeking to rise in station will typically seek to do this by providing a better education and better opportunities for their children. These households will invest in self-improvement, more for their children than for themselves, but very often in order to provide better conditions for their children they will have to improve themselves (we might call this the "Horatio Alger Effect"). Funds that formerly went for entertainment and for drink will now go to education and self-improvement, and preparing the children for a better life (see figure 6.1).

When a household decides to rise in the world, it adopts an investment strategy. It begins to invest in human capital development, especially education and training, and the development of communications skills. It will come to require transportation that is more flexible. It will have to rearrange its living quarters, to provide space for the new activities of learning and acquiring new skills. When a sizable number of households adopt this strategy, they will begin to benefit from interacting with each other. Even though they are competing, they will also provide support for each other. These "network effects" will increase the effectiveness of the efforts at self-improvement. Then, as more and more households seek to rise, there will be new markets created for products that contribute to self-improvement. Much of this will be education—courses, classes, night schools, and books, newspapers, and other media. Communication will become increasingly important, as will all forms of education. In turn, these will require inputs, which will be supplied by capital goods industries.[12]

This (albeit simplistic) story of the growth of consumer demand helps explain one of the most significant regularities in all of economics, depicted

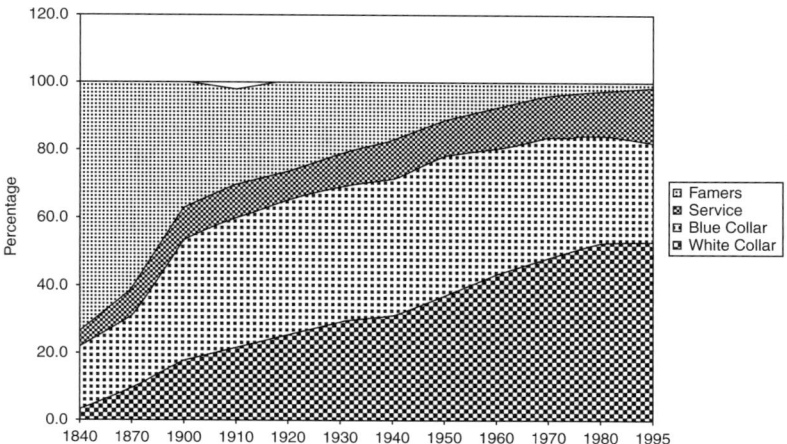

Figure 6.1 Occupations as a percentage of the labor force.

by the Engel Curve. The Engel Curve was originally developed to explain the decline in the relative importance of food in the consumption bundle of households as their incomes rise, an observation consistent with the discussion above. It has since been expanded into a statement of the gradual diversification of consumer demand as income grows, and in particular the increasing share of income spent on manufactured items, and then service items (Houthakker 1957). The important feature of the Engel Curve is that households do not spend reasonably permanent increases in income on commodities in the same proportion as they have in the past. There is a distinct hierarchy of needs and wants (Cornwall 1977, 100–102), so that "as per capita real income increases each increment of consumers' demand tends to concentrate on a particular group of goods and services. This group of goods and services gradually changes from one level of income to another. Hence, as income increases, the tendency is not to increase proportionately the consumption of already bought goods and services, but rather to buy new goods and services or to satisfy old needs with different (and hopefully better) goods" (Pasinetti 1981, 77).

This clustering of goods and services, in a hierarchical fashion with respect to income, essentially revolves around the complementarities between the goods that together form a particular "lifestyle." As income increases, there is a point at which households feel they can alter their existing pattern of consumption and "invest" in a new lifestyle (provided this income growth could be confidently projected into the future). An addition can be made to the family home that requires a new furnishing, a second TV, and so on. This disproportionate growth in the bundle of commodities that occupy a household's demand is crucial to the endogenous evolution of markets since it will allow new industries to spring up, replacing as an engine of growth those industries whose demand has reached saturation levels given their "earlier" position along the aggregate Engel Curve.

This theory of consumption, based on the evolution of demand through the Engel Curve, allows for a sociological theory of consumer behavior. It provides a role for consumer learning in the formation of tastes and preferences through emulation and trial and error, and through the pervasive effects of advertising in "helping" to determine the commodities that make up the lifestyles that define the points which make up the Engel Curve. The general point about this discussion of social structure and the growth of markets is that expansion depends on constant and far reaching changes in the way society is organized, and the ability of large groups to move into markets to which they were excluded.

The creation of new urban centers as more people leave traditional forms of production to engage in wage labor, the replacement of family ownership and control with management hierarchies populated by entirely new classes of people—such phenomena imply new lifestyles defined by an ensemble of goods and services that must be produced. As long as social stratification is fluid and new or existing markets continue to find pockets of expansion, demand will grow. As soon as social positions begin to ossify and mobility is reduced, stagnation sets in. This will then discourage further investment and innovation that in turn reduces the forces that could potentially churn up the social order and cause markets to expand again. Social change, and especially social improvement on a large scale, is an essential, but not guaranteed, part of transformational growth.

Growth of Demand—A Formal Model

The Emergence of New Markets

We saw previously that a price-expansion of demand function could be derived on the basis of a given class structure and income distribution but this did not take into account or explain innovation. It examined the growth of demand in terms of the expansion of existing (more or less mature) markets, leaving to one side the emergence and development of new ones. New markets must be created, in some process of innovation. This might result from the development of a new product or the route explored here, it could be part of a larger movement, the effort of a fraction of the working class to rise in the world, through a competitive process of self-improvement. Self-improvement, in turn, as we saw, requires restructuring household budgets, and will have to draw on sources of finance.

Once they have established a foothold, new markets will develop following a more or less sigmoid shaped path, starting slowly, then expanding at an accelerating pace, then slowing down and finally stagnating. The latter stages, of course, are the stages of expansion for mature products.

Existing markets tend to expand in line with Engel curves; increases in the incomes of existing customers will not be spent in the same proportions. Instead, households will typically introduce new elements into the household budget. So existing markets, depending on a set of regular customers, are likely to expand at a slower pace than the incomes of their customers, unless these markets are stimulated by some major innovation. (An obvious implication is that, cet. par., growth will slow down as markets mature; sustaining a growth rate requires the development of new markets.)

Existing markets can be stimulated very simply. A cost-cutting innovation may allow a drop in price that will bring the product into the affordable region for a whole new class of potential customers. This will set off a new competitive sales drive and expansion for the firms in the industry. Indeed, this suggests a regular relationship between price and the expansion of a market. In a similar way, a product innovation may make the product useful or more useful or simply more attractive, in a number of ways, thereby creating a new pool of customers. Cost-cutting, product improvement, and specialization of product design will continually bring new groups into the market, until all potential customers have been attracted. At this point, the market will have become mature, and will normally begin to stagnate. The expansion of existing markets may largely reflect aspects of the life cycle that each market passes through, from its small, early beginnings through a phase of rapid expansion, to maturity and stagnation.

The growth of demand then can be broken into two parts: the study of the emergence of new markets on the one hand, and the life cycle of their development on the other. What has to be explained therefore, at the outset, is the emergence of new markets. (Remember that throughout most of history new products and new markets were rare. Most people's lives closely resembled those of the grandparents—and also those of their grandchildren.) New markets develop when a number of households change the composition of their budgets, add new products to their consumption patterns/lifestyles, and in particular come to "invest in human capital." New markets emerge because of households reconfiguring their budgets. Demand grows because of a certain kind of change in its composition—a characteristic feature of Transformational Growth. This may take place as follows.

A certain culturally or socially determined fraction of households develops the desire to rise in station. The reasons for this are complex, and grounded in the changes in culture as the social system develops from one of tradition and "natural order" to one of "regular progress" (Nell 1998b, 9–19). A precondition for a widespread development of the desire to rise in station is that the labor in agriculture should decline and families move from the countryside to the city. This breaks the traditional bonds that tie families to their social station. It also puts people in direct contact with opportunities and alternative ways of life and work. A further fundamental precondition is that the workplace and home living space be separated. If they are not then the whole family will tend to be fully involved with the trade, and the children will not be able to learn a different or better way of life. This separation of living space from working space will take place as energy is brought into play to drive machinery. Steam power is dirty and dangerous and loud. Children cannot be near it. Electricity is dangerous, and electric power equipment needs to be treated with circumspection. As equipment comes to be driven by steam and electricity, the home and the workplace must be separated. Households seeking to rise in station will typically seek to do this by providing a better education and better opportunities for their children. These households will invest in self-improvement, more for their children than for themselves, but very often in order to provide better conditions for their children they will have to improve themselves. Funds that formerly went for entertainment and for drink will now go to education and self-improvement, and preparing the children for a better life.

An important element in the effort for self-improvement will be time saving in the household. Households should be considered production units, producing the lifestyle by preparing food, making and mending clothing, performing daily tasks of washing, ironing, cleaning, and so on. Innovations such as detergents, improved cleaning fluids, vacuums, washers and dryers, gas and electrical heating, and lighting, cut down on the time required to run the household, and thereby provided time that could be spent on self-improvement. Looked at from the other side of the market, the movement for self-improvement opened the door to labor-saving innovations in the household. Here we have the development of a process, a set of linkages running from households changing their understanding of their social position and life options, to redesigning their budgets to allow for investment in self-improvement, leading to the emergence of new markets. To make this effective on a large scale will require finance, so it also offers opportunities for financial institutions to develop. These changes in household spending patterns then lead to additional demand for capital goods to make it possible to supply the emerging markets, with the effects then running back to the productivity of households.

First demand changes composition, leading to the emergence of a new market. This new market has to be supplied, leading to new investment. A shift in demand, of course, also leads to a falling off of demand for some traditional products, with falling prices and profits in those industries, that frees up resources to shift capacity to the new area. Note, however, that a shift from an established product to a new one can also lead producers of the old to improve their product and intensify their marketing—the shift could stimulate investment in *both* old and new. In any case the new investment(s) will embody the latest technology, so are likely to be more productive than the old. This will provide the first increase in income, leading to increased demand, which in turn will lead to increased investment.

A direct consequence of successful self-improvement will be a rise in the productivity of labor, especially of supervisory and managerial labor. Hence, there will be a second increase in income, also resulting in an increase in demand, in turn calling for additional investment. (Some families who seek self-improvement and ascent in the world may fail. But this failure will not affect the development of the market. It merely means that their productivity and income will not increase.) As is evident, this develops into a cumulative process, each round of self-improvement expanding the new markets, leading to new investment, which raises industrial productivity, while the self-improvement raises labor productivity. Both give rise to higher incomes, which lead to further investments in self-improvement.

As the new group of successful families emerges, it will become aware of itself, and increasingly develop a new lifestyle. This will be partly functional, that is, will help to consolidate the productivity gains, but it will also partly be a display of class position and privilege. It will mean further development of new markets, for products especially designed to play a role in this new lifestyle. Once again, as these further or subsidiary markets develop, there will be a need for investment, so for new capital goods, to build up the capacity to produce for these markets.

Modeling Demand Growth

Now it's time to consider the economy as a whole. To do this we combine a relationship between the real wage and the growth of demand with the well-established real wage—rate of profit tradeoff (cf. Nell 1998a, 477–478). The model has four variables: growth of demand, growth of output, growth of productivity, and the real wage. There is an equilibrium condition, that growth of demand equal growth of output, and then we can define three behavioral relationships.

First there is what Joan Robinson called the "wage-accumulation" curve, the wage-profit tradeoff adjusted by the saving ratio. This relationship is inverse, and following the argument in Nell (1998a), it is likely to be linear. It will shift with changes in productivity. Second there is the wage rate—growth of demand relationship already discussed, which includes an effect on productivity. This will be an increasing function, with a sigmoid shape. At low levels of the wage there will be some growth of demand, but it will be low, and will increase only slowly; then at higher levels it will accelerate, and rise steeply, leveling off at still higher levels. Third, we can adopt some form of Verdoorn-Kaldor relationship, relating productivity growth positively to growth and real wages. This gives us three equations:

$g = g(w/p, x)$ $\quad\quad\quad\quad g'_w < 0, g'_x > 0$, assumed linear
$w/p = w(g, x)$ $\quad\quad\quad w'_g > 0, w'_x > 0$, assumed sigmoid in shape
$x = x(g, w/p)$ $\quad\quad\quad x'_g > x''_g < 0, x'_w > 0$ up to a point, then $x'_w < 0$

For a given w/p it is assumed, plausibly enough, that there is some level of g beyond which x will no longer increase. It is also assumed that, for a given g, at some level of the real wage, x (productivity) will reach a maximum and begin to decline. These assumptions effectively bound the level of x, and so ensure that the system of equations will have a solution. Given a few reasonable restrictions it can be shown that these three behavioral equations have a unique, positive solution, which is stable by normal criteria.[13] Note the analogy with businesses where each level of earnings is associated with a rate of growth of spending on capital goods. Higher earnings mean higher profits, so resulting in a higher rate of profits, giving rise to a higher rate of growth. The same holds here. The real wage-growth of demand function tells us that for each level of the real wage there will be a corresponding level of investment in self-improvement leading to a corresponding rate of growth of demand by households. Households invest in self-improvement; because they are doing so, they are eligible for credit and can increase their spending, particularly their spending on self-improvement. The function is economy wide. At higher levels of the real wage there will be higher rates of growth of demand for two reasons. First, demand growth will be higher because each household may be able to sustain a larger investment in self-improvement, and second, because more households can be drawn into the effort to rise in the world. We must be careful about the interpretation: the solution to these equations is not a long-period equilibrium. Far from it, the reason that demand is growing is that families are trying to improve themselves. Innovation is taking place. On the other hand it is not short run; it covers a long enough stretch for training and education to result in higher levels of productivity. So the time periods might perhaps be a full business cycle. This model can be used to explore an important question in the history of growth and technology. If innovations have been introduced simply because they reduce costs, we would expect them sometimes to be labor-saving, sometimes to save on equipment and capital goods. Overall, there would seem to be no reason to expect any particular bias. In fact, there has been a very pronounced bias: technical development has been overwhelmingly labor-saving, but capital-using. That is, machinery and equipment has been substituted for labor.

COLLECTIVE GOODS AND THE RISE OF GOVERNMENT

The desire of a set of households to rise in the world leads them to change the pattern of their consumption. More particularly, it leads to investment in education and training and to spending on communication. It will tend to lead to households relocating, especially moving to suburbs. One consequence is to lead businesses to invest more. Nevertheless, another takes the economy in a new direction. For it means that the spending of increases in income will now be chiefly directed to what may be called collective goods and interactive services. It is not just that markets grow, but new kinds of markets develop, generating new kinds of problems. So far we have considered only two players, households and businesses, both private. Now the implications bring in a new player, government.

That is, one person can eat a sandwich, or wear a shirt, without significantly affecting or involving anyone else, apart from the normal market processes. However, for education there must be not only teachers and students, but also subjects and disciplines. Indeed, there must be right and wrong answers and that implies a collectivity of minds. For a writer there have to be readers—and vice versa—but also there must be subjects and styles. No one can make a telephone call unless someone else answers. No one can travel without a destination. My health and yours are interconnected concerning communicable diseases. Normal market processes, for these goods, involve multiple consumers acting in coordination, or even organized into networks, and there may be networks of suppliers. As a result, these goods tend to call for more intensive government regulation, and draw more intensively on government services.

This should not be confused with the familiar idea of public goods. These latter are defined as goods or services that are nonrivalrous (and/or nondepletable, not quite the same thing), and nonexcludable.[14] A lighthouse is a good example. If one ship uses it, that does not prevent another from doing so. Nor does it use up the lighthouse, leaving less for later ships. Moreover, once put in place and working, no ships can be excluded, that is, prevented from using it. A bridge or a roadway is nonrivalrous (at least within limits) and nondepletable, but toll barriers can be erected, permitting exclusion. Collective or interactive goods often do not meet these criteria. Access can easily be denied, so fees can be charged. Similarly with education: access to the class can be denied; and at a certain point the classroom is full; if this person is in the class, that one can't be. (Although it is not true that the more one person gets from the class the less there will be for the others; on the contrary, the more some students get, the more the rest are likely to benefit.) One ship can use the lighthouse, whether or not any others do; one person can cross the bridge alone. (Although both bridge and lighthouse are means to a destination.)

However, no one can make a telephone call alone, or travel without going somewhere. Commuter travel, in particular, moves between the places of home and work, each socially defined. No one can take a class or learn a subject without participating in an enterprise of many minds. No one can use money without others also doing so. No one can take out insurance unless others do so. Education, communications, transportation, FIRE,[15] and entertainment—and even aspects of health—are collective experiences.

Collective goods, as these examples show, are often cooperative. Nevertheless, they can also be competitive, as with what Hirsch called "positional goods." Seats at a sports game or in the theater are positional; those with a better view are more desirable and command a higher price. The same is true of rooms in a hotel, travel packages, and desirable real estate. Location is everything, and these goods are therefore rivalrous, may be depletable—this year's World Series will never happen again—and are certainly excludable. Positional goods meet none of the criteria for being public goods, but they are clearly collective goods, and, as we shall see, like cooperative collective goods, call for more intensive government regulation, and interact strongly with other collective goods and with government services.

Let's consider some of the implications: food, clothing and shelter, and many forms of energy are goods that can be consumed privately, by individuals or households. That is to say, the act of consuming these goods need not necessarily involve or require the cooperation of other individuals or households. (This is also true of some traditional public goods.) When per capita incomes are low, the greater part of household budgets will be devoted to these goods. However, education, entertainment, communications, transportation, and most forms of modern health care do necessarily involve or require the coordinated cooperation of others. When per capita incomes increase, household spending will tend to shift to these categories.

These kinds of goods often, perhaps usually, have network externalities. That is, the more the members joining a network, the greater will be the benefits to each. A typical case is a telephone exchange. Service stations are another. Governments may need to supply or at least regulate such goods, in order to make sure that pricing for private profit does not result in an inadequate supply. Such goods, collective goods, also typically require regulation. They involve coordinated action by numbers of people, and regulation may be needed to ensure coordination. Moreover, the technology may be complicated or dangerous. Government oversight may be necessary. For all these reasons, such goods call for more government spending.

Government economic activity in general responds to, or provides a foundation for, private economic activity. Private activity rests on public infrastructure like roads, bridges, harbors, sewers and on basic collective services (usually with network externalities) like public health, police, justice, defense, and education. The government may provide these services and infrastructure directly or it might simply underwrite them and contract them out. In either case, the amount of government spending required will stand in some kind of proportion to the amount and nature of the private activities.

Define a coefficient of government spending as the amount of G called for per unit of private economic activity. The general claim suggested is that collective goods have a higher coefficient of government spending than private goods. The shift from a craft economy to mass production has resulted in the rise in the ratio of G to Y. Of course, rather than regulating private production of collective goods, governments may undertake their provision. In that case, G/Y would increase even more. That is, as private businesses and households shift to collective goods and interactive services, Government will not only do likewise, but it will also in general be called on to spend more in a variety of ways.

Let us look at this more closely, for there is another feature of collective goods that contributes to the rise in G/Y. Among the major categories of government activity that have been affected are education, defense, police and justice, medical services, pensions and social security, and transportation. These tend to interact strongly with private sector collective goods and with each other. The analytical point here is that interactions increase with the square of the number of actors. For example: mass production leads to urban concentration; this increases interaction between people and requires increased policing and courts, and also increased attention to public health. If there are ten additional urban workers, potential interactions increase by one hundred (actual interactions will normally be fewer); costs of policing and public health will then increase in proportion to the number of interactions, rather than the number of actors. More travel both requires and facilitates better communications; more travel requires better education—and contributes to it. Better communication leads to better education and vice versa, and both stimulate the desire to travel. Better communication, and better transport leads to wider choice of places to live and locations of workplaces, so that the real estate market develops. Better education leads to higher productivity and to more rapid technical change, which, in turn, reduces the ability of the family to provide education, and so requires a further increase in public education. As people live longer and learn more, they demand better health and medical services; they also need pension and social security, especially as they leave the land and move to the cities.

All of these interact with government services; increased transportation requires more and better traffic control, communications calls for regulation, as does education; urbanization requires public health measures, and so on.

In the craft era, the ratio of private sector collective goods to all goods was low. As it increased, interactions increased faster, but the initial impact on government was not large. As the craft economy developed into mass production, however, the ratio of collective goods increased greatly. The interactions both between private sector collective goods, and between such goods and government services, increased exponentially, so that G/Y rose dramatically. This is portrayed in the diagram. In the early stages, even a large rise in the collective goods ratio leads to only a small increase in G/Y. Nevertheless, later, as the mass production era unfolds, even a modest increase in the collective goods ratio will bring a large rise in G/Y.

Finally, the rise in government also can provide—and has provided—a significant contribution to the growth in demand.[16] As we have seen, the same process that leads to growth in household demand, and competition among households to rise in the world through investment in self-improvement, leads to a shift in the composition of expenditure, in which collective goods increase in proportion to private goods. This in turn leads to further interaction with government services. Note that two distinct patterns of interaction can be defined. The first is between activities requiring collective goods; these interact, which means that an increase in the number of such activities implies an increase in demand that is proportional to the square of the increase in activities. The second is between such activities and government services, likewise implying a multiplicative increase in demand. Together these changes require a larger size of government in relation to total output. The relative increase in government spending then raises the overall growth of demand.

A New Look at the ELR and the Long Run

A sizeable literature has developed by now, working out the idea of an ELR for Advanced Capitalist Economies (ACEs). The ELR is an automatic stabilizing program that expands in a contraction and contracts in an expansion, while hiring and releasing labor at a fixed basic wage rate. Its countercyclical movement tends to stabilize employment and output, while it acts as a buffer stock with respect to labor, stabilizing the (lower end of the) wage scale. So far, the discussion has chiefly focused on the short run; the present approach allows an extension to the long.

The creation of an ELR will not only provide countercyclical demand, it will also tend to create a *new* pool of workers, who will be drawn into the labor force by the guaranteed opportunity to work.[17] The ELR will add to output largely by producing socially beneficial goods and services which would not be privately profitable, such as environmental maintenance and cleanup, teacher assistance, home improvement in poor neighborhoods, assistance to public transport services and maintenance, aid to the elderly, public health services, and the like. Such goods and services are likely to contribute to improved overall productivity. ELR workers also maintain and improve their skills, and at the same time support consumer demand.

The new workers drawn in allow the ELR to make a net contribution to growth. By devoting a portion of its resources to retraining and to remedial education, an ELR program could help to raise a proportion of the long-term unemployed to working or lower-middle-class status, thereby creating a net new market for consumer goods. That is, the improved skills will increase the productivity of those who have gone through the ELR programs, putting them in a position to move into better jobs. As a result, they will be able to command consumer credit allowing them to undertake a pattern of consumption appropriate to a higher lifestyle than they enjoyed before. If their training has been successful, this will constitute a permanent addition to consumer demand.

AN ELR FOR THE DEUCES

An obvious extension of the project is to explore the possibilities it offers to DEUCEs (Developing Economies under Capitalist Enterprise). Here the problem of unemployment is fundamentally different. In the ACEs there is enough real capital—factories, farms, equipment, organizations—to employ, that is, offer jobs to, the available labor force. Unemployment is largely a Keynesian problem of inadequate effective demand. However, in the DEUCEs a major problem is shortage of various forms of real capital. In particular, it is likely that there will be too few properly equipped factories, shops, and service businesses to offer jobs to the urban population. Moreover, the businesses that exist may be poorly organized and administered. In addition, there may not be enough arable land to provide a living for the rural population and what there is may be cultivated inefficiently. Even worse, a sector of large farms or plantations may be run with modern technology, and these may undercut the small, inefficient (but sometimes environmentally friendly) traditional farms. If this is the case, the effect is likely to be to drive population off the land to the cities.

The Keynesian demand problem may be found in these countries, but it is only part of the story; even if there is strong demand, jobs cannot not be offered because of the shortage of *capital*. The unemployed are a "reserve army." This is the Marxian problem. The point can be seen by considering how an ELR might affect a capital-shortage economy if it operated in the normal manner. Suppose the ELR offered training and literacy programs, and provided jobs in cleaning up the environment and improving sanitation and public health. The programs would be useful and would add to demand. But creating such additional demand could, in fact, cause problems, for in the face of capital shortage there would be no way for supply to respond. The likely result would be to drive up prices relative to money wages. That is, the ELR would create additional demand for goods, but in the absence of capital to provide jobs, there would be no corresponding rise in output or in the demand for labor. Thus the effect could be to drive down real wages, reducing normal household consumption more or less in proportion to the additional demand created by the ELR.

So the ELR will have to perform a different function in such economies. Countercyclical demand creation will not be so significant. Stabilizing wages may be important, however. Nevertheless, the main contribution it can make will be to create a pool of trained labor *and* help to provide capital to give permanent employment to that labor, for example, in worker-managed firms.

The approach to the growth of demand developed above, provides a framework in which this problem can be addressed, though only a sketch can be offered here. In a developing country the ELR cannot put too great a strain on existing capacity; it may not be able to offer a job to everyone who wants one at a given time, not because there isn't plenty of work to be done, but because of the danger of driving up prices. However, it can establish a queue, and take in and train job seekers successively.

Establishing an ELR designed first to train workers and then set them up in new enterprises, will have as its initial effect introducing a new set of families into the urban upper working or middle-class consumer market. This expansion of the consumer market will call forth supply, so new capacity will have to be built. The initial size of the ELR must not be too large; it will have to be within the power of the capital goods sector to supply the equipment to expand the consumer sector's capacity. In addition, of course, the building of that new capacity will increase employment in capital goods and construction sectors, putting further pressure on the capacity in consumer goods sectors.

Once established, the ELR can be used to train laborers (often newly arrived from the countryside) in appropriate and needed skills. This training should be aimed at raising the level of skills, and, ultimately, of productivity in the country's industries, to the world level. The ELR will therefore have to work closely with the major industries—and with agriculture, too—to make sure that the training it offers is appropriate. It will also have to encourage industries to upgrade their technology; so it will also have to function as a management consultant and supplier of technical advice, even of technology. In effect the ELR will be designed to *retrain and upgrade* the existing labor force, as well as provide training and remedial education to the unemployed.

The effect of retraining workers and sending them back to industry and agriculture will be to increase productivity in both consumer and capital goods sectors. This will raise growth and also make it possible to enlarge the ELR program. At this point, the ELR can enter the venture capital business; it could not only offer training programs, but it might also provide various kinds of services and new products, many of which might draw on or make use of advanced technologies. (These could be in addition to or might even largely displace the more conventional ELR offering of socially useful but largely nonmarketable goods and services.) If these new goods and services seem to be marketable, either to the public or to local businesses and governments, it could spin them off as worker-controlled enterprises, thereby helping to create new sectors. Many of these, of course, could be expected to fail. But even a few successes may be more than enough to justify the program.

So the ELR should be phased in and developed gradually, creating and stabilizing a steady growth of demand for basic consumer goods, including especially consumer durables. A pace should be chosen that will allow for the construction of appropriate capacity, and for the corresponding expansion of government services and social infrastructure—where some of this latter can be built with the help of the ELR workforce. (And the industries establishing this new capacity can be aided by government low-interest loans, and can be provided with workers trained in the ELR, thus shifting them into private sector employment, and making room in ELR programs for unemployed new arrivals from the countryside.)

The size of the ELR in these conditions will be limited by the capacity of the consumer goods industries, while the speed with which it can be expanded will be limited by the capacity of the capital goods industries. It has not been possible to do more here than outline the way an ELR might function. Clearly this will need further analysis.[18]

The ELR could thus become the guide and provide the stimulus for a market-based balanced expansion of productive capacity in capital-constrained economies. Planning and government management could then be chiefly devoted to establishing the right programs of training, of introducing new or improved technologies and products, and expanding the program at the right pace. But once the ELR is creating new markets, and at the same time training new workers, and putting them into place with venture capital, the growth of the economy will be given a foundation.

LIMITATIONS ON ENDOGENOUS GROWTH

The preceding discussion presents the transition from a craft to a mass production economy as fuelled by endogenous processes of demand creation. The risk for any theory of endogenous change, though, is that it may be very mechanistic, presenting industrialization as an inexorable process, resistant to limitations. The emphasis on various learning processes in the discussion above, however, helps the TG story avoid such mechanistic overtones, and indicates why the transition from craft to mass production was so staggered and stretched out over time. While Transformational Growth refers to system-wide changes in production technology, these system-wide outcomes only eventuate through incremental adaptations at the micro level by individual firms and industries to the evolution of demand. Moreover, we can identify specific limiting factors that can undermine the endogenous forces of expansion.

One such limiting factor is the particular relationship between capital using and capital producing sectors. Transformational Growth does not completely eliminate craft methods of production from an economy, but rather concentrates them in the capital goods industry. As mass markets for consumer goods develop, as we have argued above, this translates into demand for specialized, often custom-made pieces of capital equipment, which encourages the adoption of craft technology in the firms making the equipment. A piece of capital such as a high speed lathe may be used in a mass production process, but may have itself been produced under craft conditions. This means that the capital goods industry, particularly its core sector of machine tool producers, cannot easily expand production in the short run beyond its existing productive capacity. Over time, as they produce more equipment and raise capacity across the economy including the capital goods sector itself, such limits can be overcome. However, at any given point in time, an economy is constrained by the productive capacity of this core sector, and the craft-like technology it employs.

Another limiting factor on self-sustaining growth involves the hierarchy of goods in the Engel Curve. In particular, manufactured commodities are not evenly spread throughout the Curve's range. As income grows, consumption demand is increasingly directed to services, which are not capable of supplying through mass production technology and division of labor. For any given household, the rise of services in the consumption bundle reduces the possible feedbacks that may eventuate through division of labor and the cumulative spread of mass production technology. Manufacturing loses its power as an engine of growth with the decline of manufactured goods relatively as components of consumption. Thus growth of markets, due to the pattern of consumption over time, has an inbuilt tendency to lose its motive force.[19]

Industrialization can also slow down through changes in the way that productivity is distributed. In the competitive phase of capitalist development, productivity gains obtained through the gradual encroachment of mass production are distributed through price reductions. This spreads the benefits across a wide number of consumers, including people on fixed incomes. In the oligopoly phase of mature capitalism when economies of scale have been realized in a wide number of industries, firms increasingly use productivity gains to raise the real wages of their own workers to "purchase" industrial peace,[20] or else to engage in oligopolistic competition— marketing, after sales service, product differentiation, and so on—rather than direct them to productivity enhancing activities per se. This concentrates the income (and thereby consumption) effects of productivity growth in a smaller number of people who are largely well-paid unionized workers, so that the potential demand effect may not be as great as when productivity growth was passed on to consumers.

If these contractionary factors come into play, the endogenous demand relationships that were a positive force generating cumulative expansion in the growth phase become a negative force generating a vicious cycle of decline. Endogenous demand is a two-edged sword. Under the craft system, the level of employment in terms of the number of workers employed did not vary, since the integrity of the work teams had to be maintained. Producers would respond to a downturn in demand by cutting prices and reducing the effort of work teams. With employment relatively stable and real wages rising, the craft system thus had an inbuilt mechanism for restoring demand. In the era of mass production, however, downturns are met through a decline in total employment, with work effort relatively stable and prices inflexible downwards. At the aggregate level, this only exacerbates the problem of demand deficiency, leading to further reductions in employment so that downturns can lead to chronic stagnation (Nell and Phillips 1995). This obviously provides scope for government intervention to act as a circuit breaker when such a downward spiral takes hold. The automatic stabilizers built in to a system with big government can arrest the decline (Minsky 1986) and restore the conditions for self-sustaining growth.

CONCLUSIONS

Neither conventional nor alternative approaches offer much help in understanding the growth of demand. Indeed, most contemporary thinking does not even recognize the phenomenon or the need for an explanation. In the long run, it is held, supply determines demand. That is why growth theory has so strongly emphasized the supply side.

But when finance is available, demand can develop separately from supply. Moreover, as households see the possibilities of self-improvement, they will develop their skills and innovate. This will both change the composition of demand and lead to the formation of new markets, and to expansion of demand generally. This growth needs explaining.

There are two parts to an explanation. The easiest is the explanation of the growth of demand in a market, following the introduction of a new product. This follows a sigmoid path, tracing out the product cycle as it moves through the income distribution. But more important is the introduction of new products, changes in the composition of demand. New products that service existing desires are easily explained, drawing on the programming approach to household budgets. Explaining changes in the composition of demand is more challenging.

Here the clue comes in understanding the changes in household budgets. The most important are those which occur when a fraction of households begin to try to rise in the world. These would-be Horatio Algers invest in self-improvement and thereby change the composition of demand. Since the change in composition stimulates investments, this in itself leads to demand growth. But the effect of self-improvement is to increase productivity, and so incomes, leading to further demand growth.

As these Horatio Algers develop, they shift their demand more and more to collective goods, as these are the goods that will help them to rise in the world. Collective goods, in turn, interact; network externalities tend to prevail in them. But these goods, in turn, require more and more government services; they have a higher government service coefficient than purely private goods. Further, they interact with government services, which further intensifies the demand for Government. Hence, as the ratio of collective goods to private rises, the ratio of G/Y will rise even faster. But a higher level of G/Y, in turn, tends to raise the rate of growth. A higher rate of growth in turn can be expected to increase real wages, leading to still further changes in household budgets, as households seek even greater self-improvement. This is a long-term cumulative process, leading to both perpetual demand growth and higher productivity. And it can provide the theoretical basis for adapting the ELR for service in developing economies that suffer from capital shortage.

To sum up, there has been a growing interest in theories that seek to explain capitalist expansion through recourse to internal "engines of growth," rather than exogenous forces such as population expansion or autonomous technical change. The popularity of Romer's Endogenous Growth Theory within a neoclassical framework is testament to this. Yet, such theories have tended to concentrate on supply-side changes, especially in the area of technological change and productivity. But technologies that raise productivity are only viable if they have expanding markets to sell to and therefore a theory of the growth of markets needs to be developed to give a complete picture. This is provided by the theory of Transformational Growth, which locates the growth of markets in the dynamic interaction between household and industrial production and consumption. When this relationship is fleshed out we discover endogenous processes on the demand side that can explain the emergence of mass markets that complement the emergence of mass production in a mutually self-reinforcing manner.

Notes

1. Sraffa, P. (ed.) "Notes on Malthus's Principles of Political Economy" *Works and Correspondence of David Ricardo,* vol. II, Cambridge: Cambridge University Press. Ricardo: "All men will allow then that savings may be so rapid and profits so low in consequence as to diminish the motive for accumulation and finally destroy it altogether", 8. Population growth governs accumulation, 302. Malthus: "On the supposition...of a *given* consumption, the accumulation of capital beyond a certain point must appear at once to be perfectly futile...even taking into consideration the increased consumption...among the labouring classes...from the abundance and cheapness of commodities...this cheapness must be at the expense of profits [leading to] a very rapid diminution of the motive to accumulate," 326.
2. A reduction of the unproductive classes—and so of their consumption demand—in relation to the value of the whole produce is repeatedly argued to lead to a fall in the rate of accumulation (302, 326–327). It is suggested that a rise, if not too great, might, in the right circumstances, raise the rate of accumulation. Maintaining the proportion, of course, means that unproductive consumption must grow at the rate of accumulation. How this is to be ensured is not explained (431–436).
3. Rather than being an account of growth, the Harrod-Domar formula might be considered a dividing line between two divergent *modes of operation* of a mass production economy (Nell, in Nell and Semmler 1989; Nell 1998a). One is an excess capacity regime, in which demand always has a tendency to fall short of capacity, or rather, in which capacity is always running ahead of demand. The other is an excess demand regime, in which capacity is always running short. The first is typical of modern capitalism, the second of Soviet-style socialism.
4. The multiplier-accelerator model is very close to the Harrod-Domar one, but differs in that it includes *time lags* in formulating its investment and saving functions.
5. Normal capacity will be built to service the expected normal level of demand; so new capacity will be added in the light of expected demand growth. It is the latter which calls for explanation. The crucially important implication of the multiplier-accelerator analysis, however, is that the aggregate demand–aggregate capacity balance tends to generate *an unstable cumulative process.* That is, given the normal growth of demand to which normal capacity is adapting, a deviation from this in either direction will tend to set up a self-sustaining process that will continue moving in that direction. Expansion of capacity will generate even greater expansion of demand; contraction in investment will further contract demand. This is central to understanding macroeconomics, but it offers no help in explaining the *normal* growth of demand.
6. In the Cambridge view, short run models of effective demand have investment determining profits and so that the level of activity is demand-determined.

But in the long run, they allow that profits may determine investment, so that supply determines demand. (New Keynesians would agree, substituting "saving" for "profits.") The argument here suggests that the direction of causality assumed in the short run is also correct for the long run.
7. Strictly speaking, there can be no "consumption out of profits." Consumption is spending by households, whereas profits are the income of business. Business must *distribute* a portion of profits to households, for example as dividends; then households may consume all or a fraction of that dividend income. In the case of the self-employed, a portion of the apparent profits must be designated as salary. Unusually large draws must be considered on a par with dividend payments.
8. This would restrict the model to consideration of steady growth, in which variables were unchanged from period to period.
9. Of course the two interact, but separating them makes it possible to isolate the influence of demand growth, clearly a long-run question, while showing at the same time that interest costs are a short-run matter (Nell l998, chapter 10, 11).
10. For a related argument see Hicks 1989, 10–11, *et passim*. Hicks' point is that Marshall's *flow* equilibrium for a particular period is inadequate; in most markets both suppliers and demanders may be interested in stocks, which requires admitting speculation over a sequence of periods. The point here is that the anticipated balance *over* time has to be considered in determining the best course of action at any *given* time. But the argument here concerns the growth of capacity, which is different from the holding of stocks. Current supply and demand are flows, and growth of supply and growth of demand refer to rates of change of flows. Stock-flow arguments may be superficially similar, but should be kept separate.
11. But it does not follow that the long run will be characterized by steady proportional growth. On the contrary, in a class society there is good reason to think that, in general, steady proportional growth will not be attainable (Nell 1986; 1991; 1998). A very simple argument shows this: suppose there are only two classes, a wealthy class and a poor class, but both work and both own property. (The first group would be "owner-operators" in early capitalism, receiving "wages of superintendence" as well as profits; in a later era they would be professional managers owning stock. The second would be workers with pensions and savings.) The rate of interest will be the same on capital, whoever owns it. But the possession of wealth will confer advantages in the earning of salaries; the wealthier will be in a better position to acquire skills and influence. So salaries will be higher than wages, in proportion to the difference in per capita wealth. The wealthy will be in a better position to save and to invest in human capital. Under these conditions, the wealth of the richer class will tend to grow faster that the wealth of the poorer, thereby ensuring that the gap between the salaries of the managerial class and the workers also widens. Given that the consumption patterns of the rich and the poor will differ, the markets serving the rich will be expanding faster than those serving the poor.
12. Think of the increase in education at all levels in the early years of the twentieth century, the emergence of night schools (like the New School),

the popularity of books on self-improvement, the development of guidance and vocational education in the public schools, the rise of new professions like Personnel Management. All of this was part of the emergence of a new middle class.
13. Here is a simple, linear version:

    $g + G - aw/p + hx$
    $g = bw/p + jx$
    $x = cg$

    where $a, b, c, h, j > 0$, and G is the maximum growth rate. The solution is :

    $w/p = G(1 - jc)/[a(1 - jc) + b(1 - hc)]$

    and it is sufficient for $w/p > 0$ that $c, h, j < 1$.
14. "Nonrivalrous" and "nondepletable" tend to be considered the same, since both imply that the marginal cost of serving an additional customer is zero. But zero marginal cost is a supply side criterion; whereas rivalry is a matter of demand. The neoclassical concern is that public goods lead to market failures; the exact nature of the goods is not significant. By contrast, the issue for Transformational Growth is that an increase in collective goods changes the proportions and character of the economy.
15. FIRE stands for finance, insurance, and real estate, all of which are collective, the latter involving "positional goods."
16. Government growth proceeded at a higher rate than GNP growth during the first half of the postwar period, tending to pull the economy up. Government purchases of goods and services grew at 4.24 percent from 1948 to 1973, compared to GNP growth of 3.67 percent, and government employment grew at 3.62 percent, compared to civilian labor force growth of 1.57 percent. This was the "Golden Age" of the modern economy. By contrast, in the second half of the postwar era, up until the Clinton Boom, government growth was slower than that of GNP, 1.80 percent from 1973 to 1993, compared to GNP growth of 2.36 percent. The government labor force also grew at 1.8 percent, slower than the approximately 2 percent growth of the civilian labor force. So, in the later period, the government tended to act as a drag on the economy's growth.
17. So long as at least some of the activities carried out by ELR workers can be legitimately considered an addition to output—whether GNP or a measure like Net Economic Welfare—the economy is unambiguously better off with an ELR than with an Unemployment Insurance program of the same size. Moreover, the presence of an ELR tends to attract new entrants to the labor force, further increasing both employment and output.
18. A first step in developing policy proposals will be to provide good models of the role of the ELR in leading the growth of demand, and to identify the chief sorts of bottlenecks and problems that may develop. A second step might explore the likely barriers that may emerge in the capital goods sector—drawing for example on the work of Adolph Lowe, and the studies of the "traverse" that followed. What kinds of new products and new

technologies could be advanced? What opportunities for venture capital projects? How well could worker controlled enterprises function in the competitive environment? It would be important to develop adequate statistics, along with economic and social analysis, to assess the various dimensions along which an ELR and its training programs might have an impact.
19. See Cornwall and Cornwall (1994) for a growth model that incorporates these features of consumption patterns and their implications for economic expansion and state policies.
20. Henry Ford's "$5 a day" was an early example of this strategy (Ford 1922, 126).

REFERENCES

Andrews, J. N., and R. Michels. 1937. *Economic Problems of Modem Society*. New York: Ronald Press.
Andrew, John N., and Rudolf K. Michels. 1938. *Economic Problems of Modern Society*. New York: Ronald Press.
Argyrous, G. 1996. "Cumulative Causation and Industrial Evolution: Kaldor's Four Stages of Industrialization as an Evolutionary Model." *Journal of Economic Issues* 30(1) (March): 97–119.
Bernstein, P. 1986. *The Great Depression*. Cambridge: Cambridge University Press.
Bernstein, Michael A. 1987. *The Great Depression: Delayed Recovery and Economic Change in America, 1929–1939*. New York: Cambridge University Press.
Cornwall, J. 1977. *Modem Capitalism*. Oxford: Martin Robertson.
Cornwall, J. and W. Cornwall. 1994. "Growth Theory and Economic Structure." *Economica* 61(282): 237–251.
Foley, Duncan and T. Michl. 1999. *Growth and Distribution*. Cambridge: Harvard University Press.
Ford, H. 1922. *My Life and Work*. Sydney: Doubleday & Page.
Hagemann, Harald. 1992. "Traverse Analysis in a Post Classical Model." In *Beyond the Steady State*. Edited by Halevi, Laibman, and Nell. London: Macmillan.
Halevi, J., D. Laibman, and E. J. Nell. (eds) 1992. *Beyond the Steady State*. London: Macmillan.
Hicks, Sir John. 1989. *A Market Theory of Money*. Oxford: Clarendon Press.
Hirsch, Fred. 1976. *Social Limits to Growth*. New York: Pantheon.
Houthakker, H. 1957. "An International Comparison of Household Expenditure Patterns Commemorating the Centennial of Engel's Law." *Econometrica* 25A(4), 532–551.
Ironmonger, D. S. 1972. *New Commodities and Consumer Behavior*. Cambridge: Cambridge University Press.
Kaldor, Nicholas. 1960. *Essays on Economic Stability and Growth*. New York: Free Press.
———. 1961. "Capital Accumulation and Economic Growth." In *Theory of Capital*. Edited by F. A. Lutz and D. Hauge. New York: Palgrave.

———. 1966. *Causes of the Slow Rate of Growth of the United Kingdom*. Cambridge: Cambridge University Press.
Kuznets, S. 1953. *Shares of Upper Income Groups in Income and Savings*. New York: National Bureau of Economic Research.
Lancaster, Kelvin. 1966. "A New Approach to Consumer Theory." *Journal of Political Economy* 74(2): 132–157.
Landes, D. S. 1972. *The Unbound Prometheus*. Cambridge: Cambridge University Press.
Lowe, Adolph. 1976. *The Path of Economic Growth*. Cambridge: Cambridge University Press.
Malthus, Thomas Robert. 1836. *Principles of Political Economy*. London: W. Pickering.
Marx, K. 1886. *Capital*. Vol. 1. Translated by Ben Fowkes. London: Penguin.
Minsky, H. 1986. *Stabilizing an Unstable Economy*. New Haven: Yale University Press.
Nell, E. J. 1989. "On Long-Run Equilibrium in Class Society." In *Joan Robinson and Modern Economic Theory*. Edited by G. W. Feiwel. London: Macmillan. Reprinted in E. J. Nell 1991, *Transformational Growth and Effective Demand*, 323–344.
———. 1992. *Transformational Growth and Effective Demand*. London: Macmillan.
———. 1998a. *The General Theory of Transformational Growth*. Cambridge: Cambridge University Press.
———. (ed.) 1998b. *Transformational Growth and the Business Cycle*. London: Routledge.
Nell, E. J. and R. Majewski. "Leviathan's Wallet: Transformational Growth and the Government Budget," forthcoming. (Unpublished manuscript).
Nell, E. J. and T. Phillips. 1995. "Transformational Growth and the Business Cycle." *Eastern Economic Journal* 21(2): 125–142.
Nell, E. J. and W. Semmler. 1989. *Nicholas Kaldor and Mainstream Economics: Confrontation or Convergence?* London: Macmillan.
Pasinetti, L. 1981. *Structural Change and Economic Growth*. Cambridge: Cambridge University Press.
Pressman, S. 1994. "On Transformational Growth." *Review of Political Economy* 6(11): 107–132.
Robinson, Joan 1956. *The Accumulation of Capital*. London: Macmillan.
Romer, P. M. 1994. "The Origins of Endogenous Growth." *Journal of Economic Perspectives* 8A(1): 3–22.
———. 1986. Increasing Returns and Long-Run Growth." *Journal of Political Economy* 94(5): 1002–1037.
Rosenberg, N. 1982. *Inside the Black Box*. Cambridge: Cambridge University Press.
———. 1976. *Perspectives on Technology*. Cambridge: Cambridge University Press.
Young, A. 1928. "Increasing Returns and Economic Progress." *Economic Journal* 38(152): 527–542.

CHAPTER 7

The Euro Crisis and the Job Guarantee: A Proposal for Ireland

L. Randall Wray

It is now more than clear that highly indebted members of the European Monetary Union will not be able to service their debt. There is no alternative to debt relief. A few of Europe's leaders finally have started to recognize this inconvenient fact. However, they are not likely to approve any generalized approach to saving Europe. Instead, they want to drag out a resolution as long as possible because any admission of the full scope of the problem means that most of the big banks are hopelessly insolvent. So they will first deal with Greece and watch as the crisis slowly but surely spreads to the bigger nations—Italy and Spain will be next. Meanwhile, they impose deathly austerity on the debtors trying to squeeze the last drops of blood to feed what reporter Matt Taibbi calls the blood-sucking vampire squid (he refers to Goldman Sachs but the description fits all the biggest banks).

The picture of the European debtors as profligate consumers certainly cannot apply to Ireland and Iceland. In both these cases, the nations adopted a neoliberal attitude toward banks that was pushed by policymakers in Europe and America, with disastrous results. The banks blew up in a speculative fever and then expected their governments to absorb all the losses. The situation was similar in the United States but in our case the debts were in dollars and our sovereign currency issuer simply spent, lent, and guaranteed $29 trillion worth of bad bank decisions. Even in our case it was a huge mistake—but it was "affordable."

Ireland and Iceland were not so lucky as their bank debts were in "foreign" currencies. By this I mean that even though Irish bank debt was in the euro, the government of Ireland had given up its own currency in favor of what is essentially a foreign currency—the euro, which is issued by the European Central Bank (ECB). Every euro issued in Ireland is ultimately convertible one-to-one to ECB euro. There is neither a possibility of depreciating the Irish euro nor is there the possibility of creating ECB euros as necessary to meet demands for clearing, unless the ECB accommodates. Ireland is in a situation similar to that of Argentina a decade ago when it adopted a currency board based on the US dollar. Even with a budget deficit that never reached 3 percent of GDP, it was doomed when markets shut off the supply of US dollars. While Ireland is not completely shut off, its borrowing costs exploded as the interest rate it had to pay on euro debt rose far above what Germany (for example) had to pay. It is a widely recognized rule of thumb that a nonsovereign borrower cannot afford to pay an interest rate that is much above the growth rate. With Irish prospective growth rates at very low levels (and worse now given the likely collapse of the entire European economy), the debt is quite simply impossible to service.

And yet the authorities demand more austerity, to further reduce growth rates. As both Ireland and Greece have found out, austerity does not mean reduced budget deficits—because tax revenues fall faster than spending can be cut. Is there an alternative path?

In this piece I will argue that there is. First I will quickly summarize the financial foibles of Iceland and Ireland. I will then—also quickly—summarize the case for debt relief or default. Then I will present a program of direct job creation that could put Ireland on the path to recovery. Understanding the financial problems and solutions puts the jobs program proposal in the proper perspective: a full implementation of a job guarantee cannot occur on the current financial arrangements. Still, something can be done.

QUICK OVERVIEW: HOW WE GOT HERE

Voters in Iceland wisely rejected their government's attempt to foist on them the cost of bailing out foreign creditors. Iceland's oversized big banks had made bad loans throughout Euroland and, when they failed, uninsured depositors were on the hook. Governments in countries like the United Kingdom and the Netherlands bailed out their depositors and demanded that Iceland reimburse them. However, Icelandic voters have now rejected that proposition twice. They felt they have suffered enough already from a financial crisis created by largely unregulated financial institutions that lent indiscriminately in foreign currency. Iceland does not use the euro and its tiny economy cannot be expected to cover all the euro-denominated debt run-up by private financial institutions. Those foolish foreigners who took risks by holding uninsured euro-denominated deposits in Icelandic banks with no access to a government backstop in euros should take the loss. In my view, the voters have responded in a rational and responsible manner. After all, that is what market discipline and sovereignty are all about. If a saver does not like risks, she should hold only safe assets guaranteed by a sovereign power.

What about Ireland—which faced a similar situation? Should its voters have rejected a taxpayer bailout of foreign creditors? Like Iceland, it faces a crushing debt because its government took on the liabilities of its oversized banks who also had lent indiscriminately throughout Euroland. However, unlike Iceland, Irish bank liabilities are denominated in the currency used in Ireland, the euro.

Ireland abandoned its sovereign currency when it joined the euro. Effectively, it became like a US state—think Louisiana—within the European Monetary Union (EMU). This means it has little domestic policy space to use monetary or fiscal policy to deal with crisis. If we go back to 2005, Ireland's government had the second lowest ratio of debt to GDP (national output or income) in the EU-15, with only Luxembourg having a lower debt ratio. The government paid an interest rate similar to that paid by the French and German governments; it had a strong AAA rating on its debt. In fact, it was running a huge government surplus of 2.5 percent of GDP (similar to that run by the Clinton administration in the late 1990s in the United States).

Spring 2011. The government deficit ratio was about 12.5 percent of GDP and credit default spreads on the government's debt (equivalent to betting on default) reached almost 43 basis points over those of Germany, and it paid 6 percentage points higher to borrow than Germany did (on March 22 the spread on two year bonds hit a record 835 basis points—8.35 percentage points—over the rate on equivalent German debt). See figure 7.1.

Here's the problem. There is a fundamental relation between economic growth and ability to pay interest to service debt. To be safe, a government should not pay an interest rate that significantly exceeds its growth rate. If we compare Ireland to the situation of Germany, because the Irish government pays 6 percentage points more, it needs to grow 6 percentage points faster than Germany does. To be sure this is a rough rule of thumb and

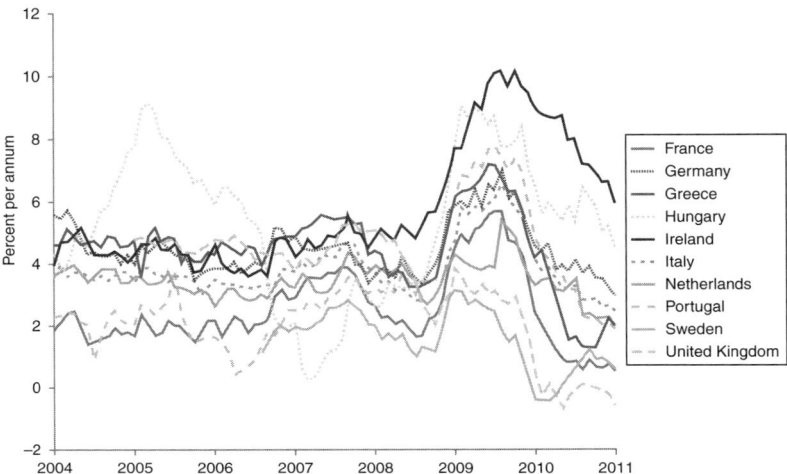

Figure 7.1 Monthly overdraft loans to nonfinancial businesses, 2004:1–2011:1.
Source: Author's calculations.

there is some leeway. But the prospects for Ireland to grow that much faster than Germany—say 8 percent growth rate for Ireland versus 2 percent for Germany—approach a zero probability.

Indeed, the conventional way to generate government revenues needed to service debt is to cut government spending and raise taxes—which will only hurt Irish growth. Further, what Ireland needs is to increase the flow of euros in its favor through its foreign balance, that is, by reducing imports and increasing exports to the EMU. The conventional prescription is slow domestic growth to reduce imports and enhance international competitiveness. This, too, further reduces domestic growth even more below the interest rate paid on government debt.

Finally, with the exception of the BRICs (Brazil, Russia, India, and China), recent economic data across the globe have not been good—and it looks like even the BRICs are slowing. It is clear that Europe is imploding—it is unlikely that growth will be much above zero this year. And while recent US data look better, I still expect a "double-dip" recession to be triggered by renewed financial crisis, perhaps coming from Europe this time. That makes it harder for Ireland to export its way out of debt—which is the least painful path. I do not see alternatives that are without substantial suffering.

Unfortunately, slow growth of the economy usually means slow growth of tax revenue. It is fairly easy to imagine a scenario in which domestic austerity actually makes the budget deficit worse, which raises interest rates on government debt. A vicious cycle can be created, with debt service blowing up as growth continues to slow and interest rates rise with credit ratings agencies downgrading government debt.

What I am going to say next sounds controversial—but it is a point I've been making for nearly a decade and a half. Ireland transitioned from a government budget surplus of 2.5 percent of GDP to a deficit of 12.5 percent of GDP, which I am arguing is a disaster. The US government has had a nearly identical transformation (from 2.5% surplus in the late 1990s to a deficit peaking near 12.5% of GDP) but it faces no insolvency constraint and no default risk. The reason this is controversial is that we do face deficit hysteria in the United States and a credit ratings agencies disposed to downgrading US government debt. Congress nearly refused to extend the self-imposed debt limit on the federal government—and it is still possible that the government might get shut down if Congress refuses to raise the limit in the future. So it might look like the United States and Ireland are in a similar pickle.

But they are not. All problems in the United States are self-imposed. Irish problems are largely imposed by "markets"—by market assessment that there is a very real chance of involuntary default. That is why Irish borrowing rates are so high, while US government interest rates actually fell(!) after the downgrade. The only path to US default is political—failure of Congress to raise debt limits. (Yes, we went through that, and we could have another standoff. It is difficult to rule out political stupidity but I think Congress will not allow default to actually happen.) The path to Irish default is "economic"—spiraling interest rates with low growth rates.

If Ireland had its own sovereign currency, the size of the government deficit or debt ratio would not be relevant to ability to pay. I will return to that below. But since Ireland gave up its currency in favor of the euro, it is not in the position of a United States or a Japan or a Turkey. It has far less domestic policy space—to run up budget deficits to boost growth, and to set low domestic interest rates. Nor can Ireland devalue the currency—the value of its euro is set at equal to the euro used throughout the EMU. As we have seen, crises in various EMU nations (Greece, Portugal, Spain, Ireland) do not cause the euro to depreciate. That might sound counterintuitive but what matters is that there are relatively safe havens for those who want to buy euro-denominated debt, such as Germany. The "periphery" nations have to pay big premiums over the interest rates paid by Germany—and the euro remains (too) strong.

Let us look at how Ireland got into this mess. Ireland was the "paragon of virtue" just six years ago—its total outstanding government debt was just eight months of tax revenue (publicly held debt was only 21% of GDP) and it was actually running budget surpluses. Then the financial crisis hit. That would have worsened the budget balance significantly—and probably would have generated a budget deficit. However, the government chose to guarantee its banks—which were vastly oversized relative to the size of the economy. That "busted the budget" and generated the current problems. In important respects, Ireland reproduced the Icelandic problem, with similar results.

As we know, the people of Iceland have voted to undo the bank bailout. The question is how Ireland might respond to the will of its voters. Any rational response should try to undo the mess created by guaranteeing bank debt.

A report by Finnish bank expert Peter Nyberg avoids naming names (by contrast, the US official report on the crisis—the Financial Crisis Inquiry Report—does so) but says that guaranteeing the banks was based on "insufficient information." Well, that information is now sufficient to conclude that the bailout was a mistake. It needs to be unwound. The documents must be made public. The guilty need to be prosecuted. Funds need to be recovered. Guarantees of crooks need to be withdrawn.

So how should the government deal with loan repayments to the EU? I would encourage the government to unwind its guarantees of bank debt. If this cannot be done, then Ireland must have a bail out and debt relief provided by the ECB or the EMU through some other entity. That is actually in the interest of the EMU since much of the bank debt guaranteed by Ireland's government is held externally by EU banks. The last resort alternative is default on debt and possible expulsion from the EMU. That will be painful. There isn't anything Ireland can be expected to do without support from the EU—except for default. Greece is now paving the way—to show how default can be done. The EU is going to accept writing down Greek debt. That probably will not prove to be sufficient. But it opens the possibility for Ireland also to cut a deal.[1]

Ireland can also learn from the Icelandic example. Both are heavily indebted because their banks were far too large and made too many foreign loans. A difference is that Iceland still has its own currency. However, its banks made loans in foreign currencies. But in important respects, so did Irish banks since the euro is a foreign currency from the perspective of Ireland. Iceland's citizens are pressuring its government to undo the bailouts. Ireland's population can learn by example.

The Irish voters should demand accountability of government, including investigation of the bailout of banks. Government should pursue debt relief on all fronts. Voters should resist austerity programs. If all else fails, they should demand either default or withdrawal from the EMU (in practice these probably amount to the same thing).

And they should demand jobs at decent pay. A Universal Job Guarantee program funded either by a newly sovereign Irish government, or by the ECB or some other EMU institution is necessary to help revive the economy and to relieve the suffering caused by high unemployment. Let us now turn to a comprehensive jobs program.

Toward a Universal Job Guarantee

Ireland needs jobs. A universal job guarantee is the best approach. The jobs would pay basic wages and benefits with a goal to provide a living wage. It would take all comers—anyone ready and willing to work, regardless of education, training, or experience. Adapt the jobs to the workers—as the late Hyman Minsky said, "Take the workers as they are" and work them up to their ability, and then enhance their ability through on-the-job training. In this section the details will be discussed.

The program needs to be funded by the central government. Wages would be paid directly to the bank accounts of participants for working in the program. Some national government funding of nonwage costs could be provided. I would decentralize the program, to allow local governments and not-for-profit service organizations to organize projects.

Now here is the problem. A sovereign government with its own currency can always financially afford such a program. Ireland could fund such a program with its own sovereign currency. In current circumstances this is posing a problem because Ireland abandoned its currency in favor of a foreign currency, the euro.

The big advantage of a sovereign currency is that government can "afford" anything for sale in its own currency. Government then spends through "keystrokes," crediting bank accounts.

Before all the Zimbabwean hyperinflation warriors attack, let me say that too much government spending can be inflationary and can create pressures on the currency. But, by design, a job guarantee program only hires people who want to work because they cannot find higher paying jobs elsewhere. It sets a wage floor but does not drive wages up. As such, it can never cause hyperinflation—it hires "off the bottom" at the program fixed wage, only up to the point of full employment. It never drives the economy beyond full employment.

For a sovereign currency nation, the interest rate is a policy variable and has no impact on solvency. Government can keep rates low (it sets the overnight rate directly, and can, if it desires, issue only short maturity bonds near to that rate) and pays interest through "keystrokes" by crediting bank accounts with interest. It can never run out of keystrokes, and so will never fail to make interest payments unless it chooses to do so for noneconomic reasons.

For Ireland, this is a very serious problem. It does not have a sovereign currency. It cannot control its borrowing rates, which are set in markets. Nominal interest rates should not exceed nominal GDP growth rates. But as we know, markets have pushed rates as high as 10 percent. For Ireland to service debt at 10 percent interest rates, it would need Chinese growth rates. That seems unlikely.

In the event that Ireland stays on the euro, and is not able to fully resolve its debt problem, is there anything she might do with respect to job creation? I will come back to that at the very end: yes, Ireland can adopt a limited job creation program, and can use creative finance to fund it.

What is the best way to guarantee long-term stability for the Irish economy? Full employment with reasonable price stability—something a universal job guarantee program can deliver. Let us turn to details.

THE JOB GUARANTEE: PROGRAM DESIGN AND BENEFITS

The benefits of full employment are numerous and include production of goods, services and income; on-the-job training and skill development; poverty alleviation; amelioration of many social ills associated with chronic unemployment (health problems, spousal abuse and family breakup, drug abuse, crime); community building and social networking; social, political, and economic stability; and social multipliers (positive feedbacks and reinforcing dynamics that create a virtuous cycle of socioeconomic benefits). A "Job Guarantee" program would restore the government's lost commitment to full employment in recognition of the fact that the total impact would exceed the sum of the benefits.

The program has no time limits or restrictions based on income, gender, education, or experience. It operates like a buffer stock: in a boom, employers will recruit workers out of the program; in a slump it will allow those who lost their jobs to preserve good habits, keeping them work-ready. It will also help those unable to obtain work outside the program enhance their employability through training. Unemployment offices will be converted to employment offices, to match workers with jobs that suit them and to help employers recruit staff.

Although the program must be funded by the federal government, its implementation can be decentralized. All local governments and registered nonprofit organizations can propose projects; proposals will be submitted to a newly created office within the national government's labor ministry for final approval and funding. The office will maintain a website providing details on all pending, approved and ongoing projects, and final reports will be published after projects are complete.

Participants will be subject to all national work rules, and violations will lead to dismissal. Anyone who is dismissed three times in a 12-month period will be ineligible to participate in the program for a year. Workers will be allowed to organize through labor unions.

Workers won't have to leave their communities to seek employment. The program will meet workers where they are and take them as they are: jobs will be available in local communities and will be tailored to suit employees' level of education and experience (though with the goal of improving skills). This will prevent communities and sometimes larger cities from being deserted. Project proposals should include provisions for part-time work and other flexible arrangements for workers who need them, including but not restricted to flexible arrangements for parents of young children.

The program could provide for flexible working conditions such as part-time and seasonal work and other arrangements as desired by the workers. The package of benefits would be subject to congressional approval, but could include health care, child care, payment of social security taxes (or other retirement benefits), and usual vacations and sick leave. The wage would be set by congress or parliament and increased from time to time, similar to how the national minimum wage is usually legislated.

The advantage of the uniform basic wage is that it would limit competition with other employers as workers could be attracted out of the Job Guarantee (JG) program by paying a wage slightly above the program's wage. Obviously, higher skilled workers and those with higher educational attainment will be hired first. In an economic boom, employers will lower hiring standards to pull lower-skilled workers out of the program. The residual pool of workers in the program provides a buffer stock of employable labor, helping to reduce pressures on wages—and as wages for high-skilled workers are bid up, the buffer stock becomes ever more desirable as a source of cheaper labor.

All participants will obtain a social security number (or equivalent) and will maintain a bank account in an approved bank. Weekly wages will be paid by the national government directly to participants' accounts. The government will also provide funding for benefits as well as approved expenses up to a maximum of 10 or 25 percent of wages paid for a project (to cover the cost of administrative materials and equipment; the exact percent would be set centrally, and could vary by type of project). Because the primary purpose of the program is to create jobs, the national government should cover only a relatively small portion of nonwage costs.

Estimated spending will be 1–2 percent of GDP (perhaps higher in a deep recession and lower in an expansion), with economic, social, and political benefits several times larger. Net program costs will be even lower, since with the institution of a JG program spending on unemployment compensation and other relief will be reduced—this program will pay people for working, rather than paying them not to work. The promise of increased national productivity and shared prosperity should far outweigh any fears about rising deficits. To fulfill this promise, we need to put workers back to work.

The JG will not only help achieve full employment but will also ensure that all of society's needs are satisfied regardless of whether they constitute profitable business opportunities or not. More generally, it can be used to provide goods and services that are too expensive for low-income households or that markets do not provide. Examples include social services (child and elder care, tutoring, public safety), small scale public infrastructure provision or repair (clean water and sewage projects, roads), low-income housing and repairs to owner-occupied housing (following the lead of Jimmy Carter's Habitat for Humanity), and food preparation ("soup kitchens," local bakeries). The JG won't compete with private businesses and jobs but will rather fill the gaps left by the private sector. Only community needs and imagination would limit the ability to provide adequate and useful jobs. Forstater (1999) has emphasized how JG can be used to increase economic flexibility and to enhance the environment by creating green jobs in the framework of the program. In addition, for a country that relies on tourism, the JG can be used to enhance the environment and public infrastructure in a way that promotes tourism. Similarly, projects can also enhance the general economic environment to promote exports if that is desired.

While neoliberals and their ancestors have managed to taint the memory of the US New Deal's job creation programs, the truth is that these programs provided lasting benefits. The naysayers actually began to fabricate falsehoods about the program and its participants from the very beginning. With corporate funding and ready access to the media, they painted a picture of lazy tramps leaning on shovels. But the evidence is still plain to see for any visitor to the United States, in the form of public buildings, dams, roads, national parks, and trails that still serve America. (A similar story can be told about Australia, for example, which also engaged in public works programs during the Great Depression.) For example, workers in the Works Progress Administration (WPA).

> Shouldered the tasks that began to transform the physical face of America. They built roads and schools and bridges and dams. The Cow Palace in

San Francisco, La Guardia Airport in New York City and National (now Reagan) Airport in Washington, D.C., the Timberline Lodge in Oregon, the Outer Drive Bridge on Chicago's Lake Shore Drive, the River Walk in San Antonio.... Its workers sewed clothes and stuffed mattresses and repaired toys; served hot lunches to schoolchildren; ministered to the sick; delivered library books to remote hamlets by horseback; rescued flood victims; painted giant murals on the walls of hospitals, high schools, courthouses, and city halls; performed plays and played music before eager audiences; and wrote guides to the forty-eight states that even today remain models for what such books should be. And when the clouds of an oncoming world loomed over the United States, it was the WPA's workers who modernized the army and air bases and trained in vast numbers to supply the nation's military needs. (Taylor 2008, 2)

The New Deal jobs programs employed 13 million people; the WPA was the biggest program, employing 8.5 million, lasting eight years and spending about $10.5 billion (Taylor 2008, 3). It took a broken country and in many important respects helped to not only revive it, but to bring it into the twentieth century. The WPA built 650,000 miles of roads, 78,000 bridges, 125,000 civilian and military buildings, 700 miles of airport runways; it fed 900 million hot lunches to kids, operated 1,500 nursery schools, gave concerts before audiences of 150 million, and created 475,000 works of art. It transformed and modernized America (Taylor 2008, 523–524).

We do not want to overemphasize public infrastructure investment, however. In many of our highly developed nations, the needs today are at least as great in the area of public services, including aged care, preschools, playground supervision, cleanup of public lands, retrofitting public and private buildings for energy efficiency, and environmental restoration projections.

A new universal direct job creation program would improve working conditions in the private sector as employees would have the option of moving into the JG program. Hence, private sector employers would have to offer a wage and benefit package and working conditions at least as good as those offered by the JG program. The informal sector would shrink as workers become integrated into formal employment, gaining access to protection provided by labor laws. There would be some reduction of racial and gender discrimination because unfairly treated workers would have the JG option, although JG by itself cannot end discrimination.

Finally, I would also like to emphasize that a JG program with a uniform basic wage would also help to promote economic and price stability. The JG will act as an automatic stabilizer as employment in the program grows in recession and shrinks in economic expansion, counteracting private sector employment fluctuations. Furthermore, the uniform basic wage will reduce both inflationary pressure in a boom and deflationary pressure in a bust. In recession, workers downsized by private employers can work at the JG wage, which puts a floor to how low wages and income can fall.

A sovereign nation operating with its own currency with a flexible exchange rate regime (i.e., when it doesn't peg its exchange rate to another currency or metal, such as a gold standard) can always financially afford a JG program (Wray 1998). So long as there are workers who are ready and willing to work at the program wage, the government can "afford" to hire them. Let's look at an example, using US currency and institutions. Just like households have checking accounts at their local bank, the banks have "checking" accounts at the Federal Reserve Banks. Unlike households, the government makes payments by crediting bank accounts. When the government pays $500 to Mrs. Smith, it credits the account of Mrs. Smith's bank at the Federal Reserve Bank by $500. The bank where Mrs. Smith has an account then credits her account for $500. Technically, this amounts to money creation. Tax payments on the other hand result in a debit of bank accounts or, in other words, destroy money. If in each period the government credits more accounts than it debits through tax payments, a deficit results. In no sense is the government spending on JG constrained either by tax revenues or the demand for its bonds.

Nor will spending on the JG program grow without limit as some project. The size of the JG pool of workers will fluctuate with the cycle, automatically shrinking when the private sector grows. In recession, workers shed by the private sector find JG jobs, increasing government spending and thereby stimulating the private sector so that it will begin to hire out of the JG pool.

A floating exchange rate provides the "degree of freedom" that allows the government to spend without worrying that increased employment and higher demand will threaten an exchange rate peg—by possibly increasing domestic inflation and/or increasing imports. As discussed above, government deficit spending amounts to net money creation and if a country is pegging its exchange rate this may lead to a pressure on the exchange rate peg. Thus, with a flexible exchange rate, fiscal policy is "freed" to pursue other objectives, rather than being held hostage to maintenance of the peg. This is not to imply that the government will necessarily avoid any consideration of impacts on exchange rates while forming fiscal and monetary policy. However, if achievement of full employment is believed to conflict with maintenance of a constant exchange rate, the government in a floating currency regime *can* choose full employment. On the other hand, on a fixed exchange rate, a government that has insufficient foreign exchange reserves may not be able to "afford" to spend to promote full employment if that might lead to loss of reserves.

The problem, of course, is that Ireland does not have a floating exchange rate, and it does face affordability problems because it adopted the foreign currency—the euro.

DEVELOPING A LIMITED JG FOR IRELAND

Given its high indebtedness and the fact that it does not have its own sovereign currency, Ireland cannot today implement a universal job guarantee. It must worry about effects on the budget and trade balances (since it cannot devalue relative to the euro). There are some steps that can be taken to minimize such effects. We will outline those and then will turn to a novel way to finance a bigger program.

A nation with a sovereign currency and floating exchange rate has a significant degree of domestic policy independence—both in terms of fiscal policy and in setting of interest rates through its monetary policy. This is because it can choose policy to achieve domestic stability while allowing its exchange rate to adjust to enhance external stability. Ireland, a small and relatively open nation with a pegged currency, however, is severely constrained—its interest rate is set by markets as a markup over the interest rate of the strongest euro nation—Germany. "Sound" fiscal policy is required to prevent assessed risk from raising borrowing costs. The best recommendation to such a country is to move toward a floating exchange rate with its own sovereign currency. However, I realize that this is not yet an option for Ireland. Can an effectively nonsovereign nation (i.e., one without fiscal and monetary policy independence) implement a JG program?

First, let us see how Ireland can reduce impact on prices, the exchange rate, and the trade balance as it implements JG. It will need to limit the program's impact on monetary demand, which can be done by setting the program's monetary wage close to the minimum wage in the formal sector—which may not be a living wage for many families. However, poverty still can be reduced if the JG total compensation package includes extra-market provision of necessities. This could include domestically produced food, clothing, shelter, and basic services (healthcare, childcare, eldercare, education, transportation). Because these would be provided "in kind," JG workers would be less able to use monetary income to substitute imports for domestic production.

Further, production by JG workers could provide many or most of these goods and services—minimizing impact on the government's budget as well as on the trade balance. These could be supplied at low or no cost to poor families even if they do not participate in the program.

Still the JG program will impact monetary demand—some of which will leak to imports. Further, production by JG workers might require imports of some tools or other inputs to the production process. Careful planning by government can help to minimize undesired impact. For example, import of required tools and materials can be linked to export earnings. Because production techniques used in a JG program are flexible (JG production does not have to meet usual market profitability requirements—see Forstater 1999), government can gradually increase "capital ratios" in line with its ability to finance such imports. Further, JG projects can be designed with a view to enhance the nation's ability to increase production for export. The most obvious example is the provision of public infrastructure to reduce business costs and attract private investment. In Ireland's case the most likely area to enhance inflow of euros is the tourist sector.

A phased implementation of the program will help to attenuate undesired impact on formal and informal markets, while also limiting the impact on the government's budget. Further, starting small will help the government to obtain the necessary competence to manage a larger program. For example, Argentina limited its program by allowing participation by only one head of household from each poor family with dependent children. If desired, the program can start even smaller than that, allowing each family to register a head of household, but allocating jobs by lottery so that the program grows at a planned pace (10,000 workers the first year, 20,000 the next year, and so on until it provides a universal job guarantee). The phased implementation can also be done on the basis of selecting the best projects proposed by individual community organizations that will employ a given number of heads of households from the community (again, with selection of workers by lottery). Decentralization of project development, supervision, and administration can reduce the administrative burden on the central government while also ensuring that JG projects meet local needs. Generally, JG production should not compete with the private sector.

In the economic downturn we have seen some local communities resorting to the creation of "local currency units" sometimes called LETS systems. In depressed conditions, local business will often accept local currencies as better than no sales at all. Argentina's provinces had experimented with "patacones," regional currencies used to finance government spending. Even California under Governor Schwarzenegger had used "vouchers" to pay employees. Ireland could use these examples to develop a novel method of funding government spending—including wage payments in the JG.

Many economists are coming to understand that "taxes drive money"—the reason that "fiat" money is accepted is because the government promises to accept it in payments made to the state, chiefly tax payments. That does not mean that taxes are the only reason that euro is accepted, but with the tax systems of the euro-using nations standing behind the currency, it is widely accepted. We can use that understanding to develop two alternatives for Ireland.

The first would be to develop a new currency—let's call it the punt—to be used for government payments of wages in the JG. All levels of government would agree to accept the punt in payment of taxes, fees, and fines.[2] Assume that at government pay offices the punt is accepted at par for euro tax debts. Let us further presume that punts would be supplied only through government payment of wages to JG workers. Since JG workers as well as anyone with a tax due could use the punts to pay taxes, they would soon circulate widely. The government would not make the punt convertible to euro—it would not supply euros when punts are presented—but in private transactions they would trade at close to par because in payment of taxes they are equivalent.

The government can never run out of punts, so it can make all JG wage payments as they become due. The problem is that government will receive a mixture of punts and euros in tax payments—and so far as servicing its euro debt (at least to foreigners) goes, only euro works. In terms of euro, the government's debt problems could get worse. That would depend on the punt spending on the program (say, 2% of GDP), the size of the government spending multiplier (non-JG jobs would be created, too), and the resulting increase of tax liabilities. It is conceivable that a punt-financed JG program would not worsen the euro debt problems because it would stimulate the economy sufficiently so that all the punts created would be less than the additional taxes due. But that would depend on complex dynamics and is not a foregone conclusion.

Of course, if the government unilaterally converted all outstanding euro debt to punt debt its problems would be resolved—but that is effectively a default and would lead to political repercussions. (It is not clear that creation of the punt to pay JG wages would be permitted, either.)

The second alternative would be to pay JG wages in euros and to float bonds to raise the euros as needed. The current problem is that markets are concerned about the possibility of a default on Irish government debts, which is why interest rates are so high. The government can eliminate default risk if it issues special bonds that are acceptable in tax payment. There would be a guaranteed coupon—say 3 percent—so that a 100-euro bond could be used to pay taxes of 103 at the end of the year. This could be combined with limitations on the size of the JG program—that is, the funding raised through the bond sale would determine how many jobs would be created.

In conclusion, Ireland needs both debt relief and jobs. While a universal JG is the best approach, it may not be "affordable" on current arrangements. A sovereign, floating currency is required to ensure affordability. Meanwhile, Ireland can undertake a limited program even on conventional financing arrangements. Or, it could experiment with one of these two unconventional approaches. It could also approach official international lenders, or the ECB, but I am doubtful over the wisdom of the first (Ireland does not need more debt) and the likelihood of approval of the second.

Notes

1. Indeed, after Greece got its deal, Ireland began to insist it should get similar treatment: http://www.reuters.com/article/2012/02/08/ireland-ecb-idUSL5E8D89QY20120208.
2. In an interesting development, Bristol, UK, has created a local currency that can be used in tax payment: http://www.bbc.co.uk/news/uk-england-bristol-16852326#story_continues_1.

References

Forstater, Mathew. 1999. "Full Employment and Economic Flexibility." *Economic and Labour Relations Review.* Volume 11.

Ginsburg, Helen. 1983. *Full Employment and Public Policy: The United States and Sweden.* Lexington, MA: Lexington Books.

Harvey, P. 1999: "Liberal Strategies for Combating Joblessness in the Twentieth Century," *Journal of Economic Issues* 33(2) (June): 497–504.

———. 2000. "Combating Joblessness: An Analysis of the Principal Strategies that Have Influenced the Development of American Employment and Social Welfare Law during the 20th Century." *Berkeley Journal of Employment and Labor Law* 21(2): 677–758.

———. 2002. "Human Rights and Economic Policy Discourse: Taking Economic and Social Rights Seriously." *Columbia Human Rights Law Review* 33(2) (Spring): 364–471.

Mishel, L. 2011. "Education Is Not the Cure for High Unemployment or for Income Inequality." *EPI Briefing Paper #286*, Economic Policy Institute. January. www.epi.org.

Reich, R. 2011. "The President's Jobs Plan (Not)." *Huffington Post* July 12.

Taylor, N. 2008. *American-Made: The Enduring Legacy of the WPA: When FDR Put the Nation to Work.* Old Saybrook, CT: Tantor Media.

Tcherneva, P. and L. Randall Wray. 2005. "Gender and the Job Guarantee: The Impact of Argentina's Jefes Program on Female Heads of Poor Households."

Working Paper No. 50. Center for Full Employment and Price Stability. December. www.cfeps.org.

Wray, L. R. 1998. *Understanding Modern Money: The Key to Full Employment and Price Stability.* Cheltenham: Edward Elgar.

———. 2011. "The Job Guarantee: A Government Plan for Full Employment." *The Nation* June 27.

Contributors

George Argyrous is senior lecturer with the Australia and New Zealand School of Government in Sydney, Australia. He has published papers in a variety of areas including government budget policy, labor market interactions with the welfare system, the dynamics of technological change, and written on the history and philosophy of economics in a range of journals including *Cambridge Journal of Economics*, *Journal of Economic Issues*, *History of Political Economy*, and *Economics and Philosophy*.

Mathew Forstater is professor of Economics at the University of Missouri—Kansas City, director of the Center for Full Employment and Price Stability, and research associate with the Jerome Levy Economics Institute. He is the author of *Little Book of Big Ideas: Economics*. He is also the author of numerous journal articles, working papers, and policy reports on unemployment, full employment, green jobs, money, and competing approaches to debt and deficit. He received a PhD from the New School for Social Research.

Scott T. Fullwiler is associate professor of Economics, James A. Leach Chair in Banking and Monetary Economics, and codirector of Social Entrepreneurship. He is also a research associate with the Center for Full Employment and Price Stability in Kansas City, Missouri. His academic research has focused on the details of monetary and fiscal policy operations, macroeconomic policy, interest rates, and large-scale macroeconometric models. He has published numerous journal articles, book chapters, and working papers, and recently coedited *Institutional Analysis and Praxis: The Social Fabric Matrix Approach* (2009) on applying systems-theoretic approaches to economic policy analysis. He is also frequently invited to present his research at regional, national, and international conferences. At Wartburg College, he teaches Advanced Macroeconomics, Financial Management, Financial Modeling and Valuation, and Bank Management. Fullwiler received his PhD in Economics from the University of Nebraska.

Contributors

Philip Harvey is professor of Law and Economics at Rutgers University. He received his PhD in Economics from the Graduate Faculty of the New School for Social Research in 1976 and his JD from Yale Law School in 1988. He is the author of *Securing the Right to Employment* (1989) and coauthor with Theodore Marmor and Jerry Mashaw of *America's Misunderstood Welfare State* (1989, 1991). His most recent article, "Back to Work: A Public Jobs Proposal for Economic Recovery" (2011) discusses the advantages of direct job-creation as a means of delivering an economic stimulus to a market economy in recession. Copies of this and many of Professor Harvey's other published articles can be downloaded from his web site www.philipharvey.info.

Fadhel Kaboub is assistant professor of Economics at Denison University, Ohio, and research associate at the Levy Economics Institute of Bard College, New York, the Center for Full Employment and Price Stability; and the International Economic Policy Institute, Ontario, Canada. He has taught at Drew University where he was also codirector of the Wall Street Semester Program; the University of Missouri—Kansas City; and Bard College at Simon's Rock.

Dr. Kaboub's research is in the post-Keynesian and post-Institutionalist tradition in the fields of macroeconomic theory and policy, monetary theory and policy, and economic development, with particular emphasis on job creation programs and social justice through full employment. Dr. Kaboub's regional expertise is on the economies of the United States and the Middle East and North Africa (especially Tunisia). His work has been published in the *Journal of Economic Issues, Review of Radical Political Economics, Review of Social Economy, International Journal of Political Economy*, and *International Labour Review*. He is also a regular contributor to the social justice column published by *Street Speech*, a newspaper of the Columbus Coalition for the Homeless. He has been a member of the editorial board of the *Review of Radical Political Economics* since 2006, and has been the book review editor of the *Heterodox Economics Newsletter* since 2007.

Michael J. Murray is assistant professor of Economics at Bemidji State University and a research associate with the Center for Full Employment and Price Stability. He received a PhD from the University of Missouri—Kansas City. His current research focuses on simulations of various Employer of Last Resort proposals, heterodox price and production modeling, and the economics of Adolph Lowe. He has published in the *Review of Radical Political Economy, Journal of Economic Issues*, served as a book reviewer for the *Heterodox Economics Newsletter*, and contributed to edited volumes.

Edward J. Nell is Malcolm B. Smith Professor of Economics at the New School for Social Research in New York. Professor Nell concentrates on macroeconomic theory and policy, methodology, growth theory, business cycles, inflation, and unemployment. He currently heads the New School's Program on Transformational Growth and Full Employment, which collaborates closely with the Center for Full Employment and Price Stability. Professor Nell was a key figure during the Capital Debate of the 1960s. He is the author of *The General Theory of Transformational Growth, Transformational Growth and Effective Demand, Prosperity and Public Spending*, and numerous other books and articles.

Nicholas Reksten is a PhD student in the Economics department at American University.

Jon D. Wisman is professor of Economics at American University in Washington, DC, where he teaches graduate courses in the history of economic thought and economic methodology and undergraduate courses in macroeconomics, European economic history, American economic history, economic development, and labor economics. He has twice been selected by American University as the Outstanding Teacher of the Year. His research spans a broad spectrum of domains from history of economic thought and methodology to labor and other social issues. He has published in a wide variety of economic and social science journals, including *Review of Social Economy, Journal of Economic Issues, Social Research, World Development, Review of Political Economy, International Journal of Social Economics, American Journal of Economics and Sociology, Peace Review, Forum for Social Economics,* and *Revue d'économie sociale*, as well as contributed numerous book chapters. He edited *Worker Empowerment: The Struggle for Workplace Democracy*. At present, he is working on a book tentatively titled: *We All Must Work: Creative Destruction and the Pursuit of Happiness*. During 2002, he served as president of the Association for Social Economics.

L. Randall Wray is professor of Economics at the University of Missouri—Kansas City as well as research director, the Center for Full Employment and Price Stability, and Senior Scholar at the Levy Economics Institute of Bard College, New York. A student of Hyman P. Minsky while at Washington University in St. Louis, Wray has focused on monetary theory and policy, macroeconomics, financial instability, and employment policy. He has published widely in journals and is the author of *Understanding Modern Money: The Key to Full Employment and Price Stability* (1998) and *Money and Credit in Capitalist Economies* (1990). He is the editor of *Credit and State Theories of Money* (2004) and the coeditor of *Contemporary Post Keynesian Analysis* (2005), *Money, Financial Instability and Stabilization Policy* (2006), and *Keynes for the Twenty-First Century: The Continuing Relevance of the General Theory* (2008). Wray is also the author of numerous scholarly articles in edited books and academic journals, including the *Journal of Economic Issues*, *Cambridge Journal of Economics*, *Review of Political Economy*, *Journal of Post Keynesian Economics*, *Economic and Labour Relations Review*, *Economie Appliquée*, and the *Eastern Economic Journal*. Wray received a BA from the University of the Pacific and an MA and PhD from Washington University in St. Louis. He has served as a visiting professor at the University of Rome, the University of Paris, and UNAM (Mexico City). He was the Bernardin-Haskell Professor, UMKC, Fall 1996, and joined the UMKC faculty as professor of Economics in August 1999.

Index

advanced capitalist economies (ACEs), 148
aggregate demand, 33, 39, 50, 51, 53, 63, 95, 111, 115, 128, 155 (*see also* Keynesian demand)
agrarian societies, 134
Argentina, 3, 4, 73, 74, 83, 86, 94, 162, 174, 176

big bank, 161, 162
big government, 153
BRICS, 164
budget deficits, 162, 165

Cambridge growth models, 129
capital accumulation, 93, 96, 97, 121, 122, 158
capital goods, 96, 103, 113, 121, 127, 142, 143, 144, 150, 151, 157
  capital goods industry, 138, 152
central bank, 67
  European (*see* European Central Bank)
Civilian Conservation Corp (CCC), 118, 119
collective goods, 125, 144, 145, 146, 147, 148, 154, 157
consumer behavior, 132, 133, 139, 158
consumption, 24, 77, 98, 99, 102–108, 111, 115, 117, 118, 119, 120, 127, 128, 133, 134, 136, 139, 144, 149, 150, 152, 153, 154, 155, 156, 158
craft economy, 146, 147
craft technology, 134, 152
creative destruction, 17, 21, 27, 181

debt
  consumer, 68
  crisis, 60
  default
  national, 1, 60, 63, 161
  non-sovereign, 162–168, 175, 176
  reduction, 68
  sovereign, 161
  student, 15, 16, 30, 32
defense, 146, 147
deficit, 42, 50, 51, 53, 60, 63, 74, 78, 86, 88, 89, 93, 162, 163, 165, 166, 172, 179
deregulation, 14, 60
Developing Economies under Capitalist Enterprise (DEUCE), 149

economic growth, 9, 35, 36, 51, 67, 68, 97, 103, 105, 106, 112, 123, 158, 159, 163
education, 5–6
  attainment, 19
  demand for educated population, 19
  educational achievement gap, 6
  educational stagnation in the United States, 13–17
  evolution of, 7–13
effective demand, 2, 4, 70, 95, 98, 112, 122, 127, 137, 149, 155, 159, 181
Employer of Last Resort (ELR), 1, 25, 26, 27, 31, 32, 60, 62, 63, 65, 66, 67, 68, 69, 98, 112, 113–121, 125, 148–151, 157, 158 (*see also* job guarantee)

184　　　　　　　　　　　　　INDEX

employment:
　as a human right, 3, 40, 43, 46, 50, 55, 56, 57, 176
　emulation, 115, 139
　endogenous growth, 151, 154, 159
　Engel Curve, 139, 140, 152
　expectations, 6, 75, 111, 113
Euro, 83, 84, 161, 162, 163, 164, 165, 166, 167, 168, 173, 174, 175
Europe, 1, 7, 8, 36, 37, 58, 161, 164
European Central Bank (ECB), 162
European Monetary Union (EMU), 161, 163
Eurozone, 60, 162, 163
excess capacity, 155
exchange rate, 63, 64, 73, 76, 83, 84, 172, 173

Fairmodel, 74, 75, 76, 77, 78, 79, 82, 83, 84, 94
Federal Reserve, 33, 38, 67, 79, 121, 172
finance
　Internal finance, 131
Financial Crisis Inquiry Report, 166
financial fragility, 88, 89, 90, 93
fiscal policy, 40, 63, 95, 163, 172, 173
Foley, Duncan, 129, 158
Forstater, Mathew, 1, 3, 4, 23, 32, 38, 61, 62, 65, 69, 70, 71, 74, 94, 98, 99, 113, 120, 121, 122, 124, 170, 174, 176, 179
France, 9, 29, 164
Fullwiler, Scott, 3, 63, 69, 73, 76, 79, 80, 88, 89, 94, 179
functional finance, 1, 3, 63

Germany, 9, 10, 162, 163, 164, 165, 173
Goldman Sachs, 161
Great Depression, 27, 61, 68, 74
Great Recession, 25, 59, 61, 68, 97, 104
Greece, 161, 162, 164, 165, 166, 176

Hagemann, Harald, 96, 121, 158
Harrod-Domar Model, 128
Hicks, John R., 97, 122, 156, 158

households, 4, 13, 30, 46, 89, 90, 134, 135, 137, 138, 139, 140, 141, 142, 144, 146, 147, 148, 153, 154, 156, 170, 172, 174, 176
human capital, 7, 8, 9, 10, 11, 12, 13, 18, 21, 24, 25, 26, 28, 29, 35, 138, 141, 156

Iceland, 161, 162, 163, 166
inequality, 6, 9, 14, 16, 17, 29, 33, 34, 35, 36, 37, 59, 67, 97, 176
inflation, 1, 13, 32, 33, 45, 46, 49, 51, 53, 63, 67, 70, 73, 74, 75, 77, 78, 80, 81, 82, 83, 91, 93, 94, 112, 115, 124, 167, 172, 181
innovation, 69, 96, 97, 103, 122, 130, 132, 133, 136, 140, 142, 144
　financial, 68
input-output models, 99, 102, 107, 110, 112, 120
investment, 2, 4, 8, 9, 11, 18, 34, 52, 75, 93, 98, 99, 100, 102, 104, 106, 107, 108, 111, 112, 113, 114, 116, 118, 120, 121, 122, 126, 127, 128, 129, 130, 133, 138, 140, 142, 143, 144, 148, 154, 155, 156, 171, 174
Ireland, 58, 161–168, 173–176
Italy, 161, 164

Jefes de Hogar Program, 4, 84, 94
job guarantee
　benefits of, 2
　buffer stock, 45, 46, 48, 51, 62, 70, 73, 76, 79, 80, 83, 84, 93, 119, 148, 168, 169
　cost estimation of, 65–67
　foundations of, 2, 39, 62–65, 73–74, 98
　as a retraining program, 6, 7, 25–26, 28, 31, 98, 115, 120, 148, 150
　and social justice, 3, 4, 38, 60–62, 67, 68, 71, 124, 180
job insecurity, 20–22
jobless growth, 103, 104, 112

Kaldor, Nicholas, 126, 129, 136, 158
Keynes, John Maynard, 5, 32, 33, 36, 95, 122
Keynesian demand, 149
Keynesian unemployment (*see* unemployment, Keynesian)
knife-edge, 129

labor productivity, 32, 96, 97, 98, 102, 103, 104, 105, 111, 115, 120, 143
labor-saving inputs (*see* technological change)
Leontief, Wassily, 112
Lerner, Abba, 63, 70, 74, 94
Lowe, Adolph, 96, 97, 113, 123, 157, 159

Malthus, Thomas Robert, 127, 128, 155
manufacturing, 10, 11, 22, 29, 65, 97, 98, 152
market fundamentalism, 60
Marx, Karl, 96, 105, 111, 121, 123, 134, 149
 laws of motion of capitalist process, 96
 mass production, 131, 133, 134, 136, 137, 146, 147, 151, 152, 153, 154, 155
Mill, John Stuart, 96
Minsky, Hyman P., 44, 56, 60, 62, 63, 68, 70, 88, 89, 90, 159, 167, 181
modern money theory (MMT), 1, 51, 57, 63, 71, 94, 124, 177, 181
monetary policy, 33, 61, 63, 75, 76, 79, 94, 122, 172, 173
Moore, Basil, 63, 70
multiplier-accelerator models, 128, 129, 155

Neisser, Hans, 96, 123
Nell, Edward J., 3, 4, 70, 74, 94, 98, 122, 125, 128, 131, 132, 133, 138, 141, 143, 153, 155, 156, 158, 159, 180
New Deal, 4, 33, 41, 42, 43, 50, 57, 64, 68, 115, 118, 119, 170, 171

Non-Accelerating Inflationary Rate of Unemployment (*see* unemployment, natural rate)

Pasinetti, Luigi, 95, 99, 112, 121, 123, 139, 159
positional goods, 145, 146, 157
post Keynesian growth theory, 125
poverty, 24, 31, 45, 47, 59, 62, 67, 68, 70, 168, 173
price stability, 1, 2, 4, 39, 45, 46, 64, 67, 68, 73, 82, 84, 93, 119, 120, 168, 171
productivity, 2, 21, 27, 30, 31, 32, 33, 38, 63, 77, 79, 125, 132, 133, 136, 142, 143, 144, 147, 148, 149, 150, 152, 153, 154, 170
 of capital, 128, 129
 of labor, 96, 97, 98, 102, 103, 104, 105, 111, 115, 120, 143
profit motive, 112, 115
profits, 63, 89, 98, 99–106, 110, 111, 114, 115, 116, 117, 118, 120, 127, 128, 129, 130, 142, 144, 155, 156
public goods, 5, 29, 145, 146, 157
Public Works Administration, 42

recession, 21, 22, 23, 59, 64, 80, 82, 83, 84, 85, 87, 88, 89, 90, 91, 92, 93, 97, 106, 110, 121, 135, 164, 170, 171, 172
regulation, 145, 146, 147
reserve army, 149
Ricardo, David, 95, 96, 97, 123, 127, 128, 155
Robinson, Joan, 103, 123, 129, 143, 159
Romer, Paul, 154, 159
Roosevelt, Franklin Delano, 40, 41, 52
 Universal Declaration of Human Rights, 43, 46, 55, 56, 57

Say's Law, 126, 127
Schumpeter, Joseph, 21, 96
Semmler, Willi, 155
Smith, Adam, 5, 8, 28, 29, 31, 136

social security, 32, 42, 52, 53, 55, 56, 57, 147, 169
social stratification, 140
societal welfare strategy, 40–41
Solow, Robert, 126
sovereign currency, 161, 163, 165, 167, 168, 173
Sraffa, Piero, 123, 155
structural change, 69, 95, 98, 120, 123, 159

taxation, 9, 56, 64, 123, 128
Tcherneva, Pavlina, 3, 4, 83, 86, 94, 95, 121, 124, 176
technological change, 2, 7, 11, 14, 17, 18, 19, 28, 30, 95, 98, 115, 122, 154, 179
technological progress, 95, 96, 97, 102, 103, 104, 105, 111, 121
transformational growth, 94, 122, 125, 133, 134, 136, 140, 141, 151, 152, 154, 157, 159, 181
traverse analysis, 97, 122, 158
Troubled Assets Relief Program (TARP), 66

underemployment, 1, 3, 17, 22, 28, 61, 66
unemployment
  Keynesian unemployment, 95, 103, 110, 120
  long-term unemployment, 7, 17, 19, 22, 24, 61
  mass unemployment, 135
  monetary costs, 24
  natural rate, 1, 70, 73, 75, 84
  social costs of, 1, 24–25
  Structural unemployment, 97
  technological unemployment, 96, 97, 103

Verdoorn-Kaldor, 143

wage
  Basic Public Sector Wage (BPSW), 118, 119
warranted rate of growth, 128
Washington Consensus, 60
Works Progress Administration (WPA), 4, 32, 33, 41, 42, 171, 176

Young, Allyn, 136, 159

2 4 6 8 9 0 1 Printed in the United States of America